Untethered

Creating Connected Families,
Schools, and Communities to
Raise a Resilient Generation

Doug Bolton, PhD

AVERY

an imprint of Penguin Random House

New York

AVERY

an imprint of Penguin Random House LLC
1745 Broadway, New York, NY 10019
penguinrandomhouse.com

Most Avery books are available at special quantity discounts for bulk purchase for sales
promotions, premiums, fundraising, and educational needs. Special books or book
excerpts also can be created to fit specific needs. For details, write
SpecialMarkets@penguinrandomhouse.com.

Library of Congress Cataloging-in-Publication Data has been applied for.

Hardcover ISBN 9780593713341
eBook ISBN 9780593713358

Printed in the United States of America
10 9 8 7 6 5 4 3 2 1

Book design by Ashley Tucker

For Kathy, Angelique, Matthew, and Anna.
My community.

CONTENTS

AUTHOR'S NOTE

This is a book filled with stories of people—often people who are struggling through their hardest moments. Writing about these moments felt sacred. I hope that my telling of these stories honors their journeys. I've tried to represent these stories accurately and with sensitivity, but they are filtered through my own experience and memory. I reached out to the former students and parents featured in this book to check certain details and ask for permission to use their stories. I let them know that I would not use their real names and would change identifying details to protect their privacy. I was unable to track down some students, while others gave me permission to use their real names and share their unaltered stories. When I reconnected with students and parents, we relived their stories together. Many shared how they hoped that their stories could be helpful to others who are hurting. Those conversations were an unexpected gift, allowing me a glimpse into their lives, often decades later, and to reexperience the depth of their wisdom, gratitude, and generosity.

Two Boys, Two Very Different Lives

On my last day as principal of North Shore Academy, as I was looking through old pictures and putting them in boxes, my eyes fell on a class photo from 2001. It was taken during my early days as a middle school psychologist. Staff and students were sitting on a picnic table in a courtyard, squinting into the sun. My eyes landed on the faces of two boys who couldn't have looked more different. Nick's back was straight, his head up, blond hair glowing in the sun. His grin was big and aiming to please. At eleven years old, his innocence was on full display. Danny was slouched, his thick brown hair appearing to weigh on him, his eyes barely making contact with the camera. He wore a heavy flannel shirt on a warm, sunny day. His sullen look revealed a deeper sadness. At thirteen, he was already world-weary.

Although they each felt the sting of a life marred with loss and rejection, they had a charisma that drew people to them. In the years that followed, both boys would struggle with drug use and were known well by their local police departments. They rebelled against authority with a passion that seemed primal. Nick's aggression would come to define him. Danny's defiance was quieter but seemed more powerful. They would fight even small limits with a purpose and vigor that others reserved for more mortal threats.

I attended a wedding for one of them and a funeral for the other. One thrived and the other died. After all of these years, I feel complicit in both.

◆

This is a book about how children's lives can veer off course, and what we can do as adults to help them find their way back. It is a road map for healthy child development. As parents and educators, we have never needed a road map more urgently. Over the past decade, children's mental health challenges have reached epidemic levels. Our children are melting down at home and in school at unprecedented rates. As a society, we have taken detours that have led our children astray. And we are all complicit.

This road map can help us find our way to parenting and educational practices that promote children's behavioral and mental health and wellness. It is a road map that brings us back to embracing the power of community, to weaving together what is unraveling. It is not a new path. In fact, in many ways it dates back to our beginnings as a species, when living and thriving in communities was a matter of survival. And yet, even with all of our modern comforts, we are still at our healthiest when we are embedded in a thriving community. Healthy communities not only enhance our wellness, they buffer us from the impact of trauma and are the guiding force in helping us heal from both emotional and physical injury. Our ancestors understood this and built on this wisdom, passing it on from tribe to tribe and family to family. In recent generations, however, our reliance on the power of community has been receding as we have embraced the false promise that scientific, economic, and technological advancements hold the keys to wellness. Although the improvements in material comforts are both profound and impactful, we are increasingly losing something foundational to our well-being as a species: the ability to contribute to, and benefit from, being tethered to an interdependent community.

The parent-child relationship is at the center of a child's community, creating a template for how a child learns to trust and engage with others, building on-ramps or roadblocks to accessing the powerful support of others. Being part of a healthy community—at home, in school, or on teams—is at the core of human development and wellness. As we rely less and less on community, it is our children who are most acutely experiencing this cultural loss, struggling with unprecedented depression and anxiety, leading to behavior problems at school and at home. They are melting down emotionally like never before.

As adults, we have the power to change this. Creating communities steeped in the values that have kept our species on course for several millennia does not require additional resources, just an understanding of the power of community to make each of us physically, mentally, and behaviorally healthier. As a psychologist, as a principal, and as a parent, I have worked for more than three decades with thousands of children and families to help them redraw their maps. In doing so, I realized that, in each of these roles, I had gone off course myself. I was following outdated research, buying into common yet toxic parenting and educational practices. I believed that behavior was rooted in motivation, and to help children behave better, I needed to create menus of punishments and incentives to help them grow and develop. As I began to look at the research, and reflect on my experience as an educator, psychologist, and parent, I realized how wrong I was. A huge body of research points in the same direction: growth and development are rooted in our ability to foster communities of belonging—in our homes, in our schools, and beyond. Believing in, and creating, these healthy communities is simple in theory but complex and messy in practice. But the cost of disconnection is ultimately catastrophic for children. And we contribute to this disconnection, unwittingly, every day.

The Crisis Facing Our Children

It is not alarmist to say that our children are in crisis. The data tells the story. Our current generation of children is experiencing unprecedented rates of mental health problems. In the decade before COVID, rates of childhood depression rose by 60 percent and the number of children and adolescents seen in emergency rooms for suicidal ideation or behavior rose by 50 percent. More frightening to me as an educator, the suicide rate for children is significantly higher in the months when school is in session. Something about our schools seems to be pushing children to the brink of their coping ability—and, for some, beyond. As we know, for many students, COVID exacerbated their stress, making them even more vulnerable to mental health challenges.

It is even more tragic that we know what is causing this epidemic, and how to cure it. We have been ignoring research from the past 150 years that points toward an authentic, research-driven approach consistent with traditional theories of child development that focus on compassion, common sense, and reliance on relationships. It is essential, however, that we don't confuse this path with laissez-faire parenting and teaching styles; this approach actually demands more of us as parents and teachers, but produces measurable, positive, lifelong outcomes. It is proactive, but not punitive. It is empathetic, but not passive.

It is alarming that the most common parenting and educational practices continue to ignore this research. Instead, we cling to older and more familiar practices, born out of behavioral models that saw compliance as the vehicle and punishments and incentives as the fuel to guide the healthy development of children. This obsolete model of raising children is even more damaging in the light of the escalating academic and social expectations placed upon our children that have filled the process of growing up with new levels of toxicity. In our desire to help our children become successful, we are paradoxically undermining their healthy development. Our children today are more isolated than any generation before them. They are sadder and lonelier. They are competing with more classmates for fewer spots in increasingly selective colleges, and they see their futures as defined by their test scores rather than their passions and virtues. In the past, risk factors for children's mental health were well established: trauma, discrimination, and poverty. In 2019, Robert Wood Johnson added "excessive pressure to excel" to the list of the top environmental conditions harming adolescent wellness. Society's emphasis on high achievement has become a chronic stressor for children, parents, and educators, making high-achieving children just as vulnerable to mental health crises as those who are struggling with profound historical and societal stresses. As adults, we have created systems that put children across the spectrum of experience and functioning at risk for severe mental health problems. No one is spared.

And yet, as a culture, we have been conditioned to see these problems as the result of poor motivation. In America, the fabled individualist spirit, born out of early Puritan tradition and reinforced by Industrial Revolution–era influences, suggests that the answer to even the most complex of problems is to work harder. To persevere. So when problems arise, a lack of motivation is seen as the obvious culprit. When all you have is a hammer, everything looks like a nail. We see emotional and behavioral challenges as signs of weakness of character that are fixed by improving children's motivation. When we see problems this way, we then have two choices: we can incentivize or punish. And our most common form of punishment is to exclude from the community the children who are most at risk and have the greatest need to experience the power of a connected community. In the past century, research has filled our workshop with new tools and more sophisticated ways to understand children and address their challenges. Unfortunately, we continue to reach for the hammer.

There is something compelling and reassuring about the simplicity of a hammer. But it is also harmful. When we see a child's behavior through the lens of motivation, we punish them believing that they "know better" or that punishment will teach them to "know better." However, as a parent, I "know better" than to lose my temper with my children, but I've done it anyway. More often than I would like to share in the pages of this book. I'm a psychologist who is highly informed about the costs of adults losing their temper with children and I'm highly motivated not to yell at them. Yet I do it anyway. There must be something more that is happening for all of us in our moments of struggle.

In the pages that follow, I will explore child development through a different lens and, in doing so, will propose using new tools based on the wisdom of our ancestors and the wonders of modern science, to make our relationship with our children more gratifying, healthier, and less stressful. These tools will help children develop and reach their potential by feeling more connected, less anxious, more included, less shamed, and more securely grounded. We will dive into the research that we have ignored for decades, explore the possible solutions, and see the evidence come to life through the stories of children—my own children and the students I have worked with for nearly forty years.

I spent my career working in therapeutic schools as a teaching assistant, psychologist, and principal. I joined children and families on their heart-wrenching journeys through an educational system that continued to shame and alienate them. I was inspired by the resilience of children and parents alike and encouraged by their responsiveness to these tools. As a parent, I have helped raise three children, learning new lessons from each as they found their own path to adulthood. As I struggled in each of these roles, I found that the outdated tools and practices I had learned in graduate school and from our collective parenting wisdom were failing me, creating more problems than solutions. Because these practices relied primarily on systems of punishment to gain compliance, when children struggled, I became increasingly controlling. After delving deeper into research on child development and the behavioral sciences, I was able to see with greater clarity how this understanding of behavior undermined the development of both my students, who were identified as having significant emotional and behavioral problems, as well as my own, more typically developing children. As I learned, I changed. This book shares the story of these lessons and the stories of the children and families who joined me on this journey.

Where We Went Wrong

Recent advances in neuroscience, genetics, and the behavioral sciences are forcing us to rethink many of the strategies and tools that parents and teachers have used for decades to guide our treatment of children. The science and practice of child development have been misaligned for more than a century. While research on the importance of relationships and the power of community has been around since the early days of behaviorism, no one took it seriously. If you couldn't observe it, it didn't exist. Then, in the early 1990s, we found a way to observe the power of relationships, by looking into the brain itself. Social science research had been challenging the theories of behaviorism since the late 1940s, but with the advent of this new science of the brain, traditional theories of behaviorism have been making a hasty retreat.

When children are struggling emotionally and behaviorally, we are often flooded with advice based on outdated and inconsistent parenting theories. When our children melt down, struggle to make friends, or get in trouble in school, we hear strong opinions from our own parents, friends, our child's teacher, and in the pages of many parenting books on the market. Often these suggestions are in conflict with one another.

"You need to set better limits. If you don't hold them accountable, they will think that they can get away with anything."

"You need to use incentives because positive interventions are always more effective."

"They need medication."

"Kids these days are overmedicated. You will only teach them to rely on a pill instead of taking responsibility."

"They need play therapy."

"You need family therapy."

"You need parent training."

"You need to get the school to provide services."

"Services at school will only create a stigma."

"Kill them with kindness."

"One afternoon with me behind the woodshed and that behavior wouldn't be happening."

We are often caught in a no-win situation. At the grocery store when your toddler is screaming for a candy bar and you draw a hard line, they melt down more and other customers shake their heads, frustrated that you can't control your child. If you give in and buy them candy, other shoppers shake their heads in judgment.

In schools, we are often overwhelmed by conflicting opinions from the experts. Educational teams try to integrate, among other things, educational testing to address academic achievement concerns, psychological testing to assess cognitive functioning, assessments from the occupational therapist about sensory needs and executive functioning, reports from the speech language therapist about challenges with pragmatic language, the board-certified behavior analyst about environmental reinforcers, parent requests for accommodations, the school and classroom behavior systems, the school's discipline practices, the school board's policies for behavior, and often the child's private therapist about the underlying reasons for the behavior. Then, when you are really stumped, you hire an independent neuropsychologist to do a full workup and you have a psychiatrist complete a diagnostic evaluation. Often these reports issue conflicting conclusions and different diagnoses.

Even when there is diagnostic clarity, parents and teachers are often expected to implement specific treatments that align with that diagnosis. For families with a lot of time and resources, that may be possible, but these interventions are often so sophisticated that only clinicians are able to fully implement them. Children diagnosed with anxiety are often referred for cognitive behavioral therapy. Children struggling with depression and self-harm may need dialectical behavior therapy. Children with ADHD are frequently embedded in highly structured programs of incentives and rewards. Applied behavioral analysis (ABA) therapies have been found to be effective with children with autism. I am not suggesting that therapy is not helpful—often it is necessary—but it is just not sufficient. A talented therapist can be an important tool within a much larger toolbox of people and places that will impact your child for the other 167 hours of the week.

How do we manage this complexity? I like Albert Einstein's advice: "Make everything as simple as possible, but not simpler." Our task is to distill the essence of all that we know about behavioral and mental health issues into its most basic form so that it can be accessible to everyone in a child's life. I also like to keep in mind what Michelangelo said about creating the statue of David. "David was always there in the marble. I just took away everything that was not David." Our task is to get to the essence of what is needed to help our children experience a sense of wellness. The answer is right in front of us. What is essential for wellness for those who are struggling the most is helpful for all of us. It is preventative and universal. It is the high tide that lifts all ships.

Community: Our Road Map to Wellness

Research is robust about what our children need to develop socially, emotionally, and behaviorally. Challenges almost always develop because, in the moment, they are struggling with some combination of the following three things:

Attachment: Our ability to develop healthy and enduring relationships with others.

Regulation: Our ability to effectively identify and manage our emotions.

Trauma: With childhood trauma, ongoing and profound stresses within our families continually trigger a child's stress response. As parents, our own history of trauma can echo through our marriages and our parenting. Trauma makes us hypervigilant, pushing us to constantly scan our world to identify threats. As a result, childhood trauma disrupts our ability to form healthy attachments and to regulate ourselves, often with catastrophic results.

The good news is that there is one intervention that addresses all three of these factors:

Community: Experiencing a connected and regulated community helps children learn to attach and regulate, and can both buffer and reverse the impact of trauma. Conversely, an unhealthy community undermines our ability to attach, it is wildly dysregulating, and it exacerbates the toxic impact of childhood trauma.

Every community can be transformative in the life of a child. Families and schools can have the greatest impact because this is where children spend most of their time, but the world is also filled with stories of how transformative a club, or a team, or a mentor has been in the life of a child. Almost always, people will describe the source of their ability to overcome adversity as the people and places where they felt a unique sense of belonging and connection and where struggles were met with a thoughtful, connected, and regulated response.

This has certainly been true in my life. As a child, my parents' divorce unmoored me, and to this day, I often feel adrift when I am not anchored within a caring community. As a parent, when my children have struggled, I frequently reached for the behavioral hammer, pushing my children away when they most needed me to be closer. I learned, slowly, that to engage them rather than ignore or isolate them in these moments was much more effective. I worked for twenty-one years at North Shore Academy (NSA) and was principal for the last fourteen of those years. Each day at NSA, we served about 150 students who were identified as having such intense social, emotional, and behavioral problems that they could no longer be educated in their home schools. Our goal was to give them intensive therapeutic and academic support to help them build the skills they needed to be successful. Our vision, always, was getting them back to their home schools so that they could be with their neighborhood friends and take advantage of all that their schools have to offer. I had a front-row seat, watching children who had a history of chronic failure in more traditional settings thrive as they felt a sense of belonging within the NSA community.

As mental health issues in schools began to rise with frightening intensity, I was asked by my supervisor, Heather, to prepare a presentation to special education directors from our local school districts about how to understand and address mental health issues in schools. I laughed at first. "Maybe I could talk about how to eliminate poverty while I'm at it." Then I tried to pawn the presentation off on a colleague. The truth was, I didn't even know where to start.

That's when I began to look more closely at what we created at NSA. We had seen the limits of traditional responses to students when they struggled. We explored the research from psychology, education, and neuroscience. We attended conferences where we heard about new and exciting ways to support struggling students. We also began to look closer at the staff who were most successful in our building and, as we watched, we realized that they did not adhere to the strict motivational theories that dominated the thinking in most therapeutic schools. What they were doing was in line with the research and practice that we were discovering.

We began to do things differently and realized that the concepts we were learning could apply not only to NSA students but to all children. We relied on just a few basic principles that continually drove our engagement with students and parents. As I reflected, I realized that there was no child, among the thousands that I had worked with in my career in therapeutic settings, who didn't experience challenges with some combination of attachment, regulation, and trauma. Almost to a student, they struggled with all three. I also realized that no one intervention changed the course of a student's life—it was their experience of belonging within our community that was transformative.

Every successful therapeutic program that I worked in had the same emphasis. It is the community that does the work. When the community is healthy, children get healthy. These programs helped students learn to attach through close and connected relationships. These communities were emotionally regulated so that when students struggled, they knew that the adults would not overreact or become counter-aggressive. And finally, each of these communities understood trauma. The staff had boundless empathy and compassion that allowed them to see children's behavior through the lens of their traumatic history. It is not only therapeutic programs that benefit from these qualities of community. More broadly, they are the foundations of our best classrooms and our healthiest families.

These therapeutic communities helped children with a variety of presenting concerns—anxiety, depression, suicidal ideation, addiction, noncompliance, school refusal, and aggression, to name a few. In a world more and more stratified by difference, these schools serve students across the spectrums of socioeconomic status, race, and gender identity. Within a community where children experience a sense of belonging, everyone becomes healthier. This is true for every school. All children. And really, all of us. Maybe I did have something to share with those special education directors after all.

Attachment. Regulation. Trauma. Community.

PART I

Attachment:
The Foundation of
Healthy Development

CHAPTER 1

Every Problem Is Not a Behavior to Be Punished

When my son, Matthew, was in elementary school, his classmates and their parents often described him as the smartest kid in the class. School came easy for him—until it didn't. In the spring of eighth grade, I got a whiff that something was wrong. Literally. I woke at 3:00 a.m. to the smell of smoke. I rushed to the kitchen, where I saw Matthew taking cookie sheets out of the oven, covered with paper that was charred at the edges. He explained that he was trying to make the paper look like it was a historic document for a big project he was working on. He was ashamed that he had fallen so far behind, so he didn't tell us about the assignment. He waited until my wife, Kathy, and I had fallen asleep that night to work on the project that would lead to his first (of many) all-nighters. The demands of eighth grade were ramping up and his organizational skills weren't keeping up.

In high school, it got worse. The academic rigor left him feeling overwhelmed and defeated. His active and curious brain was shutting down. He wasn't completing the work and felt ashamed walking into classes unprepared. So he skipped classes. A lot of classes. When he didn't skip, he was tardy, furiously trying to finish assignments in the hallway before walking into the classroom. Soon, getting him to school on time was a battle that we constantly lost.

I dreaded parent-teacher conferences. For two hours, twice a year, I would walk the halls of my son's high school, feeling the weight of his shame. However defeated I felt, I knew it was even worse for Matthew, who carried this burden each day. In my frustration, I had often seen him as lacking grit, unable to discipline himself to complete even basic work. I was suddenly beginning to appreciate the strength it took for him to persist in the face of such constant frustration and failure.

Each conference began the same way. His teachers said Matthew was thoughtful and engaged when he attended class. They liked him. Yet, he was often late and was always behind, if he showed up at all. With all the missing assignments, his grades consistently hovered around 35 percent.

What is a typical school's response to skipped classes and tardiness? Detentions. The belief is that the fear of staying after school or during lunch in an isolated room should motivate the student to comply with school rules. As a psychologist and principal, I knew this was common practice. I also learned quickly that detentions didn't work for Matthew. No matter how many detentions he served, the tardies and absences just kept coming.

Unfortunately, we seldom think that the punishment is ineffective even when it clearly fails to produce change. Instead, we believe that we need to intensify the pain of the punishment to make it work. So we double down with the dreaded Saturday detentions and, if that doesn't work, in-school suspensions.

Unfortunately for Matthew, the stress didn't stop after he left school because he was often met with an angry father at dinner. I learned to check the school's parent portal to see what classes he had skipped that day. My anxiety would go up whenever I clicked on the app. When I saw that he had missed classes, I felt defeated and powerless. Rather than realizing that he was feeling the same thing, I began to lecture and rant. My fear about his future expressed itself through comments that felt shaming to him. "If you can't make it to class in high school, why would we send you to college?" "You will never be able to hold down a job if you don't do the work and show up on time!" Now there was no place he could go to find peace and connection. He spent more and more time in his room. Alone.

It's not like we didn't try other things. We got him into therapy. We made schedules. We bought folders to organize his backpack, which always looked like a bird's nest of random assignments. Nothing seemed to work. We had him tested and he was diagnosed with ADHD. Medication seemed to help at first, giving him a glimpse of success before he fell back into his old patterns. When we asked the school for accommodations, Matthew informed us that he would refuse the extra time on assignments. "I should be able to do this like everyone else," he would say. But neither he nor we could understand why it was so much harder for him than it was for others.

Matthew was able to do just enough. Because of the kindness and patience of his teachers, he made it to the threshold of graduation in May of 2019. During Matthew's last week of high school, he announced that he had reached a goal that he didn't think he could accomplish. My mind took off. National Honor Society? National Merit Scholar? He was well liked by students and teachers. Graduation speaker?

Then he looked at me and said, "I made it to five hundred."

I was puzzled. "Five hundred?" I asked.

"Five hundred detentions!" he stated proudly. "I didn't think that I could make it to five hundred, but today I did!" He received a few more detentions that week, so he ended his high school career with a total of 506.

Unfortunately, he "only" served 466. That's 92 percent. At least he was getting an A in detention. However, because of his unserved detentions, he was unable to attend prom. How is attending prom related to being late to class? Were they worried that Matthew would be late for his date? He also wasn't allowed to play sports, leave campus for lunch, or attend senior week activities.

When it comes to children, we often look to punishments as the solution to behavior problems. Unfortunately, they are seldom effective in addressing the problems that lead to the misbehavior. I'm reminded of a public health parable, credited to medical sociologist Irving Zola, that I will paraphrase here:

There is a couple having a picnic by the side of a river. They hear a child screaming and flailing in the water, gasping for breath. They jump in and heroically get the child to shore. They are exhausted when they look up and see two more children drowning in the river. The couple dives back in and saves those children only to look up and see the river flooded with more children. Then, one of the adults inexplicably climbs onto shore while the other yells, "Where are you going?! I can't save these kids on my own!" The person on the riverbank yells back, "I'm going upstream to see why these kids keep falling in."

Behavior is a downstream problem that often leads to unhelpful downstream solutions. Downstream solutions are compelling because they are quick and simple. There is a behavior problem? I've got a sticker chart for that. Because misbehaviors are easy to label, and punishments and incentives are easy to implement, they become our go-to strategy. Unfortunately, such downstream responses are seldom effective because they don't address the cause of the problem. As parents and teachers, our job is to look upstream, to understand the source of misbehavior. Upstream solutions take longer to identify and implement, but in the long run, they are much more effective.

Matthew's high school looked downstream for solutions to his tardiness and absenteeism. Late to class? Go to detention. It's fast, clear, and simple. If they looked upstream, they would have seen that his punishment failed to address the problem. As it happens, Matthew was struggling with executive functioning—the skills needed to effectively plan, organize, focus, and persist to complete a task. These are skills that develop over time. The demands of school, however, did not wait for Matthew's skills to catch up, and this gap between his skills and increasing demands of school caused him (and me) to be flooded with shame. Although the testing had revealed his executive functioning gaps, it was hard to be patient and believe that these skills would, eventually, develop. Instead, at school and at home, Matthew was punished for the slower development of a part of his brain that he had no control over. Detentions, it turns out, don't solve executive functioning problems.

As I was walking down the hall during one of the conference nights, feeling powerless and discouraged, a teacher stopped me as I walked by her class. "Are you Matthew's father?" she asked.

"Yes," I said.

Her face brightened. "I love Matthew!"

I was smiling now, too. "I love *you*! Who are you?" I was so excited to find out where Matthew was excelling.

"I'm Mrs. Nelson. I'm Matthew's detention supervisor. I get to see him every day! He is so polite. I know his student ID by heart." She then gave another clue to his underlying challenges. "I hope that it's ok that I bring a little extra lunch for him because he often forgets his."

Ms. Nelson's kindness was a ray of light in an otherwise dark experience of high school for Matthew. Detention wasn't solving his executive functioning problem. In fact, it was making it worse—layering shame on top of his challenges with organization and planning.

As a society, we have been looking downstream to address problems of behavior for well over a hundred years, doubling down on incentives and punishments and drowning out the voices of researchers who have been looking upstream to gain a better understanding of why some kids exhibit troubling and persistent behaviors that others do not. The good news is that as the children's mental health crisis intensifies, upstream voices are getting louder and are now being heard.

Falling in Love with Behaviorism

Behaviorism, at its core, is a theory of motivation. There is something simple and comforting about this idea. Seeing behavior through this lens, when a child misbehaves, we have two options—either punish them to discourage the behavior or reward them to jump-start their motivation to behave in a better way. This model originated in the early 1900s with the work of psychologist John Watson, whose powerful and compelling research on animal behavior ignited the field of behaviorism. The American Psychological Association defines *behaviorism* this way:

> *an approach to psychology based on the study of objective, observable facts rather than subjective, qualitative processes, such as feelings, motives, and consciousness . . . Historically, behaviorists held that the mind was not a proper topic for scientific study since mental events are subjective and not independently verifiable.*

Understandably, the scientific community embraced behaviorism. It is logical to focus only on things that are observable. But over the last one hundred years, scientific discovery has altered the field of psychology with evidence detailing the limitations of behaviorism. For instance, we now know that brains of other mammals, while similar in many respects, are still very different from the human brain. It is also hard to imagine how we can think of behavior without considering feelings, motives, consciousness, and "mental events." Just because we can't observe a feature or a process doesn't mean it doesn't exist. Just because we can't measure these things doesn't mean that they don't impact how we interact with others. Dismissing this backstory would be akin to dismissing gravity—which we also cannot see—as a force in physics.

One core theme of early behaviorism was that withholding parental affection was essential for raising independent adults. In his 1928 book, *Psychological Care of Infant and Child*, John Watson did not mince words about his disdain for the nurturing of children when he titled the third chapter "The Dangers of Too Much Mother Love." He issued dire warnings about showing any kind of affection to a child. "When you are tempted to pet your child," he wrote, "remember that a mother's love is a dangerous instrument which may inflict a never-healing wound, a wound which may make infancy unhappy, adolescence a nightmare, an instrument which may wreck your adult son or daughter's vocational future and their chances for marital happiness." He goes on, instructing, "never hug and kiss" your child or let them sit on your lap. "If you must, kiss them once on the forehead when they say good night. Shake hands with them in the morning. Give them a pat on the head if they have made an extraordinary job of a difficult task."

Although these words may seem draconian today, his theory checked a lot of boxes at the time. It was scientific. It catered to our need for control. It was simple and easy to implement. For a long time we, as a society, embraced Watson's theory and doubled down on it, infusing it into every aspect of our child-rearing protocols. For more than a century, it has molded our parenting strategies, our educational systems, our economic theories, our approach to criminal justice, and our employment practices, to name just a few.

I share this not because our current views of behaviorism are still in lockstep with Watson's initial theory (they aren't), but because it is always helpful to understand the roots of the theories we adhere to. As we will see later in this chapter, psychologist Harry Harlow was discovering limits to behaviorism as early as the 1940s.

While Watson's beliefs about affection are well outside of mainstream thinking today, the theory has left a strong residue on how we respond when children are struggling behaviorally. When children misbehave, Watson's words come roaring back with frightening force. This theory is powerful because it appears to give parents and educators just what they are looking for in their most stressful moments with children—a sense of control. A quick and simple remedy. Withdraw attention and affection from children when they misbehave, and they will shape up. Conversely, if you offer kindness or support when a child is struggling, it will only reinforce the negative behavior, which will then become inextricably integrated into the child's personality. Or so the theory goes. This false belief has led adults to emotionally abandon children in their moments of greatest distress, creating a behavioral and relational road map that has had a powerful and devastating impact on their overall health and emotional well-being.

The Problem with Incentives

As early as the 1940s, the foundation of behaviorism was beginning to form cracks. Psychologist Harry Harlow, an animal researcher investigating the power of incentives on performance in his monkey laboratory at the University of Wisconsin, stumbled upon evidence that directly challenged some of the tenets of behavioral theory.

In 1949, Harlow was studying how his rhesus monkeys solve problems. He wanted to see how they would respond to a three-step task that involved opening a metal latch connected to a wooden frame by removing a series of pins and hooks in sequence. Harlow placed the monkeys in separate cages, each with their own metal latch. He wanted the monkeys to be comfortable with the apparatus before teaching them how to open it. Then something unexpected happened. The monkeys independently began to play with the latch without any external reinforcements. They were curious. Soon enough, they had it figured on their own. Two-thirds of the monkeys learned to open the latch in less than sixty seconds without any teaching or reinforcements.

The fact that the monkeys solved the problem of the latch without incentives seemed to contradict the motivation theory of behavior. Harlow, curious, wondered how much more quickly he could get the monkeys to solve the latch problem when he added incentives. He used the monkeys' favorite treat—a raisin—to motivate them to perform the task more quickly. Imagine Harlow's surprise when the opposite happened. With the incentive, his monkeys made more errors and, as a result, were slower to complete the task. He sounded the research alarm, urging his fellow researchers to rethink the models of reinforcement that were dominating the psychology of learning. "Introduction of reward in the present experiment served to disrupt performance, a phenomenon not reported in the literature," he wrote. But to no avail. The field of psychology didn't budge.

Harlow believed that there was another factor more important than rewards in these interactions: the desire to engage in an activity for the simple pleasure it brings, without any reward or punishment. Most parents have probably observed similar patterns in their children. Just as monkeys solved puzzles without reinforcements, children will spend hours building LEGO towers or finger painting. I can remember entire afternoons as an eleven-year-old throwing a tennis ball onto the roof of the barn behind our house, watching it disappear and then waiting for it to emerge over the eave as I would lunge to catch it with my baseball glove. This kind of incentive-less engagement is not confined to childhood. Think of all the adults who play in garage bands even though they know they will never record an album. Others refine their cooking skills, journal, and compete in athletics knowing that they will never go pro. Many of the things we most enjoy, we do without weighing the benefits of a reward. The reward is the engagement in the activity, the inherent joy of learning, growing, developing, and reaching a goal that we set for ourselves.

Decades of research followed Harlow's initial experiments, and his results have been replicated with children and adults in a multitude of settings. In the 1970s, Edward Deci and Richard Ryan dove headfirst into this research and coined the terms *intrinsic* and *extrinsic* motivation. They define *intrinsic motivation* as engaging in an activity for the inherent satisfaction of it rather than for some separable consequence.

Conversely, they define *extrinsic motivation* as a motivation to participate in an activity based on meeting an external goal, garnering praise and approval, winning a competition, or receiving an award or payment. In the 1990s, Deci summarized the decades of overwhelming research on the impact of incentives:

> *Careful consideration of reward effects reported in 128 experiments lead to the conclusion that tangible rewards tend to have a substantially negative effect on intrinsic motivation. When institutions—families, schools, businesses, and athletic teams, for example—focus on the short-term and opt for controlling people's behavior they do considerable long-term damage.*

And yet our children are flooded with incentives at home and at school in efforts to manage their behavior. For instance, we use incentives to get children to read. Knowing that reading is important for children, schools and libraries organize incentive programs to keep them reading during the summer months. In response, children beg their parents to take them to the library or bookstore so that they can get their books and earn their prizes. The good news is that it works. Children read more when they are incentivized to read. But there is a flip side to these results. In a 1982 research paper, psychologist Barry Schwartz tells the story of a teacher who noticed that once she introduced the incentive, students started choosing different books. They picked shorter books with larger print and more pictures. They also were unable to answer questions about the story after finishing the book. They got through the book quickly to get the prize, not to enjoy the story. Perhaps even more problematic, children began reading less outside of school. The process that was meant to make them more avid readers pointed them instead toward shortcuts. These lessons about incentives are consistent. If you want short-term results, incentives can work. If you want active engagement and long-term investment in a task, incentives are counterproductive. They undermine intrinsic motivation. Full stop.

Even when we know about the deceptive allure of incentives, we can still succumb to their power. I'm an older guy, and lately I've been trying to get fit in an indoor cycle class. Typically, my goal is to keep a high but steady heart rate, sweat a little, and avoid the need to use the AED paddles. One day, the instructor let the class know that there would be a reward for the rider with the highest average watts for the class. (Watts measure the intensity of the workout by combining the pedaling speed with the resistance on the flywheel.) I remember looking around at the other eleven riders and thinking, *I'm a former athlete. I think I can win this thing!* Suddenly my health and fitness took a back seat—my eyes were focused only on the prize. I cranked the resistance up and started pedaling with a newfound vigor. My heart began pumping harder than it had in years. Sweat poured from my forehead onto the mat below. My face moved from pink to crimson. At the end of the ride, I struggled to get off the bike and into my car. I missed my next several workouts, my body aching and depleted for the rest of the week. My fitness strategy and goals were no match for the reward that awaited me along with the satisfaction of winning.

It turns out that I didn't win. I think I came in tenth. I also didn't get the prize—which turned out to be a designer sports bra. True story. I knew all of the research on the misleading allure of incentives, but this knowledge was no match for the power of the prize. My goal in attending the class was to get in shape. Instead, I spent the next few mornings nursing my legs and cursing my age.

Although the research on incentives undermining intrinsic motivation is robust, they remain our go-to strategy to motivate behavior, particularly with children. What begins with sticker charts and grades in school evolves into bonuses and titles at work as part of the larger paradigm that often drives our daily lives. We learn to engage in behaviors not because they are positive or healthy but because there is a payoff. And our brains are exquisitely wired to focus on this short-term payoff, making incentives hard to resist. In the words of Barry Schwartz, "incentives demoralize what is otherwise a moral act. They change the question in people's minds from, 'Is this right or wrong?' to 'Is this worth the price?'"

The Problem with Punishments

Punishments are equally problematic because they, too, lead us to focus on what is in *our* best interest *now* rather than what is the right thing to do. Psychologists Uri Gneezy and Aldo Rustichini worked with an Israeli day care organization that had a problem with parents coming late to pick up their children. The organization had a total of ten facilities, and in six selected facilities, they decided to fine parents three dollars if they arrived more than ten minutes late. The results were shocking. In the facilities where the fines were implemented, the number of late pickups doubled. The following graph shows the data comparing the centers that fined parents for a late pickup with those that didn't. Note that the fines were implemented in week four in order to collect baseline and discontinued in week seventeen.

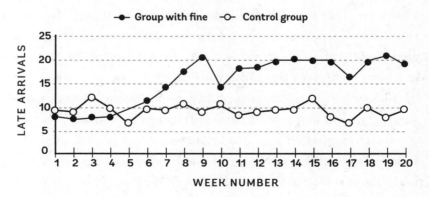

FINES

If you have young children, these results, however counterintuitive, make a lot of sense. For three dollars, I get to go to happy hour with my colleagues? I can go grocery shopping without having my toddler in the shopping cart? I can get a workout in before going home? It's easily worth the price. Realizing that the punishment for late pickups had the opposite effect, the researchers eliminated the fine, but, interestingly, the number of late pickups didn't go back down (note weeks seventeen to twenty). Prior to the punishment, you can imagine parents rushing to pick up their child so that their child's teacher could get home to their own family. Punishing parents for being late made the interaction transactional. Parents were now focused on what was best for them. It was worth the cost. And once we make an interaction transactional, as the data shows, it is hard to undo it.

The active ingredient for punishment is fear, which triggers our stress response. Clearly, the three dollars was not enough to engender fear in the parents, so the day care organization discontinued the practice. With children, however, when punishments don't work, we increase the punishment to instill greater fear. Fear, however, activates our stress response, preparing the body for action to address a threat, flooding it with stress hormones and neurotransmitter activity to activate our fight, flee, or freeze response. The more frequent our stress response activation, the more impact this has on our physical health. (I'll explore this in greater detail in Part III.) And the more we learn to be fearful of people who provide care for us, the more it impacts our mental health.

We often justify our use of punishments by saying that this is how people learn from experience. Unfortunately, stress limits our ability to learn from experience because it shuts down the reflective parts of our brain as it prepares us for a physical battle for survival (more on this in Part II). If we want people to learn why what they did was wrong, we want their brain to be at its most open, not its most threatened.

Disrupting Attachment and Regulation

When presented with incentives and punishments, our brain becomes laser focused on earning the prize or avoiding the pain. We lose the ability to reflect on the big picture and we become short-term thinkers. Incentives and punishments also focus us on ourselves and our personal needs—if I am going to be rewarded or punished for my behavior, my focus naturally shifts from "What is the right thing to do?" to "What is in my best interest?" One of the most insidious aspects of using behavioral methods to manage behavior is how we unwittingly focus children's attention on their own self-interest, undermining their developing sense of morality—what is best for the common good.

The same principle is true for adults. Bonuses rule the day in business, as organizations try to maximize profits by getting their employees to work harder and produce more. Corporations invest huge sums of money on incentives to improve their bottom lines. Incentives must work for businesses, right? Not so, says the research. In fact, the data is unequivocal. Despite decades of research that sounded the alarm that business incentives undermine performance and culture, businesses continue to use them to try to motivate performance. Thirty years ago, author Alfie Kohn described the hidden and toxic costs of business incentives at work. Incentives, it turns out, are only successful at gaining temporary compliance but are ineffective at creating long-term changes in attitudes or behavior. Further, when people expect a reward for completing a task, they underperform when compared to people who have no expectation of receiving an incentive. And the bigger the reward, the more negatively they view the task or activity they are being rewarded for. Finally, he writes, "The surest way to destroy cooperation and, therefore, organizational excellence, is to force people to compete for rewards or recognition or to rank them against each other."

In 2011, Adam Grant and his colleagues at the Wharton School cautioned against the use of financial incentives in business. After reviewing the research, they argued that employees who were financially rewarded for achieving goals were "more likely to engage in unethical behavior, such as cheating by overstating their performance." They summarize the research by writing, "the bottom line here is that financial incentives, by definition, create inequalities in pay that often undermine performance, collaboration and retention." And yet, financial incentives continue to be the backbone of business strategies aimed at improving performance and productivity. Despite decades of research warning us about the negative impact of incentives and punishments at work, at school, and at home, they still are a mainstay of most of these communities.

If the research is so compelling, why do we persist in using incentives and punishments as a way to raise our kids? One reason is that they are fast-acting responses to behavior that does one important thing for a parent or teacher at a loss about how to get a child to behave—it gives us a desperately needed *sense* of control. Having the power to inflict a punishment or grant a reward allows us to regain our footing as the adult in charge. This sense of control, however, is short lived. It undermines long-term goals, often creates feelings of shame, and can damage our relationship. But in that moment, when we and our children are emotionally dysregulated, we feel a strong sense of urgency to use our power to wrest compliance from a noncompliant child.

Punishments are not only problematic in the long run; they can also exacerbate the problems we are trying to solve in the moment. Many of our behavior plans actually lead to the acting out that we are trying to prevent. Have you ever punished a child for having a temper tantrum and the tantrum got more intense? Have you ever set up a reward system for a child, and when they didn't earn the reward, they completely fell apart? This happens often with children who struggle the most. Incentives and punishments assume that children have the skills to do what we are asking them to do and they just don't want to do it. Children want to make adults happy. When they fall short of our expectations, they feel terrible. Motivation is not the problem.

Further, we often make the mistake of trying to gain compliance by turning a child's favorite activity into an incentive/punishment experiment. We identify what our children like the most and then we threaten to take it away. You didn't do your homework? You can't play in the baseball tournament this weekend. You got into a fight with your sister? You can't go to your friend's birthday party. You didn't follow directions in class? You can't go outside for recess. Unfortunately, the activities that children like the most are often the ones that help them emotionally regulate, build resilience, and become receptive to learning. At baseball, kids get to experience teamwork, movement, persistence, and skill development. At the birthday party and at recess, they are practicing social skills.

Ironically, when children struggle, we often punish them by taking away opportunities to address the skill deficits that led to those struggles. When a child struggles with a math concept, we wouldn't exclude them from math instruction and then expect that they will do better on the next assignment. We would spend more time helping them learn the concept. In the same way, if a child is struggling with social skills, not allowing them to participate in the next game is counterproductive. They need more social skills practice, not less. If a child is impulsive and can't sit still, taking recess away is similarly self-defeating. They need more movement, not less. Children whose engine runs faster and who struggle to sit still and follow directions in class need the release of outdoor recess more than anyone. Giving them an opportunity to run and play will help regulate their brains and bodies for the rest of the day, making learning and compliance more likely, not less.

Back when I was dealing with my son Matthew's tardiness at school, a more severe punishment may have gotten him to class, but it wouldn't have taught him how to plan and organize his schoolwork, a skill that was essential to his success in college. The problem with punishments is that they only tell us what not to do—they don't teach us what to do. But we almost always know what we shouldn't do. Matthew knew that he should be on time to class. He knew that he should complete his work. He also knew that he was bright and that more was expected of him. His shame at being unable to organize his work was only intensified by the constant threat of punishment and disapproval. There were greater challenges for him that punishments simply couldn't solve.

We justify our continued use of punishments despite the research refuting its effectiveness. One of the more imaginative ways we've done so was to create a big tent we call "natural consequences" and fill it with punishments. Many people say, "I don't punish children. I use natural consequences to change behavior." The statement is an oxymoron. Natural consequences, by definition, happen naturally. Once we "use" consequences, they are no longer natural. Getting wet after going outside in the rain without an umbrella is a natural consequence. In high school, detention is considered a natural consequence for being late to class. The natural consequence for being late to class is missing out on instruction. If I am late for a meeting, I wouldn't be told that I need to sit in my boss's office for forty-two minutes after my colleagues have gone home. Natural consequences are natural precisely because they happen *without us intervening*. Any consequence we place on a child is, therefore, no longer natural.

Although punishments and rewards are the bread and butter of many child-rearing practices today, the research says consistently and clearly that punishments do not change behavior in the long run. Once the punishment or incentive is discontinued, people go back to their old behavior. Even B. F. Skinner, a leading voice in behaviorism, didn't believe that punishment helps people to learn healthier behaviors, writing, "A person who has been punished is not less inclined to behave in a given way; at best he learns how to avoid punishment."

The Allure of Compliance

As a society, we have relied on rewards and punishments as our method of maintaining order and compliance. Parenting, therefore, has traditionally focused more on children's compliance than on their development. It is true that given the right menu of punishments and rewards, we can almost always get people to behave in a particular way. It begs the question, however, whether order and compliance should be the primary focus of our parenting. Most parents and teachers would place greater value on children being engaged in activities that are meaningful, embrace positive values, and have the skills they need to solve the problems that they face in their lives. We hope our children will be independent and collaborative. Unfortunately, most of the systems we have for maintaining control and motivating children undermine, rather than support, the development of these virtues. When we flood them with fear of punishment or the allure of incentives, we disrupt these cornerstones of healthy development. Ironically, if we want children to learn how to behave differently when they struggle, we need to keep their brains open so that they can learn from their mistakes. They need to feel safe. Unfortunately, our incentives and punishments often shut their brains down when we most need them to be available to learning.

The research that provided the foundation for behaviorism was based upon studies of animal training. By observing how contingent rewards and punishments work to get animals to be compliant, it was not a big leap to also apply these theories to human behavior. Children are not pets, however. We train our animals to comply with our expectations—to be house-trained, to not jump up on visitors, to heel and sit. Children's brains are much more powerful. We want those brains to grow, and think, and engage. When we begin to see healthy child development as more than compliance to adult expectations, the fabric of behavioral theory begins to fray.

Even animal researchers have moved away from behaviorism as a way to understand animal learning. Frans de Waal, one of the world's foremost primatologists, doesn't mince words when he describes how his field of study is moving beyond the theories of Watson and Skinner to embrace new ways of seeing behavior. "Neuroscience is breaking open the black box to look inside the brain, offering accounts of how animals solve problems that rely less and less on the learning theories of the past. Behaviorism is dying a slow death, lifting its head only now and then to feebly try putting a brake on these developments."

The negative impact of punishments has been profound. Nowhere is this more apparent than in the debate about suspensions that has occurred at school board meetings around the country. In 2011, 3.5 million students in the United States were suspended. That is double the number of suspensions compared to 1975. If suspensions worked, wouldn't that number go down instead of up? For adults, the fear of incarceration is our worst punishment. That's got to work, right? And yet, there is a 76.6 percent five-year recidivism rate following release from state prison. If punishment worked, would three of every four people who experience our very worst punishment reoffend? Clearly, it is time to move beyond behaviorism, and yet, we continue to struggle to put it in the rearview mirror.

Looking Upstream

There are three main reasons why we cling so closely to punishments and rewards as our go-to child-rearing strategies. The first is that we wrongly attribute our success in life to the incentives and punishments we received as children. "My parents punished me and it worked." What we may not be considering is that we are often successful in spite of, not because of, incentives and punishments. The active ingredient of our success is that there were people in our lives who loved and supported us through the hard times. Just because we have survived a childhood filled with incentives and punishments doesn't mean that we are better for it. Often, despite our success, we are still impacted by the lasting shame or fear of punishments in our childhood. This is the ultimate and lifelong price we pay growing up in systems that reward and punish.

The lessons we learned did not need to be based in fear of punishment or losing an incentive. Brené Brown, the powerful and inspirational speaker and leader, is also a social worker who does research on shame. She found that 85 percent of people she interviewed were shamed in school in a way that changed how they viewed themselves. We survived school in spite of, not because of, that shame.

The second reason we cling so tightly to behaviorism is that it helps us feel more powerful when we are feeling powerless. When children misbehave, it makes us, as adults, feel an unnerving loss of control, shutting our brains down and narrowing our focus. We need compliance—now! A child's misbehavior is especially threatening to us. We feel responsible for them. We see their behavior as a reflection on us as parents and teachers. And, we are so invested in their future. We worry that if we don't act now, the behavior will persist throughout their lives. When we feel out of control, our brains work quickly to regain control. There is no quicker and more compelling response than delivering a punishment or offering an incentive. Even if it doesn't work, we feel a greater sense of control. This short-term illusion of control, as we have seen, often comes with a high cost to the child.

But it is important to not throw the baby out with the bathwater. Behavioral interventions can and do have great short-term utility. They are sprints that can get us through a hard moment, hopefully without inflicting too much shame or fear. But parenting and education are marathons, and with marathons, we need to deal with our anxiety of the long race ahead by not overreacting to momentary set-backs. Sprinting miles one to seven will end up hurting us when we get to mile twenty-four. The same is true for behavioral interventions. The more we engage in them as our primary strategy to help our children develop over time, the more impact there is on their long-term emotional and physical well-being. There are times when gaining immediate compliance is essential and behavioral interventions can work wonders. However, we need to understand the significant limitations and the profound long-term costs of over-relying on punishments and rewards.

So, what do we do instead? Fortunately, there was another theory of child development that was in its infancy as John Watson was developing behaviorism. A young medical student in London was discovering what many current scientists now agree is the most powerful parenting tool available. It has only taken us a century to realize it.

CHAPTER 2

The Surprising Impact
of Relationships

Most camps have a parents' weekend but at Wediko, a therapeutic summer program for children and adolescents who struggle emotionally and behaviorally, we called it Visitors' Day. When so many of the children didn't live with their birth parents, we had to be careful with our language. For most, it was a special day, an oasis of connection with loved ones in the middle of the summer. But for some, whose visitors never showed up, it would be remembered as one of their loneliest days.

At Wediko, children and staff enjoyed forty-five days of typical fun camp experiences while engaging in intense and powerful therapeutic growth. Visitor's Day was the halfway point in the summer. As the day approached, the anticipation was palpable. Art projects were being completed, welcome signs made, and each cabin was bustling with conversations about how to make the day special for their families. In cabin meetings, each camper began to talk about their home life more honestly. Amid this energy, Chantel remained silent and sullen. This was Chantel's second summer at Wediko. Visitor's Day during her first summer was frightening. She remembered. We all remembered. We worried that it could happen again.

Chantel's default expression was anger, with rare flashes of a smile and a laugh that sounded more like a cackle. She was tall, thin, and strong, her hair either groomed tightly to her head in braids or worn loose and long. When she smiled, she looked self-conscious, like she had revealed a secret. She would suck her tongue before she spoke, and when she spoke, she spoke fast, with words bursting to get out. It was usually a warning: "Stay the fuck away from me!" As we got to know Chantel better, we realized that the warning was actually: "If you get any closer, I'll get hurt."

This summer was going to be different. At least that was Chantel's intention. Applications to Wediko included an exhaustive interview process, a process that engaged the child and the family in what was the beginning of the therapeutic work. Could they talk about the really hard things in their lives? Could they imagine a different future? Could they identify things that they need to do differently? For Chantel, the interview also addressed the events of the Visitor's Day during the prior summer. Could Chantel commit to doing things differently? Could her mom make the same commitment? They said that they could and would.

In the week leading up to Visitor's Day, we talked to Chantel. "Of course I'm not going to do that shit again! How many times do I have to tell you people?" she snapped in her characteristically clipped, staccato voice. Her body expressions were staccato, too—quick, disconnected movements—turning away, then turning back. No eye contact. But still, somehow warm and connected just enough to keep the others hanging on, not wanting to let go. "Plus, my mamma said it won't be no problem, neitha." She sucked her tongue.

I was in my second year at Wediko, and I was the lead staff for the oldest girls' group. Chantel had come to trust me more than the other staff in the three weeks that led up to Visitor's Day. It was my responsibility to be sure that Chantel was going to be safe. We called her mother the week before, and she said that she was definitely coming. Our call the day before Visitor's Day, though, went unanswered.

As Visitor's Day approached, I recalled the previous summer when Chantel waited with the other campers in her cabin, as parents, siblings, foster parents, and grandparents started showing up. Children ran from the cabin to greet their families and then eagerly brought them back to introduce them to the other campers and their families. Chantel met them all as she waited, eager to show off her mom. When waiting, there is always a sliver of hope. That sliver lingered on as lunch came and went. She became agitated, pacing and swearing about her mother. The students who knew that their parents weren't coming were off on a fun trip so that they could be spared the sadness of being alone while watching other families' joyful reunions. Chantel stayed, buoyed by the promise from her mother. After three hours of waiting, it was clear to Chantel that she would be alone for the day.

Chantel left the cabin and ran through camp, threatening staff who tried to stop her. She mocked children who were with their families, she swore at their parents, she destroyed property. Staff rushed to contain her as she ran to the main picnic area, where she found a two-by-four sitting near some construction materials and began swinging. She ran between and across the blankets of families enjoying their meals. Finally, staff had corralled her into a corner of the field. A dozen staff in a circle. Chantel, holding her two-by-four, ready to strike. Bob, the supervisor of Chantel's cabin, arrived and stepped forward, arm extended, trying to reach past Chantel's rage and give Chantel access to a caring relationship to soothe her. "Get away from me, you bitch-ass motherfucker!" Chantel yelled. Then, with less conviction, "I hate you people." She dropped the two-by-four and began sobbing.

A year later, Chantel and I were finishing up another game of Uno. Taking no chances of a repeat of a year before, we decided to wait in an empty cabin, away from the others, just in case. The walkie-talkie sat idle on the table next to us. With each passing hour, Chantel got quieter. A single tear began to roll down her cheek. "She ain't comin'." Chantel walked over to a bunk bed and lay down, silent, her shoulders heaving. I have never felt so helpless.

The saying goes that 90 percent of life is just showing up. As a twenty-two-year-old, I must have understood that. I knew that nothing I could say would help Chantel—if I spoke, it would only be to help me manage my own desire to fix things that couldn't be fixed. We sat, quietly, until the last parent left. We walked back to the cabin, where Chantel, stone-faced, refused dinner and lay, face down, on her bunk.

The other girls returned to the cabin with a mix of emotions and gifts from home. They felt thrilled, loved, and for many, newly homesick. When they saw Chantel on her bunk, they set those feelings aside and went to her. Her two best friends sat with her for the rest of the night. Chantel had many nights at home when she felt abandoned. This night, her cabin made sure that she wouldn't be alone.

The Power of Presence

I remember Chantel so vividly, decades after our two summers at Wediko, because of how intensely I felt her suffering. As Chantel's anxiety over her mother showing up for Visitor's Day heightened, I experienced echoes from my own childhood with clarity that I, at the time, hadn't felt in years. Each of my siblings remembers finding out about our parents' divorce a little differently, but we all agree on a few details. We were at our cabin in the Adirondacks. I was six when I asked Mom, "Are you and Dad going to get a divorce?" It was 1970, when divorces were relatively rare. I must have sensed something between them, an unspoken yet unsettling distance or anger. I don't even remember knowing what divorce meant. She said, "Yes," and a seismic shift reconfigured our family. Fifty years later, we all still feel the aftershocks, tremors that continue to ripple through our own family lives.

Mom didn't work outside the house before the divorce, putting all of her energy into raising us. We also had a babysitter, a student from Syracuse University, who lived in the attic. Our father, a minister, was around most evenings and weekends. Someone was always available to us. That all changed after the divorce. My dad saw us only on Sundays. My mom took a full-time job and went to school part-time to become a social worker. She was seldom home. We lived on the bottom floor of a three-family house. After being brought up in a home full of adults, the four of us suddenly felt alone. We were ten, eight, six, and four at the time. I remember feeling like I had lost both parents and would cling to any moment I could have with my mother. Waiting for her to come home from work and school was the most anxiety-ridden part of my day. Her absence filled me with dread that she was never coming back.

The fact that she was always running late didn't help. I remember sitting behind the rain-streaked window, watching headlights go by, wondering which one would turn into our driveway. Our house sat on a hill. I knelt on the seat of the recliner in the bay window, chin on the back of the chair, counting. "I should only worry if she doesn't come within the next twenty-five cars." The counting began. And continued. Another twenty-five. And another.

I understood what it felt like to wait for a mother who may never show up. I had no doubt that the pain of Chantel's losses eclipsed mine. I also have no doubt that I could glimpse into her pain, an umbilical cord of loss connecting us. What I didn't understand at the time was that these disruptions in our relationships with our parents would put our physical health at risk. Years later, I was introduced to a body of research, nearly one hundred years old, that has shown that the quality of a child's attachment to their caregivers is predictive of their physical and mental health as adults. As I dove into the attachment research, I realized that the relationships between parents and children are more important than I ever imagined. Our ability to attach, I learned, is the main driver of our physical and mental health in both childhood and adulthood.

English psychiatrist and psychoanalyst John Bowlby, who pioneered the field of attachment theory, could relate. He was born in

England in 1907 to parents who were emotionally unavailable and, as soon as he was of age, sent him off to a boarding school. Bowlby often described how the lack of nurturing parents haunted him throughout his life. It also inspired him to study the impact of parental presence on children's development. Interestingly, as he was going through the pain of separation from his parents, the medical world was faced with an unexpected problem.

At the turn of the twentieth century, hospitals were a dangerous place for infants and toddlers. At the time, three prevailing ideas— Louis Pasteur's germ theory and Joseph Lister's innovative sanitation techniques—collided with Watson's behaviorism with both surprising and devastating results. The hospitals' efforts to keep children safe from germs made them, paradoxically, more vulnerable to disease. In these hospitals, infants were arranged in rows, and nurses wore masks and gloves and were warned not to touch the children to avoid transmission of disease. Robert Karen, in his powerful book, *Becoming Attached*, described the painstaking effort to keep babies safe, going so far as to assert that, "handling a baby was considered dangerous to its health." Consistent with Watson's beliefs about the negative impact of parental affection, when a child was hospitalized, the mother was only allowed to visit once a week for a few minutes for fear that she would make the child more emotional and disrupt treatment. For many children, this lack of touch and interaction proved to be fatal.

Despite adhering to the best possible medical practices of the time, children in both England and America began dying at unfathomable rates from what would later be described as a "failure to thrive" or from nonspecific infections. A 1915 review of ten infant hospitals in the US concluded that up to 75 percent of children died before their second birthday. The very best hospital had a mortality rate of 31 percent.

Armed with his own scars from childhood and increasing evidence of the physical damage separation in childhood can inflict, Bowlby began to see the medical and psychological problems that he encountered in his patients through the lens of the pain they suffered from that early separation. In contrast to Watson, Bowlby believed that "the infant and young child should experience a warm, intimate, and continuous relationship with his mother in which both find satisfaction."

Bowlby found himself drawn to children who exhibited "disturbed behavior" and began interviewing them, discovering that they had "unfortunate early histories." Eighty-five percent of children with "disturbed behaviors" had been separated from their parents in early childhood. He believed that such separation could have a devastating impact on children's physical and mental health. Decades later, the science of the brain would prove his initial hunch correct.

Remember the psychologist Harry Harlow, the one who challenged the prevalent behaviorist theories about incentives? In the 1960s, he found himself at odds with the psychological establishment once again when his work with monkeys unexpectedly led to a deeper understanding of the power of parental attachment. In preparation for his tests of cognition, Harlow wanted his monkeys to be as healthy and focused as possible. To avoid any social distractions, the spread of illness, or fighting over food, he separated them from their mothers and put them in their own cages. But rather than becoming strong and resilient, these monkeys began to fall apart physically, emotionally, and cognitively. When Harlow's graduate students would clean the cages, they occasionally left the cloths they used in the cage. The students noticed that the monkeys would cling to these cloths for dear life. The cloths seemed to provide a sense of comfort and soothing.

Believing that these monkeys were missing their mothers' nurturing touch, Harlow put two "surrogate mothers" in the cages with the young monkeys. One surrogate mother was made of wire mesh covered with the soft terry cloth that was used to clean the cages. The other surrogate mother was made of the same wire mesh, but without the terry cloth. Harlow added a twist. The mother without the terry cloth had a supply of milk. The mother wearing terry cloth didn't. He put the monkeys into the cages with both surrogate mothers and watched, recording where the young monkeys spent their time.

According to behavioral theories of the time, the importance of a child's relationship with the mother is driven by the reinforcement of the mother's milk. If behavioral theory held up, the young monkeys would prefer spending their time with the wire-mesh mother who provided the milk. Instead, Harlow consistently found the opposite. According to psychologist Karen, "Harlow's studies dealt the first scientific blow to the belief that affectional ties were based on nursing: For rhesus monkeys, at least, cuddly contact proved much more important." Harlow, himself, summarized his results succinctly: "It's as if the animals are programmed to seek out love."

Is Harlow's research applicable to humans? His observations of the importance of adult nurturing and the risks of isolation in early childhood would become hauntingly relevant just a few decades later in Romania, when the Communist rule of Nicolae Ceaușescu collapsed with his execution in 1989. When he first took power in 1965, in an effort to jump-start the economy through population growth, Ceaușescu outlawed contraception and abortion. This did produce the hoped-for population growth, but the economy didn't grow in response. The result was an explosion in the birth rate of children in families who could not afford to keep them. Hundreds of thousands of children ended up living in understaffed and underfunded orphanages. For the most part, the orphanages met the physical needs of infants. While they provided food, clothing, and shelter, the caregiving staff, each responsible for at least twenty children, had little else to give. In 1989, as Ceaușescu's dictatorship was toppled, 170,000 children were found living in these conditions. After they were rescued, researchers found profound delays in every aspect of the children's development—physical growth, cognitive development, language, social skills, and motor skills.

Just as in the case of Harlow's monkeys, the lack of loving contact had produced devastating consequences for these children.

Understanding Attachment

It was Matthew's third day of kindergarten. He and I sat anxiously on a short stone wall and watched his new classmates play. "Do you want to play with your friends?" I asked. He shook his head and sidled closer. The school bell rang and the other students began to line up in front of their teacher. Matthew climbed onto my lap, and with a pleading in his voice I had never heard before, he said, "I don't want to go, Daddy."

As the principal of a school that worked with so many students who refused to go to school, I knew that this was an important moment. I now was learning just how heartbreaking this process was for their parents. His anxiety entered my body as if through osmosis. Of course he needed to go. Of course he would be ok. But it felt like an emotional betrayal. He was so vulnerable and so frightened.

His arms locked around my neck as the class finished lining up. I stood and walked over to his teacher. Ms. Allen was tiny. Barely five feet tall, no more than a hundred pounds. I leaned down to whisper to her. "This is going to be a challenge." Her look of sympathy for Matthew was quickly replaced by determination. "We'll be ok," she said gently before she pried him from my neck, placed him on her hip, turned to her class, and said, "Let's go!"

Everything in the busy playground seemed to go quiet except for Matthew's screams of "Daddy! No!" As he disappeared around the corner, I felt like I had been a coconspirator in my child's abduction. I got to my car and began sobbing.

I waited a few minutes before calling the school. I told the secretary, "I'll stick around in case Matthew just can't make it today." She called the classroom and then gave me the news I knew was coming but struggled to believe. "Oh, he's doing just fine. He is happy and playing with his friends."

◆

Mary Ainsworth, a developmental psychologist and student of Bowlby's, had a hunch that how children managed this separation from their parents early in life could help us understand how they coped later in life. She believed that the early attachment relationship creates a template for later relationships and provides a foundation for our sense of safety in the world. When, as infants and young children, we have attentive and attuned caregivers who soothe our distress, we learn that the world is a safe and responsive place. If our caregivers are inattentive, abusive, neglectful, unpredictable, or absent, we learn as infants to be highly vigilant in an unpredictable and unsupportive world. We learn that we can't rely on others to keep us safe and to soothe us when we are upset.

To test her hypothesis, she created a study that she called the "Strange Situation." This situation for most parents, however, is anything but strange. It studies a moment that every child and parent has to navigate early in a child's life—a temporary separation from the mother. Ainsworth created a room with a play area, some toys, and chairs. A mother brought her one-year-old into the room as research assistants observed out of view. Did the child stay close to their mother? Did the child explore the room and play with toys? Then a research assistant entered the room. Did the toddler engage the stranger in the room? Did they retreat to their mother? After a few minutes, the mother would leave the room and the team would observe how the child responded to this separation. After a few minutes, the mother returned and the team would observe how the child managed the reunion. Later, both the mother and the assistant left the room, leaving the child alone. All in all, it took about fifteen minutes to complete.

How much information could you get from fifteen minutes in a one-year-old's life? Enough, it turns out, to transform our understanding of child development.

Sixty-six percent of the toddlers responded in similar ways. They felt safe to explore the room when their mother was present and, although distressed when their mother left, they were able to be soothed when she returned. Ainsworth described this type of interaction as indicative of "secure attachment." Some children, however, completely fell apart. They wouldn't leave their mother to play, were inconsolable when she left, and clung for dear life when she returned. Others didn't seem to notice that their mother left and were unmoved when she returned. Some toddlers became angry when she returned, turning their back on her or becoming aggressive. Thirty-four percent of the children behaved this way, and Ainsworth described them as "insecurely attached." (She identified four different types of insecure attachment that, while interesting and important, are beyond the scope of this book).

The real power of the "Strange Situation" study, however, would begin to reveal itself over time. Those fifteen minutes told a story of attachment that extended well beyond the children's time in the "Strange Situation." It turned out to be highly predictive of how they would cope later in life.

Byron Egeland and Alan Sroufe, psychologists at the University of Minnesota, used Ainsworth's "Strange Situation" task to identify the connection between attachment status and behavior in school. They followed children who had participated in the Strange Situation into their nursery school and eventually into elementary school. The children who were identified as more securely attached were rated as more independent, sociable, and popular, and scored higher on tests of intelligence, self-esteem, and resilience. Unfortunately, the story was very different for children who were identified as insecurely attached. Only one of eight insecurely attached children was described by their teachers as "effective." Two of three were referred for special education.

Nine of ten were described as mean, antisocial, and immature. It turned out that a child's attachment status at age three or four was more predictive of whether they would get a high school diploma than either their IQ or scores on achievement tests. Researchers were surprised to find that the connection between infant attachment and the relational and behavioral challenges they faced got stronger, not weaker, as the children in the study got older. The impact of insecure attachment on children seemed to snowball, leading to greater problems as they were entering adulthood than when they were in the early grades. Ainsworth was onto something. A fifteen-minute separation from their mother at age one was predictive of challenges in school and life decades later.

Ainsworth was curious to understand the causes of insecure attachment. She observed mother-child interactions within the home and found that, compared to insecurely attached children, the mothers of the securely attached children were much more responsive to their child's needs. They were sensitive to their needs, picking up on their cues, comforting them when they were distressed, and enjoying their time together more than parents of insecurely attached children. Ainsworth identified four scales of maternal behavior that she found were key to children's secure attachment: sensitivity, acceptance, cooperation, and emotional accessibility. These parental behaviors help a child feel safe in an unpredictable world. Once again, research was telling us that the quality of a child's attachment to a parent is essential for their emotional well-being.

But this was only part of the story. Launched in 1938, the Grant Study revealed how relationships impact our physical health, and how the quality of our attachments can either add or take away decades from our lives. George Vaillant, who led the research for more than three decades, described this ambitious and impactful longitudinal study as an attempt to understand not what makes us sick but what makes us healthy. The study recruited 268 sophomores at Harvard

University (who were all white men). The group included, among others, Ben Bradlee, who would become one of the most prominent journalists of his generation, and President John F. Kennedy. They combined the findings with the Glueck Study, which included 456 young men from Boston who did not grow up with the privilege of the Harvard cohort. The goal was to study these men over the course of their lives to see what factors led to a successful, happy, and healthy life. The battery of tests was extensive and included, among other tools, psychiatric interviews, thorough physical exams, childhood assessments, projective testing, and even handwriting samples. They continued to interview and examine these men and, eventually, their families, for decades. They are still following up with the men who are alive today, now more than one hundred years old. Based on the extensive information collected on the young men in the study, Vaillant was able to identify whether they were securely or insecurely attached as children.

The Grant Study collected an overwhelming amount of data, and Vaillant delivers one clear message about the results. What the study tells us about physical health and happiness is clear, simple, and convincing. Love matters most. In his 2012 book *Triumphs of Experience*, Vaillant summarized the data from the study in one simple phrase: "Happiness is love. Full stop."

But that was not the most shocking part of the study. Vaillant's data also pointed to another revelation: insecure attachment was associated with not only unhappiness but also tragic mental health issues and devastating physical health outcomes. Here are just some of his findings. People who were identified as insecurely attached were ten times more likely to have a *chronic* illness. They were 66 percent less likely to live into their eighties. They were 2.5 times more likely to have dementia. In his 2023 Surgeon General's Advisory, Dr. Vivek Murthy stated this even more succinctly: "Loneliness is far more than just a bad feeling—it harms both individual and societal health. It is associated with a greater risk of cardiovascular disease, dementia, stroke, depression, anxiety, and premature death."

The study also found that the men with insecure attachment experienced high levels of emotional and behavioral challenges. Those who were insecurely attached were five times more likely to be diagnosed with a mental illness and three times more likely to struggle with addiction. They earned, on average, 50 percent less over their career than their well-attached peers. Poor attachment was ravaging their physical and mental health.

Vaillant's conclusion was remarkably simple. "There are two pillars of happiness revealed by the seventy-five-year-old Grant Study. One is love. The other is finding a way of coping with life that does not push love away." Tragically, the children with insecure attachment struggle to place trust in relationships. Because caregivers were not able to provide sensitivity, acceptance, cooperation, and emotional acceptance, the insecurely attached children became adults who remain vigilant and distant. In doing so, they often reject the one thing that is most likely to make them healthy and happy.

Healthy attachment, ultimately, is the key to our physical and emotional resilience. According to Vaillant, "it is the experience of loving and being loved that most closely predicts how we react to the hardships of life. Human attachments are the ultimate source of resilience." Science journalist Jonah Lehrer, who reviewed the attachment literature in *A Book about Love*, came to the same conclusion, writing that "the feeling of love is not just a source of pleasure. It is also a kind of protection." In recent decades, with the advent of genetic research and advances in neuroscience, our understanding of the positive benefits of healthy relationships has moved from a trickle to a flood.

It is common sense that healthy attachments make us happier. What is new, and game-changing, is that our attachments impact us at a cellular level and forever change how our bodies respond to stress. Seen through this lens, the role of attachment in children's mental health takes on a whole new meaning. And, as we will learn in Part IV, our connection to one another and our connection to a broader community has deep roots in our evolution as a species. These connections provide a buffer for us, immunizing us against the impact of stress. They also help us recover, to get back onto our feet, after the challenges of life have knocked us down. They enhance our mental health, boost our physical health, and are essential for our behavioral health. When these connections are tenuous, we hurt, we hurt others, we get sick, we fall apart. When our children struggle to attach, they are at risk for all kinds of challenges later in life. As parents, teachers, and coaches, this is where we can step in and help them rewrite their attachment stories, each relationship becoming another chapter in their story of healing.

Repairing Insecure Attachment

Every parent wants to provide for their children. We want to be sensitive to their needs, to accept them for who they are, to engage with them in a spirit of cooperation, and to be emotionally accessible. And parenting is a huge challenge. There are times when all of us struggle to be present, attuned, and collaborative. Life gets in the way. Parents are pulled in many directions: demands at work, financial stresses, health issues, and caring for elderly parents. For some parents, life is even harder. Trauma, mental illness, substance abuse, postpartum depression, poverty, and divorce are just some of the challenges that can make us less available to connect with our children. I can't imagine a mother caring for her children more than my mother did, and yet divorce, graduate school, and work made her unavailable to meet many of the needs of her children. We had to figure out a lot on our own.

I remember Sophie, a seventh grader at NSA who was struggling in school, consistently defiant, and verbally abusive to adults. She refused to do any academic work and consistently disrupted class. When I met with Sophie and her mother at their intake meeting, I learned that Sophie's father had never been a part of her life. When I asked about Sophie's early life, her mother began to choke up as she told the story. "Just before I had Sophie, my mother—my best friend in the world— was diagnosed with brain cancer. My dad was never around, and I didn't have any siblings—it was always just the two of us. When I was pregnant with Sophie, I would go from a prenatal meeting with my ob-gyn to the cancer ward, where I sat with my mom during chemo. She was dying when Sophie was born. I was always at the hospital. Four months after she was born, my mom died. I was so sad for so long." There was no way that Sophie's mom could be emotionally and physically available to Sophie while losing her own mother. The timing of Sophie's entry into the world couldn't have been worse.

At NSA, our job was to help Sophie revise her template. To do that, she needed many doses of connection with everyone around her—her family, her teachers, her classmates. Every day, despite her challenges, staff welcomed her into the classroom with an authentic joy. They shared with her a belief in her goodness. They empathized when she was upset. They laughed with her often. Classmates embraced her. Moment by moment, she felt more valued and more connected. It was a slow process, but Sophie made it back to her home school. Even though she left NSA in eighth grade, Sophie and her mother continued to reach out to share her high school journey and celebrated with us when she graduated. The key to helping children reverse the impact of early insecure attachment is to give them as many doses of healthy connections as possible. The more insecure the attachment, the more doses are needed.

Insecure attachment, it turns out, is not a life sentence. As Lehrer writes, "the human attachment system is responsive to changing conditions. That means that we can still learn how to love, even if our childhood was marked by loss and insecurity. Attachment is not a fixed state, or a permanent diagnosis. It is a continual process, a working model of relationships that can always be revised." He goes on to write, "it's never too late. Love never loses the capacity to transform what it touches." We are always one relationship or one connected community away from relationships of attachment and belonging that can lead to positive and powerful changes to our physical and mental health. For children, these communities are ready-made for them: family and school. As children get older, teams, music groups, school clubs, church groups, and theater troupes can become those communities. As family members, as educators, as coaches and tutors, we all have the opportunity to create communities of belonging where our children will not only benefit in the moment from the power of connectedness, but within these communities, they also learn the social skills necessary to create a future full of healthy attachments.

Providing positive social experiences does so much more than enhance children's self-esteem—it actually changes the wiring in their brains and the expression of their genes. Because children spend most of their time in school and with families, children's classrooms and homes do most of this wiring. Neuroscientist Richard Davidson wrote, "teachers change students' brains." He goes on to explain that "the more exposure kids have to love, the more exposure kids have to kindness, the more they will have that tendency to love and be kind. Just like language, children are born with the propensity for love and kindness and the more it is nurtured, the more it will be developed." The same is true, of course, within our families.

Healthy relationships also open our minds for learning. The understandable worry for schools is that if we spend more time building relationships, we will lose important instructional time. Building relationships, however, does not come at the cost of academic rigor. Louis Cozolino, Ph.D., an educator and neuroscientist, suggests that the opposite is actually true. "It is the nature and quality of teacher-student relationships that create the possibilities of learning. Secure relationships trigger brain growth." Strong relationships, it turns out, are essential for academic rigor.

The great news for educators and parents is that, working together, we can create these communities for children that not only impact their wellness today but can set the stage for a lifetime of physical and mental health. Schools have children for thirty hours per week, forty weeks a year, for thirteen years. Who else, besides parents, has this opportunity to embed children in healthy communities? And, at least until adolescence, children are with their families most of the rest of the time. If we do this right, we can wrap children in, as Ainsworth describes, sensitive, accepting, and cooperative communities where others are emotionally accessible, setting the stage for a lifetime of connection and belonging. Or, we can continue to marry our educational systems and parenting practices to the outdated behaviorist theories of the past. The challenge of systems built from the behavioral models is that the spirit of attachment and belonging is extended to children only when they are compliant and high achieving. When they struggle, the typical response is to shame them through public punishment, or to exclude them through time-outs or suspensions. We don't learn how to develop healthy attachments when relationships are contingent on our behavior. We need to do it differently. In the next chapter, we will explore some ways to foster secure attachments in children who struggle to connect the most.

CHAPTER 3

Lifelines: Attachment Strategies

R yan was hard. He was mean. He wore a constant scowl on his face, signaling others to stay away. His clothes were baggy, his hair unkempt. He bullied both students and staff. If you dared speak with him, he would respond with a biting comment, making you think twice about trying it again. He was changing the culture of his classroom and our school. And he was only in the seventh grade.

A quick look at his file told us part of his story. His parents divorced when he was little, but he was old enough to remember his father's violence. When his father died suddenly a few years later, the family fell into deeper poverty, having to move frequently and constantly feeling the threat of eviction. Given all of this disruption, he continued to change schools—transitions that he did not manage gracefully. Fights and suspensions became the norm.

It didn't take much imagination to fill in the gaps in these events. His attachment history was littered with loss and fear. His mother, who was as caring and engaged as any mother in our school, was overwhelmed by the challenge of providing for and protecting her children. Ryan wore his insecure attachment as a suit of armor, and he was always looking for a battle. He seemed to feel safest when he was fighting.

The irony about bullies is that they are often insecurely attached. Their bullying allows them a feeling of control over relationships so that they will not be vulnerable to the pain of further loss. It also gives them a sense of empowerment in a world when those in power have been abusive.

I was Ryan's therapist. I knew that my first job was to find a way to like him, which wasn't easy. He regularly demeaned and embarrassed me, making up names for me, refusing to follow my directions, publicly and loudly suggesting that I was a pedophile. I also knew that I needed to be authentic. If I pretended to like Ryan, he would see right through me and struggle even more to trust me. It was a fine line.

Ryan seemed to soften—a little—when we would meet individually. I let him be in control of the sessions. Sometimes we played chess. Sometimes we talked. Sometimes he would allow me to ask questions about his relationships with other students. Other times, he refused to come, angry with me for setting limits on his language or outbursts of disrespect. Trying to keep my balance through the unpredictable waves of Ryan's attachment felt like surfing big waves on a small surfboard.

Slowly he began to talk about how people in his life let him down and how hurt he felt. He began to connect this hurt with his bullying. He revealed how frightened he had felt around his father. In class, he continued to rage and took every opportunity to hurt those around him. But in therapy, he began to express remorse.

A dramatic shift happened in ninth grade. Ryan was in a new classroom with a new group of staff. He was gradually becoming less mean and more connected, but his anger continued to linger ominously below the surface. One day when Bill, a teaching assistant, played a guitar during homeroom, Ryan asked if he could try to play it. Bill handed it over, and Ryan was instantly mesmerized. He strummed and picked. Bill showed him how to make chords and noticed that Ryan softened when he held the guitar. The next day when Ryan walked in, there were two guitars in the room. Bill had brought in a second guitar. Together, Bill and Ryan would strum in unison. They didn't talk much, but they were attuned to one another. They were connecting in a way that felt safe to Ryan. They began to put chords together to create songs. Students would gather, making requests, and Ryan would perform. He began to find a new rhythm in his relationships with others. The soundtrack of Ryan's life began to change.

Ryan's relationship with Bill, his increasing trust in me, and his developing relationship with his teacher were seeds that would, eventually, expand into a garden of interconnected relationships. His mother, no longer needing to cope with the daily trauma of domestic violence and economic instability, also became a more consistent loving force in his life. The energy that Ryan put into pushing others away was repurposed, exposing a charisma that drew people to him. His passion for music transformed from a flicker to a flame. Years after he left NSA, Ryan sent me a note. He was twenty-one, working in the music business, living in his own apartment in Nashville and driving a company car. "Who could have imagined," he wrote to me in an email, "that the kid you met in middle school would end up with a life like this?" Eventually, he became an organizer and producer for popular country bands, traveling around the world. He was right—I would never have imagined.

Children with insecure attachment often struggle to connect. Sometimes, like Ryan, they push people away aggressively through bullying and disrespect. Others are more passive—afraid to connect, they isolate themselves and reject friends and family members by being dismissive or unresponsive. Both are equally detrimental to their long-term well-being. If they don't develop the skills of connecting to others, they lose the powerful resilience that relationships provide, making them more vulnerable emotionally, physically, and behaviorally.

The challenge of connecting with children who struggle with attachment is that they don't make it easy. Their lack of trust and skill comes to them naturally—as infants, they may have lived with caregivers who, for many possible reasons, were not consistently responsive to their needs or became angry and violent when their child was distressed. The infant then feels alone in a dangerous and unpredictable world. These early relationships provide an emotional template through which they will interpret the world as they get older. As a result, they become anxious and reactive, pushing others away to protect themselves.

Luckily, insecure attachment is not a life sentence. Like Ryan's mother, we always have the opportunity to rebuild those relationships, become more responsive and consistent. Any adult in a child's life, through persistence and empathy, can help them rework that early template and begin to engage in more secure attachments. Ryan was lucky to have Bill see something in him that others didn't. Bill recognized the opportunity he had to connect to Ryan, and he seized it. The more doses of connection we experience, the quicker we are able to rewrite our attachment stories.

Father Greg Boyle, through his writing and speaking, has given voice to the importance of attachment. His parish in South Central Los Angeles is in the heart of multigenerational gang violence. He created Homeboy Industries, a place where gang members work side by side, embedded in a community of connection. The books that memorialized his experience are a testament to the power of love in the lives of those who feel unlovable. Boyle wrote, "how else, except through connection, can people be reminded of their goodness." He also shares that, "goodness is our preexisting condition . . . It is the starting point. Realizing it, not becoming it, is the task." If we look deeply enough, even in the hardest moments, we can always find goodness in children. Bill found goodness in Ryan and, eventually, Ryan found it in himself.

Helping insecurely attached children learn to connect is both challenging and complex. We have to find our way through their maze of defenses in order to discover their goodness. Below are ways, some counterintuitive, to help children connect after a childhood marked by insecure attachment.

Finding the Ridge

Just as Ryan and Bill found harmony through music, it is essential that children find rhythm with the adults in their lives. When we are in the presence of one another, we are hardwired to seek attunement. We synchronize our footsteps when walking with a friend. We mimic one another's body posture in conversation. This attunement to each other has its roots in our earliest interactions with infants. Have you ever noticed that when you hold an infant it is almost impossible not to mimic them? They smile and then we smile. They stick out their tongue and we stick out our tongue. They feel something, express it in their face, and we mimic it. Without language or the ability to self-reflect, this is how infants first become aware of their emotions. They feel something and make an expression. They see their expression mimicked on our face, telling them, "This is what you are feeling."

As I learned about attunement, I thought about Matthew when he was a toddler. His grandmother, Mimi, took care of him three days a week while Kathy and I were at work. One afternoon they didn't notice that I had arrived home from work, and I was able to watch them together for a few minutes. Matthew was holding a screw in his hand, and then dropped it on the windowsill. He was fascinated. He picked it up again, then dropped it, and watched it fall and bounce as he listened for the *click* of metal against paint. He repeated it again. And again. Then Mimi would do the same thing. This went on. And on. And on. Matthew was learning about gravity. He was learning about the different sounds the screw would make on wood, metal, and carpet. He was also learning that what he was interested in had value. He was being seen. They were attuned.

Dan Siegel, M.D., a pioneer in the field of interpersonal neurobiology, sees human development as the product of the integration of the brain, the mind, and relationships. He describes attunement as the reactiveness we have to another person, and the process by which we form relationships. "When we attune with others, we allow our own internal state to shift, to come to resonate with the inner world of another. This resonance is at the heart of the important sense of 'feeling felt' that emerges in close relationships." Children need to be in attuned relationships to feel secure and to develop. Throughout our lives, we need to be attuned to feel close and connected to others. Attunement, then, is an intuitive process between people who, because they are so present with one another, experience similar shifts in mood and energy. When we are emotionally out of step with our children, we are less aware of what they are experiencing and, as a result, we are less responsive. Some children are able to put into words what they are experiencing, building a bridge to attunement. Others are harder to read and, at times, seem unreachable. When we are dancing to the beat of different drummers, we often respond to this disharmony by becoming more distant. Or we become anxious about the disharmony and latch on too tightly.

During our children's infancy, we build secure attachment through holding and touching, making eye contact, and responding to their needs. They, too, begin to respond to us, giggling when we tickle, crying when we leave, smiling when we smile at them. As author Deborah Blum describes, "they are like tiny treasure hunters, carefully searching the facial maps around them." As children get older, the foundations of attunement show up differently. As parents, the most important tool in our toolbox is active listening. This skill requires us to be curious about the experience of our child and take the time to see the world through their eyes, reflecting what we see and hear back to them, an echo that resonates with their own experience. As they get older, children become better and better at masking their feelings from us. Listening helps them to remove their mask so that we can more fully see them. It is, perhaps, the most critical tool that we, as parents and educators, can develop and implement. Martin Buber, a theologian and philosopher, advocated living life on the "narrow ridge," a state of mind and heart where people discover the other's humanness. On this ridge, people engage with one another with genuineness, empathy, and respect. It is a place of connection, even intimacy. The ridge is a place of attunement, and listening skills are the trail markers that help us find our way there. It is through this kind of listening that our children feel most seen.

As a teenager, I learned how listening becomes the pathway for attunement. In the 1970s, my father, who had recently left both my mother and his job as a minister, wanted to respond to Buber's call. He developed the Center on the Ridge, an organization that sought to help people connect to one another more authentically. In his book, *People Skills*, my father describes listening in this way: "Listening is the combination of hearing what the other person says and a suspenseful waiting, an intense psychological involvement with the other." He goes on to describe the two listening skills that are essential for attunement: attending and reflecting. "Attending is giving your physical attention to another person. I sometimes refer to it as listening with the whole body." He describes reflective responses as "providing a mirror to the speaker." In the same way that our facial expressions show our attunement to our infant, good listening skills echo the thoughts and feelings of our child, letting them know that we understand their feelings, helping them to feel seen and heard. In our best moments, attunement helps them understand their own feelings more deeply, as our mimicking helps infants understand their feelings for the first time. This is the essence of attunement.

The challenge is that attunement is other-focused, while we are so often self-focused. I worry, for instance, that the attunement with our children will be disrupted by our focus on our smartphones. Rather than looking into the eyes of our infant and mimicking their expressions as they sit on our laps, we hold them in one hand and scroll through our social media feeds with the other. The expressions on our face, then, will not match the internal experience of our children. This is also true as our children get older. Our media distractions keep us from being in tune with one another's subtle but essential emotional cues.

Other things can be barriers to attunement. Busy schedules undermine our ability to be fully present with one another. Our own anxiety and depression can understandably make us less available to focus on the emotional life of our child or student. And in arguments, as we will find out in the next section, our dysregulation inhibits our ability to be empathetically attuned to others.

Attunement is about being present. Often this means spending time doing things that may seem tedious and unimportant in our busy world. Dropping a screw onto a windowsill, over and over. We don't have to be perfect. We don't have to be ever-present and ever-available. But we do need to be available and present often enough to help our children to feel seen, heard, and understood. This creates the foundation for our relationships and, consequently, our resilience. We need to set aside our needs and busy lives, even if it is just for a few minutes each day, to attune. Through play. Through listening. Through being present. Their bodies and minds relax and engage. They connect. They learn. They develop.

It's OK to Get It Wrong

Even when we are fully present, we can get it wrong. And that's ok. Research indicates that we often get it wrong. Resilience comes from continuing to work with our child to get it right.

Dr. Edward Tronick is a developmental psychologist who studied infant/parent interactions. His "still face" experiment, conducted in the 1970s, explored the idea of a "mismatch," the moment that a parent falls out of attunement with their baby. In his now-famous video, there is a split screen of a mother playing with her child. One camera is on the face of an infant strapped into a high chair in an office. Another camera focuses on the face of the mother playing with her child. Expressive and engaged, the mother responds to her infant, looking where she points, mimicking her facial expressions, holding her baby's hands. Suddenly, the mother turns away, and when she turns back to look at her baby, the mother's face is transformed—it is limp, passive, unresponsive. Her child notices immediately and begins to work to re-engage her mother. Smiling, giggling, and pointing, she puts on the charm that has always caught her mother's attention and prompted her mother's typical and reciprocal response. But this time, it doesn't work. The infant's distress appears as a wave of emotion and flurry of panicked activity. She begins to screech and cry before turning away. She is devastated. As I watch, I absorb the baby's distress. My heart rate quickens. I notice I'm holding my breath. I, too, want to turn away. After an interminable minute and a half, the mother finally leans in, her face comes to life, her voice is soft and caring. She is back. She holds her baby's hands, saying, "I'm here, I'm here." I can start breathing again.

Tronick demonstrated that from birth, "rather than being a passive recipient, a new baby was an active participant in relationships." He also was showing the impact of not being attuned and attentive to the emotional lives of our children. In healthy parent-child relationships, there is a continuous effort between an infant and their parents to be attuned to one another. He labeled the moments when parent and child are not attuned as "mismatches" and showed how both baby and parent become desperate to resolve them. When a parent doesn't pick up a child's signals, the child usually signals again and again until the parent realizes what the baby wants and then responds appropriately. Tronick found that 34 percent of mothers in his study recognized the baby's need after the second signal. Another 36 percent nailed it on the third try. "Infants and their mothers are constantly moving into mismatch states and then successfully repairing them," says Tronick. In his observations of parents with their infants, he found that up to 70 percent of interactions were out of sync and, as a result, we are always working to get back into rhythm with one another. Relationships are messy, and our ability to work together to repair them is essential for healthy attachment. He describes this as "interactive error and interactive repair." It is natural to be out of sync with our child. The key is always in the repair.

In infancy, then, children are beginning to develop templates for how relationships work, for how responsive the world will be to their needs. When children identify the mismatch and find a way to repair it through pointing, or a facial expression or noise, they learn that they can act on the world to make it better. Infants with parents who were not responsive to their efforts to engage and repair were not so hopeful and eventually gave up trying to reconnect with their parent. Without a parent to partner with them to resolve the mismatch, stress hormones begin to flood an infant's brain and body.

These interactions are formative. A baby's brain is being wired through these interactions to prepare them for the world they are entering. When we make efforts to be attuned, our children can trust the world to be responsive to their needs. If we are not attuned and don't persist in an attempt to resolve the mismatch, the infant experiences a sense of helplessness, feeling alone and finding it difficult to trust that their needs will be met. Tronick makes one important point very clear: We will often get it wrong. Children just need to know that we are in it with them, working together to bridge the gap when we are not aligned.

As a parent, I found Tronick's research comforting. About 70 percent of our interactions with our infants are out of sync. And it is in the process of repair that we bridge these gaps between their world and our world. We don't need to be perfect, we just need to be present and notice when we don't get it right. And when we get it wrong, our work is just to repair. Whether it is finding the right toy that our infant is pointing at or understanding why our child is so upset after a Little

League game, when we get it wrong, we always have the opportunity to make it right. And then, by making it right, our children learn how to make it right when they get something wrong. Our children are constantly watching us and learning from us. As James Baldwin said, "Children have never been very good at listening to their elders, but they have never failed to imitate them."

Knowing that when things go badly, we can make them right, is the building block of resilience. Rather than becoming frustrated at the mismatch, we can see it as an opportunity to teach them to repair. When we get it wrong, we just need to hang in with them until we get it right. The more mismatches we address, the more our children learn how to manage mismatches in their own lives. The more they experience the power of attunement.

Years before Tronick was doing his research, mid-twentieth-century psychoanalyst and pediatrician D. W. Winnicott was challenging the prevailing parenting theory dominated by prescriptive directions from behaviorism, when common wisdom was that a child's success depended on how strictly parents adhered to a reinforcement and punishment schedule. Winnicott believed differently. He acknowledged the inevitability of the occasional failure and embraced it. He believed that mothers didn't need to be perfect—they only needed to be "good enough." He went on to say that "children and babies actually benefit when their mothers fail them in manageable ways." When adults fail their children but remain present and loving and connected, then the child realizes that when life takes a hard turn, or unexpected events happen, they will be ok. If we forget to pick up our child at practice, they learn that they can find their way home. When we lose our temper with them but later apologize, they learn how to repair relationships after we have damaged them. It may be frustrating or hurtful, but it is also formative. These are the early building blocks of resilience. Tronick's research highlighted that these errors are not only "inevitable but essential" for a child's healthy development. It is in our consistent efforts to seek resolution when things inevitably go wrong, rather than striving for perfection, that primes children for connection and resilience.

If, for whatever reason, a parent is not able to be attentive and responsive to their child, other people and other communities can fill in the gaps. The plasticity of the child's brain allows for recovery. Skill development is based on repetition. The more unresolved mismatches there are early in life, the more repairs of mismatches need to happen later in life for a child to learn to trust in relationships. Mismatches between adults and their children occur throughout the span of the relationship. They also happen in classrooms between teachers and students. They happen between players and coaches. Between aunts and uncles and nieces and nephews. Our work as adults is to be attuned to these mismatches and to work, often imperfectly, with the child, to resolve them. We need to be partners. We don't need to be perfect.

Despite early childhood experiences of parents who are unable to be responsive to children's needs, insecure attachment can be reversed by attuned relationships later in life. One of the most powerful ways to do this is to be responsive to children's bids for connection.

Bids for Connection

I remember one of my favorite times as a parent was when I was walking with one of my young children and I felt them reach up and put their hand in mine. Now that my kids are adults, I often get that same thrill of connection when they text or call. In each of these moments, they stir me from what I am thinking about and turn my focus to them. That is the magic of a bid.

When we are in search of connection with another, we make a bid. Psychologist and researcher John Gottman describes bids for attention as, "the fundamental unit of connection." Bids are not just for children.

As adults, we are constantly making bids in our relationships and how we respond to one another's bids forms the foundation of our relationships. Gottman found that couples who stayed married "turned toward" their partners' bids 86 percent of the time, while those who eventually divorced turned toward their spouse's bids only 33 percent of the time. Healthy relationships require us to acknowledge, to turn toward, one another when we are seeking connection.

The tricky part about bids is that they look different for different people at different ages and in different situations. Younger children may sit on our lap or grab our hand, showing us something they are proud of. They may want to share something new they experienced. After watching a thirty-minute cartoon when she was in preschool, my daughter Anna would spend thirty-five minutes describing the whole show to us. We loved our daughter, but we came to dread her scene-by-scene re-creations of *Dora the Explorer.* When upset, younger children may throw things or yell and scream, seeking our connection. Older children may say things to provoke us, tease us, make jokes at our expense, or use sarcasm to engage us more covertly. We welcome some of these bids, but other bids may be more annoying or even anger us. We often describe the more annoying bids as "attention seeking" and our response is to do "planned ignoring" to "extinguish" the behavior. Each of these examples are moments of mismatch. Just as with our infant, our work is to try to resolve the mismatch and reconnect rather than create further distance and reject the bid and, thus, the bidder.

Children who make ineffective bids are often those who have two factors working against them. First, they struggle with the skills of making effective bids. When they have tried to make bids within a family that is unresponsive, those bids have gone unnoticed or, worse, have been met with rejection and shame. This often leads to the second issue. When children have a history of failed bids, they may seek to connect while also seeking to protect themselves. The best way to engage another person while also protecting yourself is to connect with conflict.

I watched this happen in one of our middle school classrooms. When you walked into Mr. Hayes's class, there was no doubt where he grew up. Green Bay Packers flags were on the wall. Green and yellow pennants were hanging from both sides of his whiteboard. Every Friday during football season he wore his beloved Brett Favre jersey. One of his students, Jason, struggled to connect, and he managed this struggle by rejecting others publicly. He didn't have a friend in the class and most of the staff were also wary of interacting with him. He frequently provoked other students and disrupted lessons. He also let it be known that he believed that football is a stupid game.

On a Tuesday morning, following a Monday-night loss to the hometown Chicago Bears, Mr. Hayes was greeted in class by a loud and buoyant Jason, making a "bid" for Mr. Hayes's attention. Jason couldn't contain himself. "Ha! Your team SUCKS!" he yelled, laughing and mocking. "They couldn't even make a field goal at the end! It's no surprise that a sucky teacher would love a sucky team." A teaching assistant intervened and took Jason out of the room to keep him from further disrupting class.

Two questions arise. The first is, how is this a bid? And why would Jason make a bid in a way that so clearly would annoy Mr. Hayes?

A glance at his history can give a glimpse into Jason's dilemma. An only child born to a depressed mother and a violent father, Jason's bids in infancy likely went unreturned by his mother and were met with angry outbursts by his father. Following his father's incarceration and parents' subsequent divorce when he was six, his mother soon remarried and, wanting to start a new life for herself, insisted that Jason live with his paternal uncle, who resided out of state. At a very young age, life had taught Jason painful lessons about attachment. He is caught between a strong innate and evolutionary pull to connect with others and his experience that he is unworthy of connection and that trying to connect is both futile and painful.

So how is this mocking of his teacher a bid? First, Jason knew that his teacher would feel badly about his team losing. In other words, he has empathy for Mr. Hayes. Second, his understanding of the missed field goal shows that, although he doesn't like football, he watched the game or read about it, presumably out of interest in his teacher. Finally, he used this knowledge to engage Mr. Hayes.

Why would he make a bid that pushed Mr. Hayes away? The short answer is that many of us do this. I worked with a family where the teenager's primary way of connecting with his father was by mocking him. This predictably made his father angry, but this was the only way the boy had figured out how to get a response from his father who always seemed preoccupied with work or watching sports. Similarly, I often notice myself in arguments with my wife, Kathy, saying things just to keep the conflict going, as if losing the connection is more threatening than the argument itself. For children with insecure attachment, connection through conflict is often a painful but safer way to navigate relationships. Their ambivalence about connecting leads them to reach out in clumsy or offensive ways, allowing them to stay engaged but distant, safer from the unpredictability and potential disappointment of a more intimate connection. We often find that adolescents use these provocative bids to navigate their existential challenge of separating from parents while still staying connected to them. As a result, they stay connected to us while also asserting their independence through this engaged conflict.

Our work, then, is to respond to these bids by reconnecting and teaching. If we can see the provoking through the lens of attachment, we can protect ourselves from experiencing it as a personal attack. Then, we can acknowledge the bid, engage in a discussion, and teach another way of engaging. The goal is to help Jason trust that he is worthy of connection, and, in doing so, we can help him learn to make bids that don't push others away.

Mr. Hayes soon joined Jason in the hallway. He saw this moment as a chance to connect and teach. "You are right, Jason, that was a painful loss! It sounds like you watched the game. Once we get things settled for homeroom, I want to hear about how great your Bears played." Then, after taking his licks from Jason, he could ask, "I loved talking about the game with you, but it was hard because you were so loud and mocking. Is there another way you could have let me know that you watched the game without being so disruptive?" These skills are teachable within a trusting (and patient) relationship. Every bid is an opportunity to teach and connect.

The interesting thing is that bids are all around us. Most of the time, the bids work to connect us, helping us feel seen and valued. When they are not—when they are hurtful, or clumsy—our work is to see the need behind the bid and meet that need rather than punish the behavior.

Bids are bidirectional. As adults, we, too, make bids for the attention of our children and our students. The sad thing is that the children who struggle most with attachment are the ones who typically get the fewest bids from adults and other children. Children in families and students in classrooms all notice which other children get the bids from adults. Children notice who we make eye contact with, who we laugh with, who we give responsibilities to, how our face lights up—or doesn't—when they walk into the room. For children with secure attachments, these discrepancies are tolerable since they already feel secure about their place in the family or classroom. For children with insecure attachments, these bids we make to other children only further reinforce their feelings of unworthiness and alienation.

Bids are building blocks for attachment, but they often fly under the radar of our conscious awareness. Shining a light on the bids that we make to children and the bids that we receive from them can help us be more attuned and responsive. This volleying of bids back and forth is a partnership to stay connected. Our goal is not to win the point, but to keep the volley going.

Owning Our Attachment Story

Children aren't the only ones with attachment issues—each of us carries our own attachment stories into our parenting and teaching. It is our attachment story that often determines how we respond to children who struggle most with attachment.

The journey to understand how my attachment story impacted my roles as psychologist, principal, and parent was a humbling one. My father carried himself with a quiet reserve except when he exploded in laughter during tickle fights or in anger when we broke one of his rules. My mother, as a loyal preacher's wife, was always ready with a casserole for the potluck or could be seen on the couch crafting the felt flags that decorated the worship spaces. She was also more relaxed, often becoming a coconspirator in undermining my father's rules, when he was away. Our house was the parsonage of the Methodist church that sat in the shadows of Syracuse University. It was big, with many places to play and hide. Between my mother and Jenny, a Syracuse University student and our live-in babysitter, we were given the freedom to explore the world and safe arms to return to whenever we bloodied our knees or felt left out of the neighborhood game. We summered at our cabin in the Adirondack Mountains. It was a cottage my father designed, on the shore of a beautiful mountain lake. I like to imagine that my attachment back then was secure. Then I turned six.

My parents' divorce is a black hole in my memory. It's as if two years of photographs were deleted from my hard drive after their separation. I must have spent those years feeling frightened and lost. As an adult, I saw a video taken a few weeks after we found out that they were divorcing. It was my birthday and the video shows my excitement

opening my gifts, running around on the deck of the cabin, and hug-
ging my new stuffed polar bear. Then the video shifts abruptly to a
new scene. I'm taking a big breath, wearing a cone-shaped birthday
hat, my family seated around the dining room table. As I finish blowing out the candles, my huge smile is juxtaposed with the image of my
father, unshaven in white T-shirt, sad and sullen. Before seeing the
video, I would remember this as my favorite birthday, filled with the
biggest and best gifts of my childhood. In the following years, however, I began to dread my birthday, a feeling that I experience to this
day. The unacknowledged grief that we were all feeling that day, the
last day that we were together as a family, still shows up, unconsciously
like poisoned groundwater rising from deep in the earth just as my
birthday nears.

I do remember feeling the loss of both parents. In order to stay
afloat as my family plunged into chaos, I did my best not to rock the
boat. I was small and skinny and scared. When feelings got hot, I got
quiet. As we look back now, our ways of coping with our childhood
have followed each of us into adulthood—into our work, and our families, and our friendships.

I did my clinical psychology internship at Children's Memorial
Hospital (now Lurie Children's Hospital) in Chicago. My supervisor,
Karen Gouze, was gentle but direct as we watched the video of the
family therapy session I led. "Watch," she coached me. "As the conflict
grows, you get quieter. Where did your voice go?" At first, I was defensive. I shared my clinical reasoning. "I wanted to empower them to
find their own solution." The wonderful thing about being a psychologist is that we can always reason our way out of acknowledging how
our own issues impact our work. Karen was not buying it. The losses
from my childhood had a long tail, showing up in my work as a therapist, decades later. Just as I did as a child, when the feelings got hot, I
became anxious and tried to disappear.

As an individual therapist, I was able to quickly connect with the charismatic but angry students. Given how much conflict I experienced with my siblings, I was able to tolerate their fury. I could see beneath their rage at the pain and loss in their lives. I struggled, however, with students who were quirky. I seemed less interested in the children who were less volatile. I found that I needed a certain amount of chaos to be fully present with them. I also realized that goodbyes are very challenging for me. When it is time for someone I care about to move on, the valve controlling my feelings turns off. I find myself wanting to ignore endings, and I often find myself avoiding opportunities to bring closure to years of therapy or friendship. I need to coach myself to stay present so that I can feel the loss without being overwhelmed by it.

My attachment story doesn't just take away from my work; indeed, it can enhance it. I feel like I have an unspoken connection to families that have experienced loss. My connection to my mother during her journey as a single parent helps me intuitively understand the journey of single parents. Growing up, I learned to be flexible in my relationships—always trying to find ways to keep the peace. This allows me to be adaptive and to find ways of connecting to children who are hard for others to connect with.

Reflecting on my attachment story is more difficult to absorb as a parent, yet it is even more important. When it comes to my family, I frequently find myself needing to feel in control and valued. When either of those is in doubt, it can tap an anger that arrives unexpectedly and persists. As skilled as I am at connecting with others socially and professionally, in conflict with family I often lose my temper and then retreat. As committed as I am to put my family's needs before mine, when I feel threatened, I quickly become self-focused. When I'm calm again, I feel waves of shame as I see clearly how this volatility impacts the people I love. I am always surprised at how my training in psychology and my years as a principal have not been more helpful to me as I deal with my own attachment challenges.

Being able to understand and reflect on our own attachment history is essential to helping others rewrite theirs. There will be moments when our stories make us less attuned to others. However, as we discovered in Tronick's research, it is not the disconnection that defines a resilient relationship. It is the repair and reconnection that are transformative. Our attachment stories are both our greatest threat and our greatest gift in our ability to be resilient.

Greg Boyle cautions us about the cost of not being aware of our own stories. "If we don't welcome our own wounds," he writes, "we may be tempted to despise the wounded." One of the greatest challenges we have in caring for children, as teachers and as parents, is that in order to be fully present, we need to be aware of our own pain. We need to find a way to welcome our own wounds. This enables us to be resilient in the face of children who challenge us. Otherwise, we unintentionally inflict our own histories of shame and hurt on children who desperately need us to connect, to grow, and to thrive.

PART II

Regulation: Managing Our Hardest Moments

CHAPTER 4

Why We Melt Down

He screamed when he saw me. "Fuck you, Bolton!" Dylan had just gotten off the bus and entered the building. Scott and Mike, our two deans, moved in front of him, obstructing his path to me. Though Dylan was only a freshman, he was tall, strong, and easy to spot with the dirty-blond mop of hair framing his deep-set eyes and square jaw. He had been with us for several months, and we never knew when his charm would turn into raw and unabating anger. On that day, he skipped the charm.

He pointed at me. "I'm going to fucking kill you!" His words spewed from his mouth, eyes wild. Now he was bumping into Scott and Mike, trying to push through them. I had no idea why Dylan was angry with me. He and I had a good relationship. I took a step toward him, trying to connect. Scott shook his head slightly, signaling "Not now." I moved away as Dylan lunged at me, and the three of them fell to the ground in a controlled chaos. Once on the ground, Dylan had more leverage, and more people jumped in to hold him—feet, knees, hips. He continued to scream. "I hate you, Bolton! When they let me up, I'm going to fuck you up!"

Dylan wouldn't calm down with me there, so I left. Scott and Mike, struggling to restrain his relentless fury, decided to call the police. Handcuffed, Dylan towered over one of the officers as they escorted him out of the building. I watched from a distance, knowing that if he saw me, it would escalate again quickly. As he left, Dylan yelled five words that echoed throughout the school.

"THANKS FOR THE FUCKING CHILI!"

Dylan was referred to us after a hard transition from middle school to high school. Teachers described him as impulsive, disrespectful, confrontational with other students, and disengaged academically. His early days at NSA were no different. But as we got to know him better, we also grew enamored of his wit, his strong sense of honor, and unwavering loyalty. He began to connect with students and staff, and over time was able to engage more academically. We had also begun to build a partnership with his mother. His parents were first-generation immigrants working hard to build a life in a wealthy suburb of Chicago. His father's masonry business was successful, enabling him to comfortably raise four children. Dylan's mother was a very active parent. We quickly realized that Dylan's unwavering loyalty must have come from her. She would always side with him against the school, believing that Dylan's behavior was the result of bias and mistreatment by our staff. Through her anger, we began to understand why she was so protective of Dylan. She shared her hopes and dreams that he would be the first in his family to graduate from college. She also shared her worries about him—how he struggled with his temper and how school had always been so hard for him both academically and behaviorally. Slowly, she began to trust us, and we became better partners and a stronger team. As Dylan watched his mother's trust in us grow, he, too, began to let down his guard. "I should get an office here," she once joked. "I'm here almost every day!"

One morning, she came into school to deliver the bad news in person: she had breast cancer. In the months ahead, she would face rounds of chemotherapy and radiation. We promised to do whatever we could, and within a day, set up a "meal train" with staff and parents volunteering to cook dinners for the family so that she could focus on her treatment. As the meals arrived, Dylan took pride in being the oldest son, providing in this way for his family.

Then, it was my turn to deliver dinner. A parent had made a big pot of chili with corn bread. All I had to do was drop it off at the house. As Dylan was leaving school for the day, I quickly took him into the teacher's lounge, opened the refrigerator, and showed him the pot I would be bringing over. He smiled and hugged me, almost giddy with excitement. "My family is going to love this!"

My workday was almost done when I got called to the district administration building. There was a budget issue that needed to be resolved that afternoon. I rushed back to my office and dove into the spreadsheet, trying to figure out where I had gone wrong. Lost in the numbers, I looked at my watch and realized that I was late picking up Matthew and Anna from their grandparents' house. I rushed to get them, forgetting all about the chili in the refrigerator. Forgetting all about Dylan. Until he was in handcuffs.

We didn't press charges, explaining to the officer that our goal in calling them was to make sure Dylan was safe. His mother picked him up at the police station and brought him back to school. They walked into my office, and before they could speak, I said, "I am so sorry." Dylan hung his head. "I'm sorry, too." He wrapped his long arms around me and squeezed, tight. We all sat down. His mother rubbed his back. She looked at her son, shook her head, and laughed. "The funny thing is that we had plenty of food left over from other meals. What got into you? You need to control your temper. Why would you threaten Dr. Bolton that way?"

"I don't know, Mom," he said, staring at the floor. "I really don't know."

Dylan wasn't the only one who didn't know. I was in the process of trying to understand why kids at NSA melted down so often. Theories of motivation didn't seem to hold up at times like these. Dylan wasn't motivated to hurt me or frighten me. As I began to reflect on the research I was reading, and as I watched people who were most successful with the most challenging kids, a different story began to emerge. Dylan's anger wasn't an issue of motivation. It was about emotional regulation.

Emotional regulation refers to our ability to cope effectively with our emotions. It is the key that unlocks our understanding of how we manage our hardest moments. We are emotionally regulated when there is a balance between the resources we have and the resources we need at any given moment. Physically, our bodies are constantly making adjustments to meet the needs of our environment. When we are physically dysregulated, our body is out of balance, and it reacts with an equal and opposite response. When our body temperature goes up, we sweat to cool ourselves down. When we feel restless, our body wants to move. If we are hungry, we seek food. Emotionally, we follow a similar pattern to address an imbalance. When we feel out of control, we seek control. When we feel disconnected, we seek connection.

As Dylan's story illustrates, *attachment* and *regulation* are the yin and yang of our emotional lives, each constantly interacting and impacting the other. They are complementary, interconnected, and interdependent. Dylan felt betrayed by me, and it triggered intense anger. This is not uncommon. When our relationships are threatened, we become emotionally dysregulated. Similarly, when we are dysregulated, our behavior can significantly threaten our relationships with others. It is not just Dylan, or students at NSA, who struggle with emotional regulation. We all do. Think about the last time that you lost your temper. The last time that you felt really angry or hurt. What did you look like? What did you sound like? What dumb thing did you do or say? When we are dysregulated, we all say and do things that are self-defeating and often hurt those we care most about. The big question is, "Why?"

Discovering Dysregulation

The science of emotional regulation, in many ways, began in September of 1848 with a man named Phineas Gage. Gage wasn't a scientist or doctor. He was a twenty-five-year-old foreman on a railroad crew in Vermont. Railroad workers used explosives in order to lay flat train tracks in the hilly and rocky terrain of the Green Mountains. Holes were drilled into the rocks, filled with explosive materials, and then covered with sand or clay to force the blast back into the rock. Gage's job was to use an iron tamping rod to pack the holes before the fuse was lit. One afternoon, just south of the town of Cavendish, as Gage was tamping, he accidentally created a spark, igniting the explosive and propelling the tamping rod out of the hole and directly into his face. The rod entered through his left cheek and made a clear exit through the top of his skull, landing about eighty feet away, taking with it a large chunk of Gage's brain, the area now called the prefrontal cortex (PFC). Despite this injury, shortly after the blast, Gage was able to walk with little assistance. He rode a horse-drawn carriage to town and sat, waiting for the doctor. He was even able to talk and maintained his sense of humor. When the doctor arrived, Gage said, "Doctor, here is business enough for you." Gage survived following a lengthy recovery and, other than losing his left eye, he appeared physically unfazed. Yet he was not the same man. People around him noticed emotional and behavioral changes. His friend described Gage as "fitful, irreverent, indulging at times in the grossest profanity (which was not previously his custom) . . . obstinate yet capricious and vacillating." He had changed so much that those who knew him before the accident said that he was "no longer Gage." This is how Phineas Gage was the first person to give us a glimpse into the power of the prefrontal cortex (PFC).

As it turns out, the PFC is essential for helping us successfully navigate our world. Neuroscientist Robert Sapolsky defines the PFC this way: "It makes you do the harder thing when it is the right thing to do." It is the part of the brain that helps us to get off the couch to do the laundry, create an outline before diving into writing the essay, and bite our tongue when we are tempted to say the thing that we really shouldn't say. Planning, judgment, impulse control, attention, and emotional regulation are just a few of the ways that our PFC helps us manage the challenges of our day. Because of Gage, we have known for more than 150 years that damage to the PFC causes the same problems we often see in ourselves and our children when we are melting down. When dysregulated, I, too, can become "fitful," "irreverent," and, yes, I have been known to "indulge, at times, in the grossest profanity." But we have not experienced a catastrophic brain injury. Why is it, then, that sometimes we can be so reasonable, and other times, like Gage after the accident, so mindlessly reactive?

The Things We Lose

In the 1960s, physician Paul MacLean developed a model for understanding how our brain works that he coined the "triune brain." In retrospect, given the remarkable advances in brain science since then, this model can be seen as overly simplistic, especially to a neuroscientist. Still, it can be a helpful tool, perhaps a metaphor, to help us find a path through the complexity of the human brain. In particular, it can help us understand why, at times, adults and children can act in ways that are irrational and self-defeating.

Although common wisdom suggests that the human brain is driven by rational thought, a glimpse into how we behave in our worst moments suggests otherwise. The truth is that our brain, like the brain of every other creature, is built for survival first and foremost. Self-preservation is our default setting. When our survival is at stake, we act in ways that can seem wildly irrational. Why does our rational brain desert us when we seem to need it the most?

MacLean's triune brain provides an answer. According to this theory, our brain is made up of three main parts: the cortex, the limbic system, and the brain stem. Each part has its own responsibilities and its own timeline for development.

Cortex: This is the part we usually think of when we think of our brain. It is the control center of rational thought and manages tasks like organization, language, emotional regulation, problem-solving, and retaining and accessing knowledge. In many ways, our cortex is what separates us from the rest of the animal kingdom. We are able to think abstractly, peer into the future and reflect on the past, and take the perspective of other people. The prefrontal cortex sits at the front of our brain, nestled behind our forehead. It is the slowest part of our brain to grow, not completing development until our late twenties or early thirties.

Limbic System: The limbic system is our alarm system. Its job is to keep us alive by identifying threats. It also tells us what is safe and good so that we can quickly access the things around us that sustain our survival. It is the part of our brain that holds on to our feeling memories of past good and bad experiences so we can embrace positive experiences and steer clear of repeating potentially fatal mistakes. Because its job is to keep us alive, the limbic system makes us act quickly, without waiting for the slower, more rational cortex to weigh in. In an emergency that requires us to act in a split second, if we wait for our cortex to fully assess what is going on, we will react too late. That's why so often under stress we "act without thinking." Unlike the PFC, the limbic system typically completes development in a child's early teenage years.

Brain Stem: The brain stem is located in the lower part of the brain and is responsible for all of the automatic functions that keep us alive. It regulates our heart rate, breathing, appetite, and body temperature, among other things. Importantly, it is the part of our brain that triggers our stress response, enabling our bodies to fight or flee within a split second to address a potential threat. When there is no threat, it establishes homeostasis, keeping our body systems balanced and efficient. Damage to the brain stem is often fatal because these functions are vital to our survival. It is fully developed at birth, ready to take over all of these functions as soon as the fetus leaves the womb.

Survival is our brain's main focus, and these three parts of our brain work together to ensure our safety. I picture the limbic system as the center of a seesaw with our brain stem on one side and our cortex on the other. The limbic system, based on our history of past experiences, is constantly scanning our environment, assessing whether we are safe or in danger. If it determines that we are safe, our brain stem tilts the seesaw in favor of homeostasis, allowing us to fully access the cortex so we can engage in higher-order thinking. Our brain is open for learning, connecting with others, solving problems, and thinking broadly about the world.

However, if our limbic system tilts us in the other direction, the brain stem activates our stress response system to protect us from a perceived threat. A cascade of neurotransmitter and hormone activity prepares the body to defend itself. Every system in our bodies is activated—our musculoskeletal, endocrine, respiratory, reproductive, gastrointestinal, nervous, and cardiovascular systems are all involved in a well-coordinated battle to address the threat. This is our fight/flight/freeze response. Our heart rate increases and pushes our blood to our skeletal muscles so that we can fight and flee. Our pancreas pumps out blood sugar to give us energy. Our pupils dilate, letting more light in so that we can see threats more clearly. Our breathing rate increases to get more oxygen into our bloodstream. Our digestive system shuts down to preserve energy.

Our cortex also shuts down, for two reasons. First, we don't want the cortex's slow and deliberate analysis, reflection, or information processing to get in the way of acting NOW. Second, because our bodies are gearing up to fight or flee, we need energy. Our bodies respond by shutting down those parts of our brain that use the most energy.

What body part is the most energy-expensive? Our brain. While it takes up only 2 percent of our body mass, it uses up 20 percent of our energy. To preserve energy, we shut down our cortex and the brain stem takes over.

In this process, we lose the cortical tools we need the most to think, connect, and problem solve. Some of these skills include the following:

· Listening
· Creativity
· Flexibility
· Empathy
· Memory
· Language
· Inhibition

Interestingly, if you ask most teachers what skills they need their students to be able to access to be successful in their classroom, they would list these seven qualities. Children need to be emotionally regulated in order to learn. Adults need these skills to bring our best selves to our work and our families. Prior to learning about the science of emotional regulation, I often wondered why I can behave so poorly with the people I love and care about. It doesn't matter that I'm a psychologist. When my stress response is triggered, like everyone else, I lose these very important skills. I start to resemble Phineas Gage. Kathy, my wife, will be happy to confirm this. In thirty years of marriage, I have melted down more than a few times and never during those meltdowns did I say or do the following:

· "Hey, honey, I've been doing all the talking. Let me be a better listener for you."
· "I'll bet if we are creative, we can come up with an idea that neither of us has thought of yet!"

· "We did it my way last time. I can be flexible, let's do it your way."
· "I've been so focused on me, but this must have been even harder for you."

Memory during stressful interactions is often wildly inaccurate. Our language changes. When I'm upset, the only words that come out of my mouth are four letters long—and I feel like I have to yell them. Or I'm so upset I can't find the words. And so many times, I think, *I shouldn't say/do that. It will only make things worse.* And then, sure enough, seconds later, I do it or say it. And, sure enough, it makes things worse.

In these moments, I want to be that person who is a good listener, who is creative and flexible, empathetic, remembers details of the conversation, finds the right words, and refrains from saying or doing anything that could be hurtful. I really want to be that guy! Unfortunately, my brain doesn't allow me to access those skills when I am stressed or feeling threatened. And neither can you. And neither can children. It's about our brain, not about our motivation.

And here is the rub. What do we tell children to do when they are melting down?

· "You need to listen to me."
· "You need to find another way to do this."
· "You need to be flexible. The world doesn't rotate around you."
· "You need to take the perspective of others. Imagine how they feel."
· "Tell me what happened and what you are feeling."
· "Stop doing that."

Our kids can't do any of those things any more than I can when I'm upset. They can't access the parts of the brain necessary to comply any more than I can when I am melting down. But when children struggle to access these skills in the moment, we see them as some combination of disrespectful, defiant, fragile, avoidant, or uncaring.

It is important for children to listen, to reflect, to put into words what is happening for them. The problem, however, is one of timing. We often ask them to react rationally when their brains simply aren't available for that kind of thinking. We need to wait until their cortex is back online. We need to help them regulate their brain so that they can reflect on these questions to better understand what happened, to regain empathy, to understand the impact they've had on others and then to problem solve to make the situation right. Often, that only takes time. Sometimes, just a few minutes.

Why would evolution adapt our brain to go offline under stress? Remember, it is built for survival, and we respond instinctively to immediate threats in three basic ways: we fight, we flee, or we freeze. In crisis, our brain is built to make split-second decisions—the slow and deliberate prefrontal cortex, so essential to higher-order thinking, becomes an obstacle when faced with a direct and imminent threat. When we are face-to-face with an angry grizzly bear, empathy for the bear is not helpful. Active listening and complex and thoughtful language won't do us much good, either. Flexibility and creativity—no time for those. We survive physical threats by putting all our energy into fighting, fleeing, or shutting down completely. And, in these situations, it works. It has kept our species alive for hundreds of thousands of years.

Unfortunately, when we aren't faced with a life-threatening event, the loss of these skills can be problematic, significantly impacting our relationships and our ability to cope with stress. When our stress response is triggered and our cortex goes offline, for example, our language becomes much more primitive. This shift makes sense: when we run from a burning building or from a grizzly bear, we need to communicate using simple words. "Over here!" "Run!" The words need to be quickly heard and understood, but that's all.

The problem is that our modern-day stresses rarely involve grizzly bears. Our stresses tend to be social, and the skills we most urgently need go offline just when we need them the most. When I become angry, my language becomes simple. I yell. Or I become silent, shutting down and not talking. This response would be helpful if I was in danger, but not so helpful when I am simply stressed by issues at home or at school. The fight, flight, or freeze response to relationship crises can cause big problems. Evolution has yet to catch up with the realities of our modern lives.

The Many Faces of Dysregulation

Emotional dysregulation has many faces. Classically, it is the screaming child melting down in the grocery store or fighting with a sibling. But it is also a parent yelling at their children when they are misbehaving. It shows up in other ways, too—such as in daydreaming, avoiding, and pacing. It is feeling overwhelmed and tearful, defiant, and defensive. It is the butterflies in our stomach before we give a toast at a wedding, and it is the tension in our neck we don't notice until the end of the day. It is the inflexibility that shows up when dealing with our partner or colleagues. It is found in moments when we lack the empathy for others despite caring deeply about them.

What triggers our dysregulation? Both physical and emotional factors come into play. Our bodies begin to bark at us when our basic needs aren't being met. Being hangry, for example, is a real thing. Sitting too long can make us antsy. Being tired can lead to irritability. I'm a much better parent at 9:00 a.m. than I am at 9:00 p.m. after a busy and stressful day. Unfortunately, my kids seldom see me at 9:00 a.m. and are stuck with their cranky 9:00 p.m. father most of the time. They have no idea what a good father I am.

Emotional factors involve feeling *disempowered*, *disconnected*, and *devalued*. I consider these to be the holy trinity of dysregulation. They quickly tilt the limbic seesaw in the direction of our brain stem, triggering our stress response. The three feelings have something important in common—they are all relational. This is how dysregulation is so deeply intertwined with attachment, and why the dysregulation triggers are so often relational. Dysregulation is a sign that something is wrong and that we need to address the problem. We are hungry—we need to eat. We are tired—we need to sleep. We are disconnected—we need to connect. We are feeling powerless—so we seek power. We are feeling devalued—so we try to prove our worth. This pull is evolutionary.

FOMO (fear of missing out), for example, is embedded in our evolutionary biology. It is a powerful signal that we are in danger of alienation. In our early years as a species, when we relied on community for survival, alienation from the community was certainly fatal. Social rejection, therefore, triggers existential anxiety. To protect us from this threat, evolution has equipped us with a highly sensitive emotional radar system to detect any hint of possible alienation. Often below conscious awareness and within the blink of an eye, we pick up these subtle signals of social disconnection or hostility. Then our body reacts as if our life depends on it, kicking our stress response system into high gear. Unfortunately, when our stress response kicks in, rational thought takes a back seat, and we often lose access to the social skills we need the most to repair the social divide. Rather than building a bridge to reconnect, we often burn the bridge down, escalating the conflict rather than resolving it.

Even evolution has its glitches.

Kids Do Well If They Can

Ross Greene and J. Stuart Ablon's work has helped me understand how to rethink our hardest moments with our kids and students, unraveling behaviorism while also stitching together a new way that we can respond. Greene is a psychiatrist and Ablon is a psychologist who, together, developed a process for helping children when they are melting down. I once saw a video of Greene leading a workshop for educators. The video was a bit grainy and the lighting was poor, but the message couldn't have been more simple and clear. In six words, he captured an essential truth about children that pushed me to pivot even further away from behaviorism:

"Kids do well if they can."

This resonated with me. In all of my years working with children, I had never met one who would rather fail a test than get an A. I'd never met a student who would rather get punished than get praised. He was saying that behavior is based on a child's *skill*. If they have the skill to do well, they will do well.

Then Greene, in his deliberate and folksy way, said to his audience, "Or, kids do well if they wanna." This is the mantra of people who believe that motivation is at the heart of behavior. If they *want* to do well, they will.

He was establishing a dividing line about how we understand behavior. Is behavior based on skills or motivation? If you see behavior through the lens of motivation, you incentivize and punish. If you see behavior through the lens of skills, you teach.

"Doing well," he went on, "is always preferable to not doing well." This, too, instantly rang true.

I sat back in my chair and paused the video. How could I have missed this? Every student I had ever worked with experienced shame and regret when they failed to live up to the expectations of others. It is hard to sit with a chronic sense of shame. As a result, they lied, they bullied, they cheated, they cried, they gave up.

When we follow the trail of a child's meltdown back to its origins, it almost always begins with a struggle to access the skills they need in that moment. When the skills break down, the child melts down. The behaviors are just indications that the child doesn't have the skills in the moment to show up the way they want to or need to.

This pushed me to think differently about students in their hardest moments. After a major incident, I would meet with students and scour their files. I began to notice a trend I had previously overlooked. Almost all of the students described as oppositional and defiant had one thing in common—their neuropsychological testing revealed that they had slow processing speed. This suddenly made sense to me. For children whose world is moving too quickly, oppositional and defiant behavior is a way to bring everything to a stop, to regain control over the situation. I began to understand that when a child becomes oppositional, they are feeling overwhelmed. If they are processing things more slowly, I can help to slow things down so that they do not feel so lost and behind. I can help them catch up before they dig their feet in so deeply that they can't step out.

It is not just oppositional behavior that helps children regain a sense of control when they don't have the skills to manage their world effectively. Avoidance does the same thing. Avoidance is a sign that we don't believe that we have the skills to navigate the situation, and we take control by refusing to engage.

Ablon and Greene take this idea of problem behaviors as skill deficits an important step further. The skill deficits are not a problem for a child if there is not a demand for that skill. Behavior problems occur, then, when there is a *skill deficit* and a *demand for that skill*. I, for instance, can't carry a tune. That's not a problem most of the time because I can easily avoid singing publicly. Want to see me become avoidant and oppositional? Invite me to a karaoke night. Undeveloped athletic skills aren't a problem in a physics classroom but they are in gym class. Struggling to sit still and focusing is not going to be a problem at a skate park, but it may be when reading Shakespeare.

Even if we have the skills, stress can impact our ability to access them. It is harder to stay focused on algebra after your girlfriend broke up with you and you are sitting next to her new boyfriend. It is even harder if you just learned that one of your parents had been diagnosed with cancer. For a child with ADHD it is almost always more difficult to stay focused at the end of a long day. It can feel impossibly difficult to take out the garbage when you are bedridden with the flu.

My daughter Anna is two years younger than Matthew. Unlike Matthew, I think that her prefrontal cortex was fully developed in utero. She came out of the womb with checklists for the doctors. Because of this, many learning experiences came easier to her. She seemed to breeze through the demands of school and home with few struggles or meltdowns. Until Saturday afternoons. When she was seven, I began to notice a pattern that she would become very irritable and impatient when she returned from running errands with Kathy. One Saturday I simply asked how the morning went, and she snapped, "I don't want to talk about it. Just leave me alone!" Then she ran upstairs and slammed her door. I turned to Kathy. "What happened to Anna while you guys were out?"

"Nothing," she said. "We ran our normal errands, but in the last twenty minutes, she just got really irritable."

"What did you guys do for lunch?" I asked, seeing that it was one-thirty.

"Lunch? Oh, we haven't had lunch yet." Ah-ha! Anna was hangry. I can relate. So, I did the thing that most die-hard behaviorists (and nu-tritionists) would cringe at—I made her favorite lunch. Grilled cheese, flaming hot Cheetos, and an apple. Giving her something she likes will only reinforce her irritability, behaviorists would say. You are only teaching her to scream to get what she wants, they'd insist. Never happened. Why? Because kids do well if they can. It is harder for her to do well when she is hungry. So, I took the plate to her room and she snapped at me. "Leave me alone! I'm not hungry!" I left the plate on her dresser and went downstairs. Twenty minutes later, Anna appeared with an empty plate and an apology. And she has yet to melt down in order for me to cook her favorite lunch. She knows that she just needs to ask.

No child is always oppositional or avoidant. There are times when children who are labeled defiant are very compliant. There are times when highly compliant kids become defiant. We often make the simplistic mistake of assuming issues are motivational rather than situational. We say, for example, "They were able to do fine in math yesterday and they were disrespectful today. That shows that they can control their behavior. It must be motivation." Sometimes, I'm more irritable than other times. I am late for some meetings and not others. Often, I'm patient with my kids, but other times, I'm quick to anger. If I had my way, I would never be irritable, late, or impatient. When we see these behaviors as motivational, we completely miss the point and set the stage for then justifying punishments. Rather than punish, we can look for, and address, the underlying skill deficit and why they are struggling with this skill at this moment.

I was discussing an upcoming workshop with a couple of school administrators when one of them said, "I believe in the idea that problem behaviors result from skill deficits, but, c'mon, sometimes kids are just lazy. My son won't leave his video game to practice the piano—that's not a skill, that's just being lazy." Is she right? Is there a skill deficit for her son or is it just laziness?

Do you ever struggle to move from a preferred task to a non-preferred task? That is a skill that, as adults, we often struggle with. If you are binging Netflix and you have to get up to clean the kitchen, do you ever watch another episode before you find your way to the sink?

I think it is helpful to see how this reasoning applies to us as adults. I am highly motivated to be a good father, but there are times when I lose my temper with my children. Do I lack the motivation to be a good parent or are there other factors that get in the way? I struggle to be patient when I am tired or hungry. I am a less courteous driver when I am late for an appointment. Is it possible for me to be patient when I am tired, hungry, or late? Of course it's possible. But it is so much harder.

Behaviors, then, are the result of both a skill deficit and a demand for that skill. If we have a good sense of our children's skill deficits and when the demands for those skills are either too high (frustration) or too low (boredom), then we can help our children navigate their world more successfully.

It also means that most challenging behaviors are predictable. We just need to know the skill deficit and the situations that demand those undeveloped skills. Once we knew that Anna became irritable when she was hungry, we were more intentional about planning meals ahead of time and we carried snacks when we left the house. We also helped Anna be more responsible by having her carry healthy snacks so that she could notice her hunger and eat something before she started to melt down. If we know that a child moves more slowly in the morning, we can be more deliberate about our morning routines. We can help the sleepy child to set the alarm for an earlier time or set their clothes out the night before to compensate for the delay brought on by morning lethargy. Addressing the incompatibility is twofold: teaching the skill and adjusting the demand until they have developed the skill.

I had a special education teacher once say to me, "Will does great in the morning but falls apart in the afternoon. I'm trying to think of incentives and punishments that will encourage him to do well the rest of the day." I observed that he already had the same reinforcers in the morning as he did in the afternoon—a sticker chart with the reward of a soda or extra computer time at the end of the week. Clearly the menu of incentives and punishments wasn't the active ingredient in his success or his struggles. The answer wasn't creating a new sticker chart. Why would he behave differently at different times of day? "I wonder if there is something else that is going on for him." I asked her to think about his struggles through the lens of skills. "He seems to struggle more as the day progresses. I wonder if he struggles with school stamina," she said. "He also seems to have a better relationship with his morning teachers." His struggles were predictable—they happened in the afternoon and with certain teachers. Now we could try some new ideas. If it is his school stamina, does he need more breaks as the day goes on? If he gets along better with his morning teachers, can we help his afternoon teachers develop stronger relationships with him?

Often this thinking can lead to a debate about whether we are enabling children's behavior through these accommodations. However, this is what we do when we see a student struggling with a math concept. We become curious about why they are struggling, we give them more support until they develop a better understanding of the concept. Similarly, when a child learns to hit a baseball, they begin by hitting off of a tee. When I was at NSA, a local youth basketball league asked to use our gym. Their youngest groups of children had a problem—they weren't strong enough to get the ball to the rim when they shot. The coaches did two things. They taught the children to use their legs to power their shots (improving the skill). They also added extensions to the backboard that allowed them to lower the rim (reducing the demand). No one complained that the coaches were "enabling" the children, or "not holding them accountable." They knew that the children would be able to learn how to shoot more quickly and accurately at a regulation-sized basket this way. Why would it be any different for behavioral challenges?

From Mis-Behavior to Stress-Behavior

Looking at behavior as a function of the development of skills rather than motivation requires us to try on new lenses. Stuart Shanker, a psychologist at York University in Toronto and the science director of the MEHRIT Centre, brought the hazy concepts of emotional regulation into even greater focus in his book *Self-Reg*, coauthored with Teresa Barker. His ideas were consistent with my hunch that the most compelling child development theories are also the simplest. His mantra is "mis-behavior is stress-behavior." Stress as the common denominator in mis-behavior seemed so obvious and yet so novel. I know that every time I have melted down, I've been stressed. Every time I have struggled to show up the way that I would like to as a parent or a spouse or a principal, I have been stressed. Why would it be any different for children?

Shanker breaks down stress into five categories:

1. Physical Stresses: Feeling hungry, tired, sick, hot, or cold, having sensory issues—all of these things can make us irritable. I remember hearing the term "hangry" for the first time and believing that the term was coined just for me. I'm irritable when I'm tired or sick. I become very impatient and impulsive and struggle to focus when I'm in rush hour traffic. Some children are highly sensitive to sensory issues—the feeling of their clothes on their skin or the buzzing of a fluorescent lightbulb can feel like an attack on their regulation system. I've got half a century of self-awareness that children don't have, and I still struggle to cope with my physical stressors effectively. Why would I expect a seven-year-old or a seventeen-year-old to cope better with physical stresses than I can?

2. Emotional Stresses: As children explore and gain more experience in the world, they feel emotions for the first time, and those emotions often come with varying degrees of intensity. While their emotional development gives them increasingly sophisticated skills to manage these emotions, their changing brain and body chemistry means that they are constantly needing to understand these emotions in new ways. The feeling of rejection is different at age six when you aren't invited to the birthday party than at sixteen when your first love breaks your heart and again at thirty-six when your spouse asks for a divorce. Being angry with your parents because they won't buy you candy at the grocery store feels very different from the anger of being grounded as a teenager and different again, later in life, when your parents criticize how you parent your own children. Even as an adult, emotions will catch me off guard. I can wake up sad one morning and not be sure why. Some days I feel like my career is fulfilling and meaningful, and other days I feel crushed by a sense of discouragement and frustration. My emotional life is ever changing, often without warning. How hard it must be for our children to learn to surf the waves of their emotional lives.

3. Cognitive Stresses: We experience cognitive stress when we overuse our cortex. To think and learn, we need to pay attention, ignore distractions, juggle multiple thoughts at the same time, access our memory, plan, and reflect. The brain burns through a lot of energy when we are engaged in cognitive tasks. Taking the SAT, for example, is exhausting. Students are mustering all of their energy to focus on the questions. They are also constantly inhibiting their desire to get up and move around, to talk to a friend, and to check a social media feed. For children who struggle with attention and whose internal motor runs faster than the rest of us, the inactivity of school is particularly hard. We complain about how impulsive these students can be, but my guess is that they have had to inhibit many more impulses than less impulsive children throughout the sedentary school day. For every impulsive act we see, they have inhibited dozens of others. The challenge is that cognitive stress wears us down and our cognitive resources begin to wane. Then, once those resources are depleted, it is harder to hold back our impulses. That's why at the end of the day I'm more irritable. It's also the reason why ninth-period study hall is so hard for students with ADHD (and for their teacher).

4. Social Stresses: When I asked you earlier to think of the last time you melted down, my guess is that, at its core, the immediate trigger for your meltdown was social. This is because we experience social stresses so intensely. Remember the holy trinity of dysregulation is all about our social relationships—feeling disconnected, devalued, and powerless. Also, remember how we have evolved to be a social species—threats to our relationships equate to threats to our survival, which quickly kicks our stress response into overdrive.

5. Prosocial Stresses: Prosocial stress is the stress we experience as we are trying to navigate the tricky balance between taking care of our own needs or sacrificing for the good of others. This is a moral stress, and it happens all of the time in our lives and in the lives of our children. Should I wait my turn in line or cut in front of others? Should I save the last cookie for my younger sister who didn't get one or eat it myself? For adults, it's the same. Should I go to a fundraiser for a nonprofit organization I believe in or stay home when I feel tired after a long week at work? Should I take out the garbage or leave it for someone else to do? Because we are social beings, we are constantly having to make decisions about when we sacrifice for the good of the group and when we focus on taking care of our own needs. When we sacrifice for others, we often feel frustrated. When we focus on our own needs, we often feel guilty.

School is a hotbed for all of these stresses—for adults and students. When I am home, I can get a snack if I am hungry, walk our dog when I'm cognitively overloaded, or find a space where I can be alone if social stresses are getting the better of me. At school, the students and the educators don't have these options. No wonder some children really struggle with school given how many stresses they need to manage.

When a child is struggling behaviorally, you can bet that they are experiencing at least one of these stresses. Problematic behavior is simply a symptom of underlying stressors. Unfortunately, instead of focusing on recognizing and reducing their upstream stress, we focus on trying to change the downstream behavior. Shanker has some ideas about how we can begin to look upstream.

Understanding Our Limbic Brake

When kids struggle to meet our expectations, we often call them lazy or unmotivated. Yet, often, there is another reason why they didn't follow through. The same is true for us as parents and teachers. Do *you* generally consider *yourself* lazy? Let's find out by adding some cognitive stress to the equation. Solve this problem:

> *A bat and a ball together cost $1.10. The bat costs a dollar more than the ball. How much does the ball cost?*

If you are like most MIT, Harvard, and Princeton students, you answered wrong. Or did you see that it was a logic problem and didn't even try, knowing the answer was just a paragraph away?

Most people answer ten cents. If you did, you clearly skipped the one most important lesson of all of your years in math class: check your work. If you checked your work, you would realize that if the ball costs ten cents, then the bat would have to cost $1.10 and together, they would cost $1.20. Let's face it, whether you answered without checking your work, tried and gave up, or didn't even try, most of us, when it comes to this problem, are lazy. Now, let's try to understand why.

Groundbreaking Israeli psychologists Daniel Kahneman and Amos Tversky wanted to understand why our brain so often takes the easy way out. They posed the bat and ball question to people in a laboratory setting. They were able to determine, within a split second, when someone was going to answer impulsively (or, in their language, intuitively) or give up by watching their eyes. When their pupils dilated, their brains shut down and they quickly looked to escape the task. Remember, pupil dilation is an indication of activation of our stress response system. Our limbic system, sensing danger, flees the task. But what is the danger?

In order to survive an unexpected threat, we need to be sure that we have some brain and brawn available to address that threat. The "law of least effort" helps us to always keep something in the tank in case of emergency. Our brains and our bodies shut down in order to preserve enough to fight or flee when needed. Imagine if I asked you to do as many push-ups as you can. You would do them until you collapsed. If I then told you that I would give you $1 million for each additional push-up, would you find the strength to do one or two more? Of course you could muster the strength for a few more! Much like the indicator for our gas gauge in our car lights up when we are *close to* empty, our body lets us know to stop before we are completely depleted. The gas gauge lets us know that we need to stop to refuel *before* we run out of gas. If the gauge signaled empty just as our car sputtered to a stop, it wouldn't do us any good. Our brain acts the same way.

Our hypothalamus, a core structure in our limbic system, measures our brain's blood sugar levels. Our brain, if you recall, uses up a lot of energy, and the hypothalamus is keeping an eye on how much is left so that we don't run out. In case of emergency, we need to have some physical and cognitive resources available to fight a threat. When our cognitive resources are depleted, our hypothalamus signals danger and triggers our stress response. Shanker refers to this process as activating our limbic brake—the limbic system is shutting our body and our brain down to preserve energy, keeping us safe from an unseen threat.

When I heard Shanker speak about this, he shared this image that shows how quickly performance can shut down when we hit the point of depletion. Shanker describes this as the "intolerable peak." It is the point when our performance shuts down because we are using too much energy (arousal). I often hit my intolerable peak when I am trying to work in the evening. I'm a morning person, and when I hit a certain level of exhaustion, usually around 7:30 or 8:00 p.m., I can no longer be productive. I can't even look at another email. I close my computer, choosing to wake up earlier the next morning with a full brain to finish whatever task I'm working on.

KAHNEMAN'S INVERTED-V CURVE

Other times when I try to push myself beyond my ability to cope, I slam on my limbic brake and my stress response pushes me to fight, flee, or freeze. It's not pretty. Because our limbic brake is a metaphor for dysregulation, it takes on all of the other forms of dysregulation described earlier: avoidance, defiance, anger, aggression, etc. And the more depleted I am when I start a task, the sooner I slam on my limbic brake. If I am tired, if I've had a stressful week, if I'm hungry, if I'm feeling disconnected from others, I'm much more likely to shut down sooner. Difficult conversations with a family member are much more successful on Saturday morning than at 10:00 p.m. on Wednesday night because I'm much less likely to reach the intolerable peak.

Understanding how our limbic brake works is particularly important for schools when we think about our most challenging students. Stress at home, difficulty sleeping, histories of trauma, skipping breakfast or a sugar-high-inducing meal can deplete resources before a child even walks into the school building. If they have experienced chronic failure or social isolation at school, they are close to their limbic peak when they walk into their homeroom. For these children, already approaching their intolerable peak when they enter the school building, meltdowns or shutdowns can come fast and furious.

According to Shanker, when children slam on their limbic brakes, as adults, we have three choices: punish them, encourage them to push through, or help them replenish.

Punish: Punishing someone who has already hit their limbic peak rarely ends well. The angry child gets more angry, the defiant child digs in more, and the avoidant child becomes oppositional. Their stress response, already triggered, goes into overdrive.

Push Through: There are times when we can help children push through and succeed at something they didn't think they could do. Much like finding the strength to do an additional push-up for $1 million at the cost of a rotator cuff injury, they can push through their limbic brake to accomplish a goal. But there is often a cost to reaching the point of depletion. When we push children too hard to complete a task, they can melt down, unable to meet the demands placed on them. Or, when they are successful, there is often a physical cost to pushing our stress response system beyond its limits. Either way, the quality of the product almost always suffers.

A good example of the costs of pushing through is finals week in high school or college. It's surprising that educational systems continue to expect students to create their best work when they are most depleted, overwhelmed with final exams and papers in all of their classes. Clearly, most students would perform better if these exams and papers were staggered so that they could give each one more attention. It should come as no surprise that finals week often leads to psychiatric distress, with statistics indicating that suicides peak before and during exam season. Finally, if students are successful in pushing through, they often end up feeling the physical effects in the following weeks. Because the stress response triggers the activation of our immune system, once they are through the stress of exams, their depleted immune system is no match for the common cold, and they often spend the next week in bed.

Or, we can help them learn how to replenish their energy through emotional regulation strategies—a topic we will cover in the next chapter.

◆

Struggles with emotional regulation impact every aspect of our lives. Psychologist Laurence Steinberg, a leading voice in research on adolescent development, described the importance of emotional regulation this way: "The capacity for self-regulation is probably the single most important contributor to achievement, mental health, and social success." If we want our children to be successful, we need to help them learn how to emotionally regulate.

In the years after the chili incident, Dylan continued to struggle in school. Like any developmental process, it takes time and practice to develop the skills to self-regulate. His explosive and oppositional response to relatively small issues impacted his teachers, classmates, and family. As he got older, drugs became his go-to regulation strategy, which led to bigger problems outside of school and greater struggles in school. Over time, we began to notice that he calmed down more quickly and his meltdowns were less intense. His senior year, he was chosen to deliver the graduation speech for his class. He shared his journey to manage his anger, substance use, and depression. He stood in front of the audience, proud and confident, with charming moments where he also appeared self-conscious. "I learned about acceptance and what it takes to make positive choices and mature over time," he said. He thanked the staff "for the love and support I got over the years. It's a long list." After reading the list, he shared that "for me, NSA is a second family."

When he left the podium, the crowd cheering, he opened his arms wide and engulfed his mother in a hug. After high school, he went to work with his father as a mason. His Facebook page is filled with the beautiful projects that he and his father have completed. One day, he posted two photos from his graduation day on my timeline. One was a photo of me, Dylan, and his therapist, Joanna. Smiles of pride and relief filled the frame. The second was a picture of his mom, enveloped in his arms. In the caption, he wrote, "Came across this, [sic] thank you so much for everything you have ever done for me and showed me the love and support I needed in my youth. God bless you, Bolton, and your whole family. There [sic] lucky to have a father-Husband with the most purest and kindest heart." I reflected on his journey from the police station as a freshman to the podium at graduation. It was a journey of emotional regulation, fueled by partnerships between Dylan, his parents, and the NSA staff.

Mastering emotional regulation is a lifelong journey. Luckily, Dylan had a team of people at home and school who joined him on that journey during a critical time in his life. The more we began to see students' challenging behavior through the lens of emotional regulation, the more successful we were at helping them. Now, we needed to figure out how to teach it.

CHAPTER 5

Learning to Regulate

S ome of the photos David posted on Facebook were so moving for me. His wedding and honeymoon. A celebration of seven years being sober. Meals that he and his wife cooked together, hobbies that they share. David, now in his thirties, was finally hitting his stride.

As a middle schooler, David struggled to feel connected to anyone. He was in constant conflict with his parents and distant from his older and more traditionally successful brother. In school, his face wore a constant scowl. Rather than risk the vulnerability of developing relationships, David gained status by humiliating others. This was his superpower. David wasn't big, but he was bright and remarkably intuitive. His tongue was eviscerating. He sensed the vulnerabilities of others and knew just the right words, timing, and tone of voice to rain shame down on anyone at any time. Both staff and students were fair game.

Yet, here he was, twenty years later, married, happy, and at peace. I reached out, sharing that I loved seeing his posts and letting him know that I understood how hard he had worked for this life he had created. He thanked me. "It hasn't been easy," he wrote. "I definitely think staying sober is what helped me the most these past seven years. It's been a long journey from breaking the window in the quiet room to now."

I remember the window—we all remember the window. At the time, David was furious with us. Not surprisingly, we were also furious with him. He was brutal in his incessant teasing of one of his classmates. It had been going on for weeks and the staff was fed up. David was put in the quiet room to isolate him from other students. As was the practice at the time, David was given more periods to serve with every disrespectful comment. The periods piled up. Eventually, David snapped. He picked up a chair and threw it at the large window at the back of the room. David, along with everyone else in the room, thought the window was made of Plexiglas. It wasn't. The glass shattered, leaving everyone speechless.

David's defenses seemed to shatter with the glass. For the first time, he seemed contrite and apologetic. He was ready to talk about what he was feeling, admitting that his anger was out of control. He wanted to be back in the classroom with the students he had been bullying and was ready to do the work he needed to do to return.

In addition to paying for the window and helping the maintenance crew install it, he had another project he needed to complete for the class. As a gifted artist, he could mold clay into intricate figures and blend colors and textures to create beautiful images. This was often the only way that we could get him through a class period—his hands coaxing clay into shapes as he listened and absorbed the lesson. His task to return to class was to create a collage that could explain to his classmates where his anger came from and why it so often became directed at them.

Although he rarely engaged academically, he dove into this project with both his mind and his heart. When he was finished, the class was ready for him. They were angry but open to hearing him out and considering forgiveness. He walked into class tentatively, eyes cast down, partially hiding behind his poster board. His voice started in a whisper but got louder and more confident as he explained what he had created. In the center of the poster board was the picture of a fast-moving train surrounded by images of devastation—earthquakes, tornados, floods. "My anger starts slowly," he explained, "but it continues to gain momentum. It gets faster and faster until it derails. Then it destroys things." He pointed to all of the other images around the train. "These are all of you. My anger is hurtful. I know. But when it gets going, I don't know how to stop it."

The classroom was quiet. Then, one of David's most frequent targets spoke up. "Maybe we can help you." There was a tense pause. Typically, this was David's moment to pounce—to humiliate his classmate for offering to help him. David looked down, seeming both surprised and touched. Almost in a whisper, he broke the silence. "I can use some help. Thank you."

This was a lesson in regulation and reconciliation for all of us. In Part IV, we will explore in greater detail how we helped our students recover from meltdowns. But first, we needed to stop punishing and learn to teach instead.

How We Soothe

For most of us, our time of being consistently and optimally regulated is in our distant past. We were in the womb, a dark and warm place of comfort. There were no high chairs, diapers, or car seats to deal with. We got all of our nutrition through our umbilical cord. We peed and pooped without a diaper change. We constantly heard our parents' voices and the rhythmic thrumming of our mother's heartbeat. We didn't need to be responsive to the ever-changing demands of an unpredictable physical and social world. It is no wonder that in moments of our greatest distress, we still curl up into the fetal position, hoping to return to that place of peace and comfort.

Imagine, then, the experience of moving through the birth canal and the shock of the cold, bright, sterile environment of the birthing room. Infants gasp for their first breaths, opening their eyes for the first time only to be flooded by bright lights. Sounds are no longer muffled as they hear their own piercing cries. Bombarded with sensory stimulation, they scream and shake. For the first time, adults reach out to them to help them soothe. Doctors clear out their airway, nurses clean and swaddle them and place them on their mother's chest. It is through the care of others that they begin to adjust to their new world. They experience distress and adults help them soothe. Repeat. Repeat. Repeat.

In the first months of our child's life, all of our energy is spent keeping our infant regulated (soothed). In order to help them learn to regulate, we need to be sensitive to their cues of distress, we need to accept their dysregulation, we need to work cooperatively with them to find the right tool at the right time and, finally, in order to do this successfully, we need to be emotionally available and attuned. Is it any wonder that attachment and emotional regulation go hand in hand?

So, what does this look like in practice? Most of us have a checklist in our minds when our infant begins to cry. Are they hungry? Do they need a nap? Does their diaper need changing? Do they need to be swaddled? If we get through the physical checklist and they are still crying, we move on to relational strategies. We get them in the hands of someone safe and familiar. Mother, father, grandparent. Then, if that doesn't work, we move on to rhythm. We rock them, we put them in a bouncy chair. Researcher, clinician, and teacher Bruce Perry once said that rhythm is so important because the infant in the womb was constantly soothed by the thrumming of their mother's heartbeat. It is no surprise, he suggests, that any rhythm that soothes us (music, walking, swinging, bouncing) falls within the sixty to one hundred beats per minute of the typical maternal heartbeat.

In these moments, as we are responding to our infant's needs, we are also teaching them that when they are experiencing distress, there are strategies that can help them calm down. We notice that they have a need, we address it, and they feel better. If we continue this process, as they get older, we can help them learn to recognize both the triggers of their distress and the strategies they can use to soothe themselves.

Unfortunately, we often do just the opposite. As our infants turn into toddlers, we change our approach. When the "terrible twos" arrive, we stop soothing and begin punishing. We shift our focus from comforting when they are distressed to gaining compliance and control.

Why do we stop soothing?

Not coincidentally, language acquisition begins at about age two. Our child learns to say the word "no" and to understand what we mean when we say "stop," the two words most likely to trigger a power struggle. Suddenly, we begin to see their behavior through the lens of motivation rather than regulation. When they say "No!" or don't follow our directions, we see them as "noncompliant" and we feel powerless, which triggers our own dysregulation. How can we not control a two-year-old? We can't let a toddler run our family! So we punish, pushing them deeper into dysregulation.

Regulation, however, is a skill like many other skills. Teaching children how to emotionally regulate is similar to teaching them how to button their shirt and tie their shoes. Like any skill, children need to experience dysregulation in order to learn how to master it. We need a basketball in our hands in order to learn how to shoot a foul shot. We need them to hold the shoelaces in their hands before they learn how to tie them. In the same way, we need to experience stress in order to learn to overcome it. We need to be dysregulated to learn how to regulate. And, because meltdowns are so common, there are plenty of opportunities to help them learn these skills.

When we begin to see behavior through the lens of dysregulation rather than as a problem of their character, our relationship with our child can change. We can be partners in solving the problem rather than feel like victims of their behavior. Their "aggressive" moments seem less scary. When our kids shut down and avoid, they seem less "fragile," "oppositional," and "defiant." Because we can help them regulate in these moments, we feel more empowered. A child's most challenging behavior is just an expression of their dysregulation. To change the behavior, we can address their regulation rather than worry about the flaws of their character.

Adults Regulate First

I am the cook in our house. I learned to cook because I'm a picky eater and it is probably no surprise that I raised two children who are also picky eaters. While they were growing up, our dinner routine was always the same. I would drive home from NSA, hungry and stressed. I would put down my computer bag, walk to the kitchen, and start cooking. Dinnertime was at 6:30 but my hunger was always on a different schedule. By 5:30, I'd be starving. As I began cooking, I'd feel shocked at how rude, demanding, and unappreciative my family became as I attempted to accommodate all of their different palates. I would put the meal on the table, right on time, frustrated whenever someone was just a minute or two late. Since I'd snacked on unhealthy food as I prepared my healthy meal, I was no longer hungry when dinner was ready. My anger, however, was on a slow simmer as we sat down, finally, to eat.

After months (years?) of unhappy dinners, it (finally) occurred to me that (perhaps) I was the dysregulated one. After coming home hangry and stressed a couple times too many, I decided to implement some regulation strategies of my own. To quiet my nervous system and make a more thoughtful transition from work to home, I would eat an apple on my commute and walk our dog for ten minutes before entering the kitchen. The strategy worked right away. Soon I noticed that my family was more polite, less demanding, and more appreciative. Who knew that when I was regulated, my kids would behave better?

In families, we are always in a dance of regulation and dysregulation together. Because dysregulation is so contagious, any one person can set off a family flash mob of dysregulation. However, a regulated adult also has a lot of power to regulate others, changing the music from heavy metal to classical, moving from mosh pit to waltz. But in order to do that, we, as adults, need to be able to work the stereo and know how to dance.

The first step in helping our children get regulated is to be aware of our own dysregulation. We all get dysregulated, all of the time. Like our children, we lose access to the parts of the brain that will help us soothe our child the most—the ability to listen, be flexible, empathetic, and creative, among others. Dysregulation is characterized by a false sense of urgency and exaggeration that leads us to act quickly and decisively. Although this is helpful in moments of true danger—grabbing your child before they run into traffic or fighting off a mugger—our stress response is more often triggered by benign events. Seldom is the urgency or exaggerated belief about the problem real, and yet when our limbic system sounds the alarm, the most primitive parts of our brain take over. *If he doesn't take out the garbage right now, he will never learn how to take responsibility!* Our dysregulation, based on our primitive fear for our survival, wants to "fight to the death." So we keep fighting, blind to the damage we may be doing in the process. The sooner we notice our symptoms of dysregulation—a quickened heart rate, a clenched jaw, a rush of energy to our arms and legs, the sound of our voice yelling (and swearing?), the hurtful words spewing from our mouth, the urgent feeling of needing to be in control—the sooner we can utilize our strategies to regulate ourselves and avoid the destruction of our hurtful words, our reckless actions, and our unwise decisions.

As adults, we need to manage our emotions before we can help children manage theirs. Just as they are unable to learn when they are dysregulated, we are unable to teach when we are dysregulated. Just as they are unable to listen effectively when they are dysregulated, we are unable to find the right words and tone of voice to help them understand. When they most need to be calmed, we are most likely to anger or shame them. As parents and teachers, we make our worst decisions when we are dysregulated. If we are going to help our children in their hardest moments, we need to be aware of how dysregulation hijacks our brains and leads us into our worst behavior and our worst decisions.

One of the most helpful strategies and one of the hardest things to do when we are consumed by our dysregulation is to tap out. In wrestling, "tapping out" refers to slapping your hand on your opponent or on the mat to indicate that you are "forfeiting the match due to the pain caused by the submission hold you are currently in and your belief that escape from the hold is impossible." When we are locked in a control battle with a child, tapping out is an essential skill because, often, when we are dysregulated, it is impossible to stay engaged without causing greater levels of pain. And we lose our best tool for regulating our child—our own regulated self. We can tap out by letting our child know that mom or dad is getting upset and needs a break. Then it's important that we use that time to regulate ourselves before we re-engage. If we are in the car, we can ask for a few minutes of silence to listen to music until our brain comes back online. We can also seek help from our spouse, asking them to tap in if they are more regulated than we are.

Two important things happen when we tap out. First, we are modeling for our child our awareness of our dysregulation and how to soothe ourselves before we create bigger problems. Second, we are making sure that our dysregulation doesn't add fuel to their fire. Instead of dysregulating them further, when we return, we can use our calm to soothe them: a process called coregulation.

Coregulation

Just as dysregulation is contagious, so is regulation. A dysregulated person is most likely to become regulated around other regulated people with whom they feel a sense of trust and caring. This process is called *coregulation*. When we coregulate, our quiet nervous system lets our child's panicked nervous system know that everything is ok. Then they slowly begin to calm—their breathing changes, their body begins to relax, their thinking becomes more flexible, they are able to let us know what is going on and can think through options about what to do next.

The best remedy for a dysregulated child is a regulated, quiet, soothing adult presence that speaks not to the child's cortex but to their limbic system. Remember, the limbic system doesn't have language, so we need to let their limbic system know, nonverbally, that everything is ok. Our softened tone of voice. Our still bodies. Our gentle touch. Eye contact. Sympathetic facial expressions. We are responding to the child's inner alarm and saying, "Look, everything is ok. If we were in danger, I wouldn't be this calm. You are safe."

Unfortunately, as parents and teachers, we are particularly vulnerable to becoming dysregulated ourselves. We feel an urgent pressure to fix the problem and we feel powerless when we can't. We get impatient. Our tone of voice betrays our anxiety. We yell. We cry. Our movements are fast and impulsive, trying to find the quick fix. Our limbic system tells their limbic system that they were right to trigger their stress response. The fire in both the adult and the child rekindles, then rages.

I realized that often when Matthew struggled, I would escalate rather than defuse his sense of inner panic. Rather than coregulate, I found myself becoming irritable or angry, adding fuel to his dysregulated fire. If he was running late and couldn't find his shoes, as I helped him, I would begin a shaming running commentary. I couldn't help myself. (Remember that dysregulation makes us more impulsive and less empathetic.) "You are always the one making us late." "You are fifteen years old and can't remember where you keep your shoes?" "Your room is a mess! No wonder you can't find them!" Believe it or not, none of these comments helped him locate his shoes. In fact, they were counterproductive, pushing him deeper and deeper into his lower brain and making it less and less likely that he could access his cortex to help him think through where his shoes might be.

Conflicts often escalate due to issues of compliance. This makes sense. Compliance is all about control, so a noncompliant child can quickly lead to the adult feeling powerless. Unfortunately, the child we are in conflict with is experiencing the same urgency—a need for control. Further, dysregulation undermines flexibility, so we lock into our positions, digging trenches rather than building a bridge. This is the anatomy of a power struggle. Engaging in a power struggle is mutually assured destruction. The only way to win is for the other to lose, and often, the one who is losing pulls the other down with them. When you find yourself in a power struggle, it is essential to step away, literally or metaphorically, and regulate yourself before you say or do the thing that will make it worse.

Mastering our own dysregulation is the first and, I think, the most difficult part of supporting our children through their hardest moments. When I was unaware of my own dysregulation as I was cooking dinner, I perceived others as being the cause of my stress. Once I recognized and managed my regulation, dinners became times of connection rather than conflict. When our brains are regulated, we have our full menu of skills available to us. We can be our best selves— our best spouses, parents, and educators.

Regulation Strategies

Strategy #1: Take Your Time—It's Developmental

Emotional regulation doesn't just happen overnight. Learning to emotionally regulate is developmental, and development, by definition, happens over time. In fact, the part of our brain that is most responsible for managing emotional regulation is the prefrontal cortex, which waits until we are in our late twenties to complete the task. Human development is unique in the animal kingdom—we are born as the least developed and most dependent species on Earth. As a result, parents are always compensating for this lack of their child's early development. Before they can walk, we carry them, using our legs to help them move. As they get older, we help them get dressed, using our hands to tie their shoes and button their shirts until their motor skills catch up. We organize their day. We keep track of time for them, pack their backpack and make their lunch. We don't expect them to be able to do these things when they are young, so we do it for them. Emotional regulation works the same way. When we are able to stay regulated during stressful times, our calm helps to regulate their brains. After many repetitions they, too, learn how to handle stress. Just as they watch us organize their backpack and will one day do it independently, they experience how we help them regulate, and begin to develop those skills themselves. It is like we are lending them our prefrontal cortex until they can manage these developmental challenges on their own.

As author and children's rights advocate L. R. Knost wrote, "when little people are overwhelmed by big emotions, it's our job to share our calm, not join their chaos." Our emotional regulation not only soothes them in the moment but also teaches them how to regulate so that they can cope better with stressors in the future.

The development of regulation, in many ways, is similar to watching our child develop motor skills. When a child is learning to walk, they fall, on average, seventeen times per hour. They stumble. They get up. They try again. This is how we learn to walk. However, when children stumble emotionally, we are often too quick to intervene. When we rush in to fix a broken toy, a lost friendship, or a bad grade, we rob them of the important experience of learning how to cope with life's challenges. Life is full of ups and downs, and our rush to fix their distress can communicate that there is something wrong and intolerable with distress. Distress is a human condition that waxes and wanes throughout our life. Rather than protect a child from negative emotions in the short term, our work is to help them play the long game and learn to cope well with their discomfort. We do this by being present; our calm lets them know that their feelings will pass. When we coregulate with children, they, too, learn not to panic when things go poorly. They gain belief that their distress will pass. And as their distress begins to lift, their cortex becomes more active, and they are able to think of new solutions to the problems they are managing. A broken toy? Maybe I can fix it. A lost friendship? Maybe I can reach out and apologize. A bad grade? Maybe I can study harder next time.

Strategy #2: Teach the Language of Coregulation

Our use of language is a key to helping others regulate. Language is both verbal and nonverbal. We communicate with our body posture and movement, our tone of voice, and our facial expressions. This is especially relevant when it comes to coregulating with children. When children are dysregulated, they often notice our nonverbal communication before they can access what we are saying to them. That's why our dean of students, Scott, was so effective. As a student's dysregulation was ramping up, his body was slowing down. As they began to yell, his voice became softer and his words came out slower. This nonverbal communication sent the clear message to their nervous system that they were safe.

This is the essence of coregulation. If we keep our language simple and focus on understanding what is happening for them rather than trying to get them to comply, we can resolve the issue more quickly and begin to solve the upstream problem sooner. Imagine a fourth grader working on homework suddenly throwing their pencil and shouting, "I quit! This is stupid!" I could quickly try to gain compliance by threatening a punishment. I also might pile on by adding a shaming sermon that also triggers shame and anxiety by yelling across the room, "No throwing pencils in this house! You know the deal. If you don't finish your homework, you lose your phone for the night, no video games and no shows. No quitter ever achieved anything. Successful people learn how to stick with things when they get hard." Or, I could pick up the pencil, slowly walk over to them, and in a comforting tone of voice and with a hand on their shoulder let them know I see how frustrated they are. "Let's take a break." After a few minutes we can decide what to do. Do they need some help? Could it wait until morning? Does the assignment look more doable after a few minutes away from it? As we coregulate with them, they begin to learn the skills of self-regulation. We can always add: "When I'm overwhelmed, taking a break is helpful." And, if the child is receptive, we can suggest, "How about next time you take a break before you feel like throwing the pencil?"

We model and they learn.

Strategy #3: Help Children Identify Their Own Most Effective Regulating Strategies

At NSA we started to use tools to help children understand and personalize strategies to help them deal with their hardest emotions. One of these tools was Zones of Regulation. Developed by Leah Kuypers in 2011, Zones of Regulation is "a framework and easy-to-use curriculum for teaching students strategies for emotional and sensory self-management." The framework is intended to help develop student awareness of their own emotional regulation and, with that awareness, identify strategies to calm themselves when they experience their own dysregulation. In her book, *The Zones of Regulation*, Kuypers describes how the "zones" are associated with colors.

THE ZONES OF REGULATION

BLUE Zone	GREEN Zone	YELLOW Zone	RED Zone
Sad	Happy	Stressed	Mad
Sick	Calm	Frustrated	Mean
Tired	Feeling OK	Worried	Terrified
Bored	Focused	Silly/Wiggly	Yelling/Hitting
Moving slowly	Ready to learn	Excited	Panicked
		Afraid	Enraged
Low state of alertness	*I'm in control of myself*	*I'm partly in control*	*I'm out of control*

Blue Zone: "The Blue Zone is used to describe low states of alertness . . . This is when one's body or brain is moving slowly or sluggishly." Examples of being in the Blue Zone are feelings of sadness, lethargy, boredom, or feeling sick.

Green Zone: "The Green Zone is used to describe a regulated state of alertness." This is our sweet spot—our full brain is engaged, and we are productive, fun, and easy to be with. We feel in control of our brain and our bodies.

Yellow Zone: "The Yellow Zone is . . . used to describe a heightened state of alertness . . . The Yellow Zone is starting to lose some control." In this zone, we are stressed. It is hard to sit still. We are more impulsive. We may be irritable and defiant. Or, we could be agitated in a happy or giddy way—playing around with others more than they may like or being overly goofy and distractible when we are expected to be quiet and focused.

Red Zone: "The Red Zone is used to describe extremely heightened states of alertness or very intense feelings . . . Being in the Red Zone can best be explained by not being in control of one's body." In this zone, we have really lost it. We may shut down completely, sob uncontrollably, or have a full-blown explosive temper tantrum. We feel anger, rage, panic, terror, or even feelings of uncontrollable mania or elation.

The goal then, as parents and teachers, is to help children recognize what zone they are in and, if they are not in the green zone, partner with them to identify strategies that will get them there. For example, a child in the blue zone who is tired or bored may need something more active, like taking a walk, playing with the family pet, shooting baskets, or tossing a ball. In the yellow zone, a child may identify that a stress ball is helpful, or listening to music, doing a mindfulness or breathing exercise, or talking with a friend or adult. In the red zone, children may identify that being alone in a space could be helpful, being with a trusted adult, or exercising to get rid of the excess energy.

Regulation is a multistep process. As adults, if we can teach our children and students to be aware of their state of regulation, identify strategies to help them regulate, implement those strategies, and then reflect on the effectiveness of the strategy, we can help them learn to use these tools to navigate their stress in the future.

Strategy #4: Take Brain Breaks

Pausing, it turns out, is remarkably helpful. Mindfulness activities are one of the most accessible and effective ways to pause. While I am not an expert on the power of mindfulness, I'm a big believer in it. At NSA, we implemented "Mindful Minutes" in classes twice a day. The goal was for staff and students to engage in a mindful practice together. As with any initiative, some teachers embraced these practices more than others. One teacher would sit on her desk in the lotus position, leading a structured meditation. Another put on a mindfulness video and returned to her desk to finish up her email. Another teacher would just ask the students to be quiet.

"Mindful Minutes" was an opportunity for students and staff to press their emotional reset button. In the stress of a busy day, the quiet minutes are calming. This is just as true in our living room as it is in the classroom. Mindfulness improves our awareness of our states of physical and emotional arousal. We cannot address our dysregulation unless we realize that we are, in fact, becoming dysregulated. I have found that many times we try to help children solve the regulation puzzle backward. We try to apply regulation strategies after the child has become dysregulated. The opposite is so much more effective and is the key to effectively implementing Zones of Regulation. By having greater awareness of our emotional and physical regulation, we can be preventative rather than reactive. That is one of the many powers of mindfulness—it enhances our awareness of our feelings, thoughts, and physical needs. With this awareness, when needed, we can identify strategies to help us make our way back into the "green zone." When we engage in a mindful activity with our children, the added benefit is that we, too, become more aware and more regulated.

Lisa Feldman Barrett, a neuroscientist who is among the most cited scientists in the world for her research on emotions, writes that our brains work like our bank accounts. Too many withdrawals without sufficient deposits leaves us overdrafted. The biological, emotional, cognitive, social, and prosocial stresses that Shanker has identified all make significant withdrawals from our brain's budget. They use a lot of energy and can leave us feeling depleted. There are also a lot of ways that we can make deposits to our brain budgets. Sleep, positive social interactions, healthy meals, physical activities, and helping others are some ways that we add to our brain's bank account. They give us positive energy that boosts the balance in our savings account. The more savings we have, the more regulated we are and the better able we are to manage stresses when they arise.

Until our children can keep track of their own brain budgets, it is helpful for us to monitor their deposits and withdrawals. When there is a significant withdrawal, we can follow up with a deposit, keeping those brains in homeostasis. When a child hits their intolerable peak, they have overdrawn their account and desperately need a deposit. Helping children recognize the signs that they are reaching their intolerable peak before the limbic brakes slam on is the first step. If those brakes do engage, helping children to identify activities to quickly restore is essential. We can help them. We can give them a hug, play a game, or grab a snack. When I hit my intolerable peak in the evenings, my brain depleted by a long day of work, I can't even imagine opening another email. I go to sleep, depositing more energy into my brain bank and allowing me to more fully engage the next morning.

The children with the greatest levels of stress in their lives have the most withdrawals. In order for them to be regulated, they need even more deposits than other children. Unfortunately, spending their lives in a brain budget deficit often results in the opposite. Their overdrawn brains lead to dysregulated behavior that leads to more withdrawals—punishments and shame—and fewer deposits—fewer smiles from teachers, fewer invitations from peers, less praise from parents. Their life feels like one big foreclosure.

Brain breaks are a simple yet essential way of adding a deposit to everyone's brain budget. In his book *When*, author Daniel Pink provides revealing data and strategies that support giving children brain breaks in school. In Denmark, researchers assessed how a student's performance on a test is associated with time of day. Looking at the data on two million students taking the same test over the course of the day, test scores went down consistently throughout the day. Using Barrett's model, this makes sense. By the end of the day in school, there are often more withdrawals than deposits in students' brain budgets. In Shanker's language, we would expect children to be closer to their intolerable peak later in the day after an accumulation of stresses. Here is a graph of their data:

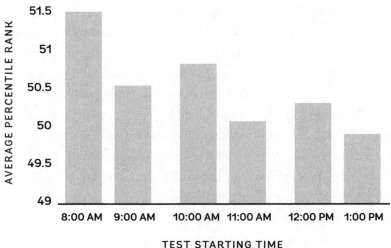

As you can see, scores go progressively down as the day goes on. However, between 9:00 and 10:00 and between 11:00 and 12:00, you see a bump. Students before the 10:00 administration and 12:00 administrations got a twenty- to thirty-minute break to "eat, play, and chat," and their scores went up compared to the group before them that didn't get a break. That may not look like much of an effect, but it is the equivalent of receiving three additional weeks of instruction, and the students who struggled the most benefitted the most.

Adult brains are no different. When we don't pause, our brain gets stressed and we are more likely to melt down ourselves. If you know that you are going to have a difficult interaction with your child, pause first. Let your brain recover, so that you can bring your best brain to these important moments with your child.

Pink suggests that breaks don't need to be long or elaborate. We just keep the following in mind:

· Short breaks can make a big difference.
· Moving beats stationary. If they can't run, stretching or walking goes a long way.

· Social beats solo. Get kids talking with one another.

· Outside beats inside. If possible, fresh air and sun are remarkably restorative.

· Disconnected beats semi-connected. We need a break from our devices, too.

Strategy #5: Give Instead of Take

Mike, our assistant dean, is a quiet man whose every movement is slow and deliberate. He is strong and thoughtful. His presence changes a room. Everyone feels calmer when he enters. He has the wisdom of a monk.

One afternoon Mike came into my office. I closed the door and listened. He told me about an interaction he had with a teacher who was struggling with how to address the behavior of one of her students. His words were simple conceptually. However, they get at the heart of how we can help our children in their dysregulated moments. They are also really hard to do.

"I told her that when I see a student who is struggling, I think about two things. I think about what I would want if I was in their situation. And I try to figure out what I can put on the table instead of what I can take away."

So simple, yet these sentences capture the essence of how we can support students who are dysregulated.

"What would I want if I was in their situation?" This approach leads with empathy. So many things we do to children when they struggle we would never want to have done to us. If I am in an argument with Kathy, it wouldn't help for her to say that I need to sit at my desk in the basement for the next forty-five minutes and fill out a processing sheet while I miss the first half of the game that I wanted to watch. That would make me more furious. Why would I think that it would be helpful for my eight-year-old? They need the same things we need when we are upset. Mike's thinking breaks down the false assumption that their melting down is different from ours. When I am in lower brain, I need time and space to regulate myself. If I have hurt others when I was upset, I know that I need to repair the damage to the relationship that I caused. Our children need the same things.

The second part of Mike's message is also profound in its simplicity. "I try to figure out what I can put on the table instead of what I can take away." When Matthew and I would argue, I would search frantically for any thread of control I could grab. It is like I had a Rolodex of things Matthew cares about, and I flipped through them quickly, trying to figure out what I could take away that would get him to comply. Car, friends, phone, guitar. Being able to take things away means being in control. But as I became more controlling, Matthew became more dysregulated. He felt devalued, powerless, and disconnected when I threatened him with the loss of something important to him. Predictably, he became more enraged. And, just as predictably, I piled on more punishments.

Mike suggests that we should do the opposite. Instead of taking things away, we should put things on the table. What things do we put on the table? Regulation strategies. "Do you want to take a few minutes and listen to music?" "Do you want to play with your LEGOs?" "Would some fresh air help?" "Would it help to take a break and get some water?" If taking a walk turns out to be helpful, then both the adult and the child know that it can be an option in the future. By trying out these strategies in the moment, then reflecting on how helpful they were, children learn what helps them and we learn how to help them. Even better, by giving them options of things they can do instead of taking things away, we are partnering with them, connecting with them, teaching them, empowering them, and valuing them. We are coregulating.

Mike's two strategies are in direct contrast to two "rules" that seem to drive so many of our beliefs about dealing with children when they are dysregulated. The first rule is, "Don't ever back down from a punishment you have given." The rationalization of this rule, I believe, is that our children need to know that we mean business. If we give in, they will never take our punishments seriously and, as a result, will walk all over us. There is another way to look at this, especially when the punishments we dole out in a moment of dysregulation seems, upon reflection, excessive. "You don't need to stick with a decision made when you were in lower brain, at a moment you were least likely to make a good decision." Also, remember that our children are learning from us. In moments of stress, we want them to be flexible. We have the opportunity to model that flexibility rather than doubling down on our inflexibility. "I know that last night I told you that you were grounded for six months, but I was upset and I wasn't at my best. Let's work together on a plan so that when you go out, I don't spend the night worrying about when you will come home."

The other rule is that we always need to enforce the limits that our co-parent or colleague has set. Why would we all have to follow the person who is in lower brain and is least likely to make a good decision? At North Shore Academy, we tried to get around this by always meeting as a team before making a decision—that way we could have multiple voices contributing to the decision. We would give it time so that everyone could be more regulated. The person who was most upset about the behavior was a partner in the decision but did not hold the trump card. We made the decision as a regulated and collaborative team. Similarly, if we, as parents, can resist the strong pull to respond in the moment, we can take the time we need to access our best brains and collaborate on a thoughtful response.

Our personal regulation strategies are like our fingerprints—unique and resistant to change. We can often identify our child's best regulation strategies by observing them. What activities tend to quiet them, and what activities tend to work them up? Some kids need movement, while others do better with quiet, sedentary activities. Our emotions follow our attention. When our attention is focused on something dysregulating, we will become dysregulated. But if we can shift that focus to something benign or soothing, we are quicker to regulate. In the early stages of dysregulation, when we can still access our cortex, distraction can be a helpful tool ("I wonder where those fire trucks are going?" Or, "Let's finish your LEGO project"). For older children, we can be more transparent with our efforts to regulate. "You seem upset about this. Before we figure out what to do about your curfew, do you want to take the dog for a walk or listen to some music?" Once we figure out how to help kids access their most effective regulation strategies, they will begin to utilize those strategies more independently. *Self*-regulation is the holy grail.

Strategy #6: Get Curious

The director of special education of a local district asked me to observe Tyler, a first grader, to see if NSA could help him. When I stepped into the back of the room, they didn't need to point him out. He stood out in a crowd. Partly because of his bright blond hair, but perhaps even more because of how he just didn't quite fit in with the other kids. His clothes were more disheveled and his hair uncombed in this community of impeccably dressed children. He seemed to always be one step behind the others, his voice just a little too loud, his movements more sudden and less fluid.

Tyler had struggled behaviorally in kindergarten, and now, in first grade, he required a 1:1 assistant to make it through the school day successfully. Even with the assistant, Circle Time was Tyler's most challenging period of the day. And he made it challenging for the rest of the class. Because he struggled to transition, he and his teaching assistant would let the classroom get settled before they entered the room, where students were sitting on the ground, ready to hear a story or share a thought. Tyler would walk in and very intentionally stand on the fingers of a student who was leaning back. Of course, he was quickly removed from class. Day after day. Our staff had a theory: he hates Circle Time. But finally, one day, as the other students were transitioning to art, his teacher asked him to stay back to talk through his behavior. She was curious, not angry. She asked, "Every day in Circle Time, when you walk in, you stand on another student's fingers. I'm curious, why does that happen during Circle Time?" Tyler, quickly and impulsively, confirmed the staff's theory. "I hate Circle Time!" The teacher wasn't convinced. She knew that there was more to the story, so she pressed on. "You hate art, too, but you don't hurt anyone in art class." Tyler paused for a minute, thinking. He looked down and said softly, "I don't know where to sit."

Suddenly, it all made sense. In an effort to make transitions easier for Tyler, he would take a break before class. He would stop by the main office with his 1:1 assistant to check if there was any mail for the classroom. This made Tyler the last student to arrive at class, where he was already feeling out of step with his classmates. The circle looked closed to him, and he didn't have the social skills or the relationships to ask the other students to move over to make room for him.

The team now had a problem that was solvable. The next thing his teacher did was equally important. She asked Tyler, "What do you think would be helpful?"

"I don't know." He paused, then looked at his teacher, and hesitantly asked, "Could I sit next to you?"

"Of course." His teacher smiled. "I'd like that, too."

From then on, the teacher saved a place for Tyler next to her and the other children's fingers were safe from Tyler's shoes. He never stepped on their fingers again. Stepping on fingers was downstream. His struggles with transitions and social skills were upstream. In order to get upstream, we need to be curious.

Being curious does a number of helpful things. First and foremost, it is our best tool to get more information. When we understand the problem better, we can find better solutions. Second, being curious is often regulating because it requires listening and it communicates empathy. "You seem really upset. Help me understand what is making you so angry" is a lot more regulating than "You cannot talk to me that way! Now you've lost your phone for the night!" Third, once a child is regulated, being curious helps them develop self-awareness. They are often clueless about their dysregulation (aren't we all), and their behavior catches them off guard. When we are curious, our children then begin to self-observe and become more self-aware. Fourth, being curious and listening helps children learn to find the words to express their feelings. Because our listening and curiosity have helped them regulate, they can better access language that will help them process why they are struggling and help us identify how to support them in the future.

Being curious can help us navigate a challenging situation in the moment by giving us essential information—the cause of the problem. Curiosity can also be our best tool when a child is struggling with a pattern of behavior. First, we begin with a trusting relationship so that they can feel safe being vulnerable with us. This is where the work of developing a healthy attachment is so helpful from Part I. Next, we need to find the right time to talk. We can't be curious and they can't be self-reflective in the moment of stress, so we need to find the appropriate time and place when everyone is regulated. We need to be ready to persist through their skepticism ("Why do you care?"), navigate their shame ("I don't want to talk about it"), and absorb their defensiveness ("Your temper is worse than mine"). We need to be authentically curious and to leave our assumptions behind.

How we start the conversation is important. "Why do you always act like such a jerk to your sister?" or "Why are you so intent on disrupting my class?" won't be a very effective way to engage in a partnership with them. The shame embedded in these questions will quickly shut the child down and trigger their defensiveness before the conversation even begins.

When planning how I will introduce the conversation, I find it helpful to ask myself, "Why is this happening now?" The behavior doesn't always happen, so I begin to wonder why it shows up sometimes and not others. For Tyler, why Circle Time and not art? For another child, I might wonder why he gets along with his sister in the mornings, but always starts an argument at dinner. I think about the times a child is able to manage situations more effectively. In school, I wonder if it could be the subjects or the time of day. What is different for them during those times? Then I will ask them, with a spirit of curiosity rather than accusation.

Curiosity is at the heart of learning. The more we can help kids wonder about what is triggering their meltdown, the easier it is to teach them how to manage their meltdowns more effectively. This process is hard work but, when done well, there is a big payoff.

◆

As I was completing this manuscript, David, the student I introduced at the beginning of this chapter, sent me a direct message on Facebook reflecting on the regulating power of art when he was trying to manage so much stress as a child. "Art was so beneficial to me in my middle school and high school years. Art calmed me. I could focus on creating figures and sculpting clay, and rid some of the negativity going on around me." His teachers saw the power of art to quiet his nervous system and let him have clay at his desk in middle school. Art continues to enrich David's life, giving it meaning and providing essential moments of calm. We are all healthier when we can integrate the things that regulate us into our lives. They become the tools we can rely on to quiet our nervous systems and open up our brains for learning and connecting.

CHAPTER 6

Wait for It: Development Is on Our Side

I n his sophomore year of high school, Matthew applied for a job. I drove him to his interview, dropping him off at the front office. This was a special milestone, another indication that he was growing up and becoming more independent. A few days later, he was offered a job as an inclusion aide for a summer recreation program for children with disabilities. Lynn, a colleague of mine, supervised the summer program and gave me an update partway through the summer. "We love him, but he is about fifteen minutes late for work every day," she said. This did not surprise me. Matthew's struggle to be on time had been a source of constant stress between us. He had a smartphone, and we bought him wristwatches and offered to wake him up in the morning. We hung a big clock on his wall. Nothing seemed to help.

When I spoke with him about his tardiness at work, Matthew became defensive. "Nothing happens in that first half hour," he said, annoyed that we were having the conversation. "I am always there by the time the kids arrive. That's what's important." I offered, unconvincingly, a novel idea. "If you are always fifteen minutes late, why don't you just leave fifteen minutes earlier?" I shared my values about the importance of responsibility, being on time for your team, and the values of conscientiousness.

He was late for work the rest of that summer.

The challenge, I realized only in retrospect, is that, although he knew how to tell time, he had not yet developed an internal sense of time. We got him watches and put clocks on the walls of his room, but he didn't think of time the way that I did. He could have a sleeve of watches on his arm, but if he didn't have a sense that time was passing and feel the nudge to check how much time has passed, he wouldn't think to look at them. The problem wasn't that he wasn't paying attention, he just wasn't paying attention to the clock ticking away. His attention was focused elsewhere.

Junior year, they hired him back. And he was on time every day. As his brain developed, he was able to track time and plan his mornings better. But he still didn't focus on everything he needed. Several times that summer, he had to be sent home because he forgot his shoes. He ran around barefoot most of the time, so getting in the car without footwear didn't signal that something was wrong.

Senior year, he was on time, wore his shoes every day, and was named a Counselor of the Year.

Watching your child develop is like watching paint dry. It happens slowly, but surely.

Developmental Empathy

Dave Gleason is a gifted psychologist and author of the book *At What Cost: Defending Adolescent Development in Fiercely Competitive Schools.* He is also a good friend. He coined the term "developmental empathy" that has completely shifted how I understand the emotional, behavioral, and social challenges that children face. He defines developmental empathy as "matching the demands we place on our children with their brain's development." Every child's brain develops differently, and when there is a good match between what we ask of children and what their development allows, they engage in the world in a way that facilitates further growth. When there is a mismatch, we are asking children to do things they are unable to do, leading to powerful feelings of dysregulation. In these moments, both the child and the adult experience incompetence and powerlessness. This is often followed by a cascade of frustration, shame, defensiveness, and avoidance.

Like all other aspects of development, children's brains develop at different rates. Development has its own timeline, and our brains are no different. Walk through any middle school in the country and you will see children who are six feet tall with facial hair sprouting walking with other children who are a foot shorter and seemingly a decade away from puberty. We don't get upset with our child when they don't reach puberty quickly. We don't create a sticker chart to motivate them to grow facial hair. We don't tell them that if they weren't so lazy, they would be shaving by now. We let them know that they just haven't hit their growth spurt yet. It will come.

Yet, it's different with brain development. As children age, we assume that they are each ready at the same time for the same cognitive tasks as every other child. Some children, who are quicker to develop, easily meet our expectations. Children who are slower to develop begin to struggle as the demands get harder. That is when we make our biggest mistake. We treat it as a problem of motivation when it is simply about development.

This was true for Matthew. With his prefrontal cortex hidden from view, we couldn't watch it develop. Sadly, children whose prefrontal cortex develops quickly follow a different trajectory than those who develop more slowly. The children who develop more quickly appear more organized, compliant, and focused, and therefore reap the rewards of a society that places a high value on our ability to meet these expectations. Children who struggle with organization, planning, persistence, managing frustration, sitting still, and maintaining attention, on the other hand, often experience heavy doses of shaming and punishing. This response to their slower development is toxic for their mental health and undermines academic achievement and emotional development. In a tragic irony, the stress of this toxic environment pickles children's brains in stress hormones, which slows rather than enhances the development of the prefrontal cortex, making it harder for the child's development to catch up.

Brain development is not a steady or linear progression. Different parts of the brain develop at different times and at different rates. The brain is constantly growing and pruning in response to its environment. This ability to adapt to our environment is essential to our survival. The longer something takes to develop, the more impacted it is by the environment. Because our prefrontal cortex has nearly thirty years of development outside of the womb, the environment has a huge impact on how it develops. Parents and teachers are the primary designers of this developmental process because they are the architects of children's environments. We can't speed up development, but we can nurture it, and we know that the brain grows best in an environment that is connected and regulated.

Children can't see that their struggles are the result of development any more than we can. But they do see the frustration they cause in adults and other children. They do experience the pain of punishment and loneliness of exclusion. They do feel the profound shame of failure.

When I was just out of college and spending my first summer at Wediko, I worked with a child named Marcus, who showed me how the world can catch children with developmental gaps off guard. Marcus was twelve years old when he came to Wediko to address concerns about his oppositional and defiant behavior. One afternoon, Marcus's group had free time followed by their favorite activity of the day—swimming and playing at the lakefront. We told the group to start getting ready. Almost in unison, they migrated to the clothesline to get their suits and towels. Not Marcus, who, fascinated, continued to peel bark from the birch trees. With five minutes to go, the other campers, in their suits and with their towels around their necks, began lining up. That's when they noticed that Marcus was still outside. One counselor yelled, "Marcus, you are making everyone late!" The rest of the group overheard, and panic set in. Losing even a minute of swim time felt intolerable. They let him have it when he finally entered the cabin. "What's wrong with you, Marcus?!" "Why do you always have to mess things up for us?!"

"No one fucking told me!" he responded, lip quivering, angry and defiant.

After Marcus changed, I walked to the beach with him. He was clearly still angry and hurt. "Why is everyone mad at ME? No one told me that it was time to go, and now everyone's yelling at me." The problem wasn't that Marcus didn't hear. The problem was that Marcus was so focused on the birch bark that he didn't process the cues that everyone else was processing. Many had planned ahead, knowing that swimming always came right after free time. Others heard the counselor tell them to start getting ready—to Marcus, their voices were simply background music. They saw other kids go into the cabin. They had an internal sense of how time was passing and how long it would take to get their swimsuits on. They were able to plan and transition. Because Marcus didn't attend to any of these cues, the first and only thing that he processed was the angry voices and dismissive looks. This happened often to Marcus. The hostility of others surprised him. Constantly. When we are frequently faced with an unpredictable and hostile world, we become defiant, we withdraw, we blame others. The world is moving too quickly, and these behaviors help us to regain a sense of composure when things feel out of control.

It Gets Easier

I learned this the hard way. In our house, we have a term for my struggles as a parent. We call them "bad dad" moments. I have a lot of them. No matter how much I read or write or speak about parenting, my own dysregulation undermines my ability to be the parent I wish to be. Luckily, I have very forgiving children.

When Matthew was eight, I had a "bad dad" moment. He joined a U9 soccer team that met for practice on Saturdays at 10:00 a.m. The morning of his first practice, he was eating cereal and watching his favorite cartoons. It was his Saturday-morning routine. Being the good psychologist and principal who understood transitions, I yelled from upstairs, letting him know that we were leaving in fifteen minutes. "Are you ready?" I asked. "Yes, Daddy!" he said. I called down again a few minutes later. "Leaving in five!"

"Ok!" he responded. Can you see where this is going?

I came downstairs and saw that he was he was still in his pajamas. Still eating cereal. Still staring at the TV set. I was angry. He had lied to me—he said he was ready and he wasn't. And we were going to be late! Suddenly, I was flooded with both the false urgency and the exaggeration that are the hallmarks of dysregulation. We needed to leave now! And if I don't teach him not to lie to me now, he will grow up to be a serial liar.

"You said you were ready!" I yelled.

"I'm sorry, Daddy," he pleaded.

"Where are your cleats and shorts?"

"I don't know, Daddy." Tears started to flow.

"Well, clearly you can't handle watching TV in the mornings anymore. No more TV on Saturday mornings!"

"No! Please, Daddy!" He was sobbing now.

Finally, he was dressed and in the car, pleading to get his morning TV back. I rushed to soccer practice and Matthew stumbled out of the car, holding back a flood of tears. I sat there for a few minutes, watching other kids get dropped off, later than Matthew, strolling onto the field. My forehead hit the steering wheel. All of this stress, all of this conflict, because I didn't want to be two minutes late for his volunteer U9 soccer coach? I had been reading about what happens when we are dysregulated and the problems of using punishment to gain compliance. Had I learned nothing?

I was lucky to have the guidance of Bill Levin, a psychologist who was also a friend and mentor. He was a consultant to NSA and met with staff to provide clinical supervision and something akin to therapy. I used him for both for more than twenty-five years. I told him about trying to get Matthew to soccer practice, about my efforts to punish him to stop him from lying, to organize himself better, and become more compliant. Still feeling powerless, I asked something like, "Should I keep him grounded from the TV for six months or reduce it to three?" Bill spoke slowly, every movement and word intentional and mindful. He paused, looked over his glasses, and said, "I think he needs your help." The words hit me hard. How could I not have seen that myself? I could see it so clearly in our students. When they struggled, they needed our support, not our punishment. They needed our help, not our shame. I just couldn't see it in Matthew.

I could hear Ross Greene's voice. "Kids do well if they can." When children struggle, it's because they don't yet have the skills to cope effectively with the demands they are facing. It's about skill, not will. But surely this doesn't apply to lying about being ready for soccer and refusing to stop watching TV. Then Greene's words nudged me again. "Doing well is always preferable to not doing well." Matthew would rather do well. He would rather make me pleased than angry. He would rather be on time than late. He would rather know where his equipment is than have to search for it. This, too, was an issue of skill, not will. But what is the skill he struggled with?

The answer was transitions, but somehow I'd missed what was hiding in plain sight. I was deceived by his fast development in other areas of his life. He was bright. He had great social skills. How could he struggle with something as simple as transitions? Even his younger sister was better at transitions than he was. Surely he was just irresponsible.

But that is not how development works. We develop different skills at different times. We have gaps. We grow in fits and starts. We regress and advance. No combination of punishments or incentives was going to help him develop faster. As you know by now, Matthew's struggles with transitions followed him into high school. He eventually developed transition skills, just a few years more slowly than most kids. It wasn't until college that he was finally able to plan and transition more successfully (and, if you saw his room today, you can only hope that the next few years of development will help him become more organized). Now, if I want a ride to the airport, he's my guy.

Although I couldn't then see that, over time, he would develop these skills, I knew that I needed to show up differently. The next Saturday morning, I handled the transition to soccer practice in a new way because I saw the problem differently. *I* needed to change. *I* needed to support him differently. Instead of assuming he should have certain skills at age eight, I worked with the skills that he had. Instead of yelling down to him, I walked up to him and let him know that we needed to start getting ready for soccer practice.

"Would you like some help getting ready?" I asked.

"Yes, Daddy."

"Let's start by turning off the TV."

"Ok."

We put his cereal bowl away. We found his cleats and shorts and shirt and shin guards. We decided to keep his equipment in his cubby and showed him where to find his shorts and shirt in the laundry. We walked out of the house and made it to soccer practice with enough time to kick a ball around together before his other teammates arrived.

He needed my help.

Matthew's struggles with organization and transitions didn't end with youth soccer, and I'm embarrassed to admit that I continued to struggle to see his challenges as developmental. When he began skipping classes in high school, and as his grades plummeted, I became more and more irritable with him. He spent more time alone in his room. My frustration was fueled by worry for his future. My anger showed up more than I like to admit. It is so hard to experience our children's struggles without becoming dysregulated ourselves. The urgency and exaggerated feelings we have are driven by a panicked belief that if we don't fix this now, they will never be successful. As I became more dysregulated, my brain shut down in predictable ways. I struggled to find empathy for him, to develop a range of solutions for this problem, to think flexibly and to identify and express my strong emotions in words he could hear. I continued to talk with Bill about Matthew and my struggle to show up as the father that I wanted to be for him. Bill again leaned forward, softened his voice, and full of empathy, he said to me, "Let him know that this will get easier for him."

This was a game changer. That's how development works. Things always get easier for us. It was soothing and hopeful. I shared it with Matthew, and this became my mantra in my quieter and saner moments. It was a message about development that we both needed to hear.

Trust Biology

Matthew graduated from high school, barely. He took all of his finals during the makeup sessions because he wasn't prepared to take the finals on time. It wasn't that he wasn't working—he was just working on the wrong things. He would spend days on a short essay or physics project, unable to shift to studying for the rest of his finals. I was worried. College was a big investment, and if he couldn't manage these demands with our help, how would he manage them independently?

College, remarkably, came easy to him. And he loved it. He attended every class, handed in his assignments (mostly) on time, and stuck to his plans for studying. He ended his first year with straight As as a premed student. He was more helpful at home. The child who was always the last one out of the house and always late was suddenly reliable and on time. I asked him what changed. "Two things," he said.

First, "It was almost like I could feel my prefrontal cortex growing." (He is, after all, my son.) Second, he said, "I always heard you and Mom when you talked about your values, but I just couldn't live up to them. Over time, I was able to live the values that you talked about." All of those talks were important after all.

My internship supervisor, Dr. Karen Gouze, once said to me in her thoughtful and patient way, "Development is always on your side." The opposite is also true. When you try to fight development, you always lose.

It is really hard to be patient. As I look back on my time with Matthew, I realize that one of the things that made it harder for me was that I didn't really trust development. My impatience and worry for Matthew wasn't unlike the panic I feel when I am making gravy for the turkey at Thanksgiving. The turkey comes out of the oven, the pan filled with juices. It's time to make the gravy and timing is essential. I start whisking the butter and flour in the pan before adding the drippings from the turkey. I stir and I stir. I know that it takes the gravy seven to nine minutes to thicken. Standing over the pan, the time moves so slowly. After about five minutes, I begin to doubt myself. It's not thickening! I must have done something wrong. I start to panic. I reach for the flour, tempted to add more, which would both thicken it and ruin it. Then, suddenly, long after I expect it to, it begins to thicken. It is ready, just as the carved turkey hits the table.

A child's brain is both vulnerable and highly adaptable. When we are regulated and emotionally connected to children, their brains develop faster. Throughout childhood, before they develop skills, children rely on us to help them. We can lend them our prefrontal cortex when theirs isn't ready for a task. Matthew needed to borrow from my prefrontal cortex longer than Anna did. He needed help keeping track of time—until he didn't. He needed help packing for a trip—until he didn't. The more that I saw his struggles as developmental, the more patient I could be with him, the more I found myself teaching rather than punishing. We became partners in his development of skills, rather than adversaries. It got hard again when his drive for independence meant that he no longer wanted my help. From that point on, I had to watch him struggle until his development caught up with the expectations of high school and college.

When we think about behavior problems, I can't think of any that don't involve the prefrontal cortex, at least in some way. So if we are worried about a seven-year-old, we can remind ourselves that they are only a quarter of the way through their developmental window. A fourteen- or fifteen-year-old? Halfway through. A twenty-one-year-old still has a quarter of their development left. One of the things that we saw at NSA was how so many of our students pulled their lives together in their early twenties after a decade of painful struggle. The growth spurt of their prefrontal cortex happened later, causing a lot of stress and heartbreak early in their lives. That heartbreak also seemed to create an even greater sense of compassion for others. They understood pain and shame, and they could then see it in others more clearly, and, as a result, many are now doing work that focuses on helping others in pain.

Many of the problems of childhood get resolved on their own because of a child's natural development, yet we have trouble being patient. When my daughter Anna was an infant, she would scream when she wanted something that was out of her reach. The piercing sound would find its way unnervingly deep within my nervous system. A few months later, when she was more mobile, the problem went away. Then it reared its ugly head again when she wanted to tell us what she wanted but didn't yet have the words. Her difficulty communicating with us led to more bursts of tears and tantrums. But as Anna developed the motor skills to move and language skills to share her thoughts, the outbursts diminished.

I spent a lot of time punishing my children for gaps in their development. I remember these moments as the most painful times in my relationship with them. And they were all ill-conceived and unnecessary. We manage some of our most important moments with our children using an outdated model. Instead of teaching our children in these moments, we frighten them. Instead of creating cultures of belonging and engagement, we create communities based in fear and compliance.

Believing in development when your child seems to be unraveling in front of you requires hope that is born of trust in our biology. It takes time to develop these skills, and different children develop these skills at different times. E. L. Doctorow, the American novelist, once wrote that, "Writing is like driving a car at night. You can only see as far as your headlights, but you can make the whole trip that way." I believe the same is true of watching children develop. It is in the constant repetition of responding in connected and regulated ways that helps our child develop. Every dysregulated moment in our children is an opportunity to help them soothe and reconnect. Each of these moments allows us to teach, to be patient, and let their own development do the work. Like driving at night, it is the constant repetition, over time, that gets us where we want to go. As Anne Lamott wrote, "Hope begins in the dark, the stubborn hope that if you just show up and do the right thing, the dawn will come. You wait and watch and work; you don't give up."

Attachment and emotional regulation are the two most important factors in the healthy development of our children. There is one thing that can quickly and ruthlessly undermine both. In the next section, we will explore the destructive power of childhood trauma. We will also learn about the surprising power of our families and our school communities to not only buffer our children from trauma but actually reverse it.

PART III

Trauma: The Long Tail of Childhood Adversity

CHAPTER 7

The Hidden Impact of Trauma

My mother died of cancer in 2015. She found the lump in her breast and after surgery, chemotherapy, and radiation, she had a few years in remission until it reappeared, with renewed vigor, in her brain. She died six years after her diagnosis. The years between her diagnosis and death were a blessing for me. Her chronic frenetic pace slowed. When I visited, we sat and watched TV together in her one-bedroom apartment for hours at a time. She let her kids take care of her after a lifetime of caring for us.

She also began to reminisce about her childhood. We heard more specifics about how hard it was for her growing up. How she never felt accepted by her parents and how my grandfather, raised in a family with strong puritanical roots, could be an overbearing man. He was a man who believed in order and planning. Then, at age forty, he learned that his wife, Sally, was expecting twins.

The babies of the unplanned pregnancy arrived in 1935 at the worst possible time for my grandparents. The country was reeling from an economic depression and was on the doorstep of a second world war. My grandparents already had two teenage children and a plan for the future. More children were not part of the plan. While my mother's twin brother became the family favorite, mom grew up feeling the weight of their untimely arrival on her tiny shoulders. "I never felt like I was valued. There was a lot of shame. My father had a terrible temper." She grew up with a fear of rejection that seemed ever-present, an additional molecule in the air that she breathed. When I asked, she couldn't recall a single person who was there for her when she was hurting as a child.

As with many people who have experienced painful childhoods, my mother was able to use her own pain to see, with remarkable clarity, the pain of others. She coped by investing in relationships, finding ways, big and small, to give comfort to those who were hurting. She became a social worker who used her abundant empathy to care for the elderly and the poor. Her focus on caring for others, however, came at a cost. Managing the needs of so many people was physically and mentally taxing. Being fiercely independent, she was reluctant to accept help, continuing to do things for others while rejecting their offers to help her. She continued to work at a frenetic pace into her mid-seventies, until the cancer decided that it was time for her to retire.

As the cancer made its way slowly into her brain, she began to change. Once bold and fearless, she became more anxious and avoidant. After a lifetime of working to make the world a better place, she had moments of seeming uncharacteristically defeated and cynical. She had expected that she would live into her mid-nineties, just as her parents had. At seventy-six, with only a few years left to live, she felt bitter about being robbed of the twenty more years she expected to enjoy in retirement. One day, as I sat with her in her apartment, she turned and said, "My parents did this to me. My childhood was toxic. This cancer started when I was little, from the stress of never feeling loved." I heard the resentment in her voice, but I found myself dismissing her comments. I knew that she was angry and mourning the end of her life. Her conspiracy theory, I believed, was fueled by painful childhood memories blending with the cancer that was quickly spreading through her brain.

After she died, I began learning about trauma. And now, years later, I believe she was right.

Embedded Memories

As a therapist at NSA, I saw trauma everywhere I looked, and I was a witness to how the pain associated with trauma affects students' behavior. I observed how Jason's early physical abuse by a parent seemed directly connected to his bullying behavior as a middle schooler. I saw how childhood sexual abuse led another student, Chelsea, to struggle with trust and anxiety. I noticed it in myself. I still struggle to manage some of the pain that dates back to my parents' divorce.

The damage caused by childhood trauma, however, extends well beyond our emotional lives. It turns out that trauma is just as devastating to physical health as it is to our mental health. It impacts every cell, and it has a long tail, continuing to affect our bodies decades after the trauma has ended. The impact of childhood trauma takes up residence in our cells, waiting patiently to show its toxic presence, emerging later as disease in adulthood.

The word "trauma" is derived from the Greek word for "wound." In childhood trauma, the "wound" is the prolonged activation of the stress response system. Gabor Maté, a physician and leader in the field of trauma, defines trauma as a "psychic injury, lodged in our nervous system, mind, and body, lasting long past the originating incidents, triggerable at any moment." Trauma can refer to a single event, but for children, it can be a collection of terrifying and disturbing events, often referred to as "complex trauma." Complex trauma results from events that are both interpersonal and invasive and occur over time with wide-ranging and long-term effects. Exposure to complex traumatic experiences can last years, and children are powerless to escape them. As Tronick and Gold write, "The trouble with the word trauma is that it is made to refer to a one-time event, while the vulnerability of trauma lies in its repetition." When traumatic events are repeated, children can feel trapped and there is the constant threat of "the next time." Complex trauma is particularly devastating because these events often happen within families. The people who are meant to protect us become the sources of harm.

Because it is so commonly used to describe less impactful events, the common use of the term "trauma" can be diluted to include events that are distressing but are also fleeting. Not making a travel baseball team is upsetting but, over time, won't result in a profound change to a child's stress response system. The same may be true for losing a pet or having a best friend move away. While the distress is very real at the moment, it is a natural response to a common event. Trauma is different. Trauma is a physical and emotional forest fire, often lit in the places and by the people who are supposed to provide safety. The stress is toxic and overwhelming, and its flames are fueled by secrecy and shame.

Although we often think of traumatic events as things that happen to other people and in other families, more common disruptions such as divorce, mental illness, substance abuse, and the emotional abuse that is triggered by adult dysregulation, are ever-present in our world. Research shows that by the time children reach the age of eighteen, a vast majority of them will have experienced at least one type of complex trauma. We often don't know the trauma that children experience, because they keep it hidden, shrouded in secrecy. Many children are suffering behind the closed doors of their houses and bedrooms. Many use hard work and perfectionism to shield the world from seeing their pain. For others, the flames and smoke show up as behavior problems—the secrecy keeps the cause of the fire hidden, but their behavior gives us insight into the intensity of their pain.

As a parent and educator, I found learning about trauma both difficult and comforting. Difficult because the impact of childhood trauma is more intense and extensive than I had ever imagined. Comforting because the negative effects of childhood trauma aren't a life sentence. We all have the power to not only buffer but to actually reverse the impact of trauma in the lives of the children and adults who we care so deeply about.

Our Body's Secret Service

To understand trauma, we need to revisit the brain.

Outside of our conscious awareness, our limbic system remembers harmful and threatening events from our past. Through sensory input, it constantly scans our surroundings to make sure that we are safe. Because danger can come upon us quickly, the limbic system is the first part of our brain to sense a threat. Remember from Part II, it can't waste time filtering all the sensory data through the slow and deliberate cortex. Our sensory system gets information first and, if there is any sign of danger, our limbic system alerts our brain stem to trigger our stress response. Because we are bypassing the cortex, it feels like we are "acting" without thinking. It would be a big problem if, when we put our hand on a hot stove, we waited until our cortex realized the burner was on, assessed the damage to our hand, and carefully considered our options. Instead, our sensory system jumps into action, communicating directly with the limbic system, and we pull our hand from the stove before consciously realizing what just happened.

The warnings of the limbic system are sometimes clear (we pull our hand from the hot stove) and other times, more vague (feeling anxious when something doesn't seem quite right). Novel events always rouse the limbic system into action until it can ensure safety and turn the controls back over to the cortex. Because the cortex is so slow and deliberative, when our stress response is triggered, we act before we think. Psychologist Dan Gilbert explains it this way: Our brains are "designed to answer the 'What should I do?' question before the 'What is it?' question." We know something is scary without knowing what it is. And we often act before we realize what we are doing.

Our limbic system is our body's secret service. It is always monitoring our environment. Its job is to keep us safe and alive. To do this, our brain is wired for prediction. It takes past experiences and applies them to the present to predict the future. It is a conservative system.

Like a smoke detector, its job isn't to be right every time. Its job, simply, is to never be wrong. Once our limbic system knows we are safe, it lets the cortex take over. But like the Secret Service, it stops everything in its tracks at the first hint of a problem. And it never stops scanning. It is always ready to trigger the stress response at the first sign of danger.

I remember the story of one of our students, Seth, who, as a young boy, was molested by his grandfather in his grandfather's house in a nearby town. Years after Seth's grandfather died, Seth found that he couldn't visit the town where his grandfather lived. It wasn't just his grandfather that triggered his limbic system. It wasn't just the sight of the house. It was the gas station on the corner. It was the exit sign getting off of the highway that would progressively unnerve him. His limbic alarm was warning him that danger was ahead. He knew that his grandfather was dead and no longer a threat to him, but his deeply rooted limbic memory of his abuse was not going to allow him to even enter the neighborhood where he was molested. His limbic GPS system was constantly rerouting him to keep him safe.

These associations are sometimes referred to as "embedded memories." They reside deep in the limbic system, and operate outside of conscious control, triggering our fight, flight, or freeze response. They are symbolic and thematic. We do not need to experience a replica of a traumatic event to trigger our stress response. Once we are in the emotional or physical neighborhood of a past event, we will experience a pull toward it if our memories are positive or a strong push away if the embedded memory is traumatic. The limbic system casts a wide net so that our brain will warn us of events that are *similar* to past dangers. The veteran of combat who cannot tolerate the Fourth of July fireworks decades after returning home is a classic example. Because embedded memories bypass our cortex, they often arrive with high intensity and without warning despite being decades and thousands of miles from the battlefield.

Children's brains, because they are still developing, are even more vulnerable to the unconscious impact of early traumatic experiences. As Bessel van der Kolk, a psychiatrist and pioneer in the field of trauma explains: "Our brains are map makers like the early explorers. The limbic system makes internal maps of the external world so that we can navigate the world in a way that allows us to be successful. The internal maps, like other maps, are based entirely on our experience. That's why childhood experiences are so important because they are the first roads that are laid down on our internal maps." When our childhood is filled with trauma, our maps are distorted, leaving us feeling lost and alone.

As a result, these embedded memories show up as behaviors that are unexpected and difficult to understand. We don't have access to a child's internal map and, as a result, we are surprised by the intensity of a behavior that seems to arise without provocation. Imagine a ten-year-old boy, practicing the violin in the living room. His father, an alcoholic who has just arrived home after drinking with friends, notices that his son's elbow is dropping as he holds his bow, making it harder to hit the notes that he is practicing. "Stop! Stop! Stop! Are you a fucking idiot? How many times do I have to show you how to position your elbow?" He grabs the elbow and squeezes it hard and tight and jerks it back. The boy can smell the scent of stale alcohol on his breath. "This is where it belongs! I knew that you would never be a musician. You are a failure at everything you do." He jerks the bow free from his son's fist with one hand and lifts him out of his seat with the other. He then whips the backs of his child's legs with the bow twice before his child can wrench himself free and run to the safety of his room. "Just run away from this like you do everything else. You are a disgrace to this family!"

Imagine the boy at rehearsal the next morning. As he is playing, the male orchestra instructor notices that the boy is missing some notes. He walks over and gently reaches for the boy's elbow to lift it into the proper position. The limbic system quickly recognizes this pattern—man standing over him while he is playing, reaching for his elbow, giving instructions. The boy, his stress response now fully engaged, isn't processing the teacher's voice saying, "Let me help you with your elbow." The boy only hears his own voice yelling, "Get away from me! I don't need your help!" It's unlikely that the boy would make the connection between his feelings of panic with his music teacher and the incident with his father the night before. His cortex was offline for both events. Certainly, his teacher wouldn't make the connection, completely unaware of this boy's home life. So they both make assumptions. The boy thinks, *I hate this teacher*. The teacher describes the boy as "defiant," "unmotivated," and "disrespectful." The limbic system has done its job—it has kept the boy safe.

But in its wake, it has left a world of damage.

The Adverse Childhood Experiences Survey

In 1995, Dr. Vincent Felitti, an internal medicine specialist, and Robert Anda, an epidemiologist, made a revolutionary discovery. They were curious whether a correlation existed between traumatic childhood events and negative health outcomes. They designed a study that they conducted with Felitti's employer, the Kaiser Permanente HMO in San Diego. Between 1995 and 1997, more than seventeen thousand Kaiser patients agreed to participate by completing a questionnaire and giving the researchers access to their medical records.

The study was remarkably simple. Felitti and Anda provided patients with a list of ten types of childhood traumatic events and asked each participant how many they had experienced before the age of eighteen:

- Physical abuse
- Emotional abuse
- Sexual abuse
- Physical neglect

- Emotional neglect
- Parental divorce
- Death of a family member
- Family member with a mental illness
- Family member incarcerated
- Family member with addiction

The scores ranged from 0–10. Because Kaiser had the participants' physical health, mental health, and behavioral health records, Felitti and Anda were able to test for correlations between childhood traumatic events and adult outcomes. After running their analyses, Felitti and Anda described the correlations between adverse childhood experiences and adult outcomes as "stunning." In a myriad of categories of mental health, behavioral health, and physical health, the higher the ACE score, the more damaging the outcome. For example, compared with people who had no ACEs, people with an ACE score of 4 or higher saw their risk of ischemic heart disease rise by 220 percent, stroke by 240 percent, and diabetes by 160 percent. Four or more ACEs were also associated with elevated mental and behavioral health problems, increasing the likelihood of depression by 460 percent and becoming an alcoholic by 740 percent, People with six or more ACEs were thirty times more likely to attempt suicide and forty-six times more likely to inject drugs. This data began shining a light on the lives of people who were struggling the most to cope with their lives. An overwhelming number of adults who needed mental, behavioral, or physical health treatment had childhood exposure to multiple traumatic events.

In addition to these correlations, the data uncovered a simple yet shocking truth. Childhood trauma is more common than they had imagined. Sixty-six percent of people in the sample reported having at least one ACE. And, if they had one ACE, they had an 87 percent likelihood of having two or more. Imagine a child whose parents divorced, one parent struggling with depression, another struggling with an addiction who also, in their dysregulated moments, yells at and shames the child. That child now has four ACEs and is vulnerable to these outcomes. ACEs are all around us.

As an educator, there is one statistic that's most chilling. According to the Centers for Disease Control's most recent data, 17 percent of people in the United States report having four or more ACEs. One out of every six children. That means that in every classroom of twenty-four students, by the time those students are seniors in high school, four of them will be at high risk of these devastating outcomes. Four students in every classroom are walking into school every day from homes and communities where they are experiencing at least four different types of traumatic events. Constantly.

In 2018, Melissa Merrick conducted the most comprehensive ACE study to date. In her sample of 214,157 adults, she found that people with low income, low educational attainment, people of color, and people who identify as gay, lesbian, or bisexual had a significantly higher likelihood of experiencing childhood adversity. Groups that are most vulnerable to experiencing ACEs are also groups who have historically been pushed to the fringes of society. The cultural pain of discrimination, alienation, and powerlessness must only intensify the impact of their own stories of trauma.

And it gets worse. It should come as no surprise that students with high ACEs are also the students who are most likely to struggle in school academically and behaviorally. Only 3 percent of students with no ACEs are identified as having learning or behavior problems in school. Students with four or more ACEs are thirty-four times more likely to be identified. The students who end up in the principal's office, the ones who are most often suspended, and the ones who are failing their classes are also the ones most likely to be experiencing trauma at home. As friend and former superintendent Dan Cates once told me, "If I want to see the kids in our district who are hurting the most, I go to the dean's office."

How Trauma Changes Our Biology

Although trauma is at the heart of so many negative outcomes, our personal secret service is working just as intended. The problem is that our stress response system is designed to be activated in short bursts. We address the momentary threat and then get back to business as usual. When someone cuts us off in traffic, our stress response gets triggered, but it quickly calms once we realize that we are safe. Our toddler runs toward a busy road, activating all of the amazing power of our stress hormones, enabling us to run faster than ever before to grab an arm before they reach the curb. Within a few minutes, our bodies go back to baseline. Our stress response is meant to be activated and then return to homeostasis. For children experiencing complex trauma, however, their stress response system seldom returns to baseline. Instead of seeing a grizzly bear and running to safety, it is as if the grizzly bear is in their living room, their classroom, and their bedroom. Their body is constantly mobilized for threat, never getting a break. Our bodies were never meant to work so hard for so long.

This is how trauma impacts our physical health. This constant activation of our stress response system wreaks havoc on our bodies and undermines our health at a cellular level. Our limbic system is on constant alert, hypervigilant for any potential threat. The more trauma we have experienced, the more activated our limbic system becomes to protect us. Back in the section on regulation, we discussed all of the body systems that get activated under stress. Stress triggers a five-alarm response within our body. Every cell in our body is activated to fight off the danger. Our respiratory and cardiac systems go into overdrive. Our pancreas pumps out blood sugar. Our immune response is activated, ensuring a rapid response to potential illness or infection. Our digestive system shuts down. Cortisol, the primary stress hormone that orchestrates all of these changes, makes the choice to slow down development so that our bodies can invest all of our energy into short-term survival. Long-term planning goes out the window. When our house is on fire, we don't worry about our plans to renovate the kitchen. We put out the fire or we get the hell out. But in the process, the fire does damage to all of the systems in our bodies that get activated.

Often the health problems seem to lay dormant, remaining hidden until later in adulthood. Like someone constantly driving their car too fast, the transmission and the brakes may seem fine for the first twenty thousand miles. But as the car ages, the transmission and brakes are quicker to fail and need to be replaced much sooner. Bodies with high ACEs respond the same way. Our cardiac system, our immune system, our pancreas, our lungs are all overworked and, eventually, begin to break down sooner. For people with high ACEs, the incidence of heart disease, asthma, cancer, and diabetes skyrocket in adulthood. For instance, if you have an ACE score of two, you have a 70 percent greater likelihood of being diagnosed with an autoimmune disease as an adult. If you have an ACE score of six or more, your life expectancy plummets by twenty years. Our stress response system always chooses short-term survival over longevity and people with high ACEs pay a very steep price in adulthood. As the Egyptian novelist Naguib Mahfouz wrote, "nothing records the effects of a sad life as graphically as the human body."

As I learned more about trauma, I began to realize that my mother may have been right. Her immune system, depleted from overuse, opened the door for the cancer to take residence in her breast and her brain. I don't think I can remember a time when her stress response was quiet—she was always on the go—until one evening in the nursing home, when she was in hospice care, just days before she died. The hospice nurse was rubbing lotion on her back. She looked up with a big smile and said, "I never thought this part would be so good." The grizzly bear had finally left the room.

CHAPTER 8

From Hurting to Healing

O ur oldest child, Angelique, was the last one to join the family. When we met her in February 2005, she was in high school. Matthew was four and Anna was two. We weren't planning on adding to our family, but once we met her, it was inevitable.

It started when Kathy and I went out on a typical date night—dinner and a movie. After some fajitas and margaritas at our favorite Mexican restaurant, we settled into our seats for a movie we expected to be both powerful and unsettling. It also turned out to be life-changing. *Hotel Rwanda* told the brutal and heartbreaking story of the Rwandan genocide that sent shockwaves throughout the world in 1994. We left the theater shaken. The car ride home was silent until I could hear Kathy quietly sobbing. I put my hand on her leg. Her body was shaking. "There must be something we can do," she kept repeating.

It turned out, there was.

The next morning at church, an announcement in the bulletin jumped from the pages. In bold print, it read, **Teenage Girl from Africa Needs a Home**. There were no more details except for the name and phone number of one of the church elders. After the service ended we drove home and called the number. Bill, a retired pastor, answered and told us a harrowing story about how Angelique, when she was only six, survived the genocide by fleeing with her older sister to the Congo and then on to Tanzania and finally to Zambia, moving from refugee camp to refugee camp, witnessing and experiencing unimaginable violence, abuse, poverty, theft, despair, and death. Finally, in Zambia, she arrived at an orphanage that she could, for a short time, call home. Then, through the generosity of the nuns at the orphanage, she had the opportunity to go to America. Despite her hopes for security and stability in her new country, Angelique was now seeking her third home in just a few years. After more than a decade of running from danger and seeking safety, she still had no place to call home. Would she feel welcomed in ours?

When ACEs Collide

One of the most insidious impacts of trauma is the erosion of trust in others. Instead of embracing relationships that can buffer stress, people who have experienced traumatic events often are reluctant to trust. Their embedded memories of past relational pain triggers their stress response when others reach out, undermining their ability to form meaningful connections. Without others to help coregulate, dysregulation can run wild, leading to one of three evolutionary entrées on the survival menu: fight, flee, or freeze.

Angelique moved into our home with all of her belongings, and all of her ACEs. Her history of traumatic experiences would show up in ways that would, at times, become unnerving for her and for the rest of us. Much of the time she was animated, engaged, funny, and eager to help. At other times she withdrew, becoming quietly but powerfully distant. Her room was her sanctuary, a place of peace and isolation. In her times of withdrawal, she was sullen and uncommunicative, sharing the kitchen without words or not responding when we would call her to dinner. It was hard to watch her face light up with others while being so sullen and distant at home. Still, she was coping remarkably well with the transition to our family. She was not demanding and was seldom defiant. As teenagers go, she was relatively easy to parent. The challenge in our family, it turned out, wasn't her ACEs. The challenge was my ACEs.

In retrospect, I can see how the echoes of our separate traumatic histories collided. *My* history of a family coming apart left embedded memories, hidden just below the surface, waiting to be uncovered. When Angelique was distant, my limbic secret service came to life, warning me of the relational threat, triggering my stress response. As she pushed us away, the deeply embedded memories of my family's sudden plunge into chaos were uncovered, and the feelings roared back with unexpected force. Decades after the divorce, I could feel the relational rug being pulled out from under me again. While my early traumatic experiences can't be compared to living through a genocide, the scars from my childhood were reopened and, like Angelique's, my stress response was activated, shutting down the parts of my brain I most needed to support her.

My internal formula looked something like this: emotional distance = loss = pain. When Angelique became distant, my limbic system, in an effort to protect me from reexperiencing my childhood pain, engaged my stress response, catching me off guard. In response, I fought or I fled. I yelled or I withdrew. Then I felt shame—knowing that Angelique needed me to show up differently for her. I was a psychologist and a principal—I was able to stay regulated and connected when kids melted down at school—why couldn't I do better at home? It was all limbic. Angelique's withdrawal made me feel powerless, disconnected, and devalued and my stress response was off to the races.

Angelique's main response to stress was to flee—she would escape to her room to avoid engaging in relationships that her limbic system told her she could not trust. Other times when she had no choice but to be with us, she shut down, seldom speaking or making eye contact. This was her freeze response. We freeze when we are powerless to fight or flee. This often shows up as dissociation—we shut our brains down, much like how our bodies go into shock in response to a physically traumatic event. This process is protective. It keeps us from becoming overwhelmed by the toxic stresses in our lives. While it does its job of protecting us from feeling the pain, it also keeps us isolated and alone.

But these difficult moments didn't define us as a family. Amidst the fighting, fleeing, and freezing, there were many wonderful times of connection, fun, and affection. We played games, we vacationed, we watched Angelique in the orchestra, in soccer, and in the theater, celebrating her successes together. We laughed. We had quiet and tender moments, too, where Angelique would share her struggles or she would cook us dinner after a hard day. Our lives were a casserole of all of these feelings, bitterness tempered by sweetness, bland moments mixing with salty interactions, the flavors merging, blending, and, eventually, providing nourishment for all of us. We didn't know how long this meal would last, but we were all at the table, sharing it together.

After six years, in 2011, we took our seats in the courtroom. The judge called us to the bench and asked us questions about our commitment to Angelique. Angelique answered questions about her desire to become a part of our family. A few minutes later, we were holding the adoption paperwork and taking photos with our lawyer and the judge. We had all chosen to become family to one another.

Angelique's past continues to emerge in her life, triggering her stress response in moments when she wishes she could be more relaxed and present. She is constantly learning to manage and rewire a hypervigilant limbic system that has taught her to be wary of relationships. I understand this journey. I am on it myself.

Over the years, Angelique and I are discovering a new rhythm together. We have shared many repetitions of calm and connected time together with fewer and fewer moments of shutting down or shutting each other out. The echoes from our past have begun to quiet. We are now more connected and regulated when we are together. We enjoy long family vacations and lengthy visits without experiencing the evocative power of our past hurts.

As we saw in Parts I and II, the more doses of regulated connection a person experiences, the more resilient they become. I believe that is what happened for Angelique and me. Unfortunately, the opposite can also be true—when we punish and exclude in response to a person's trauma-related behavior, we can do a great deal of damage. Adults can be the most powerful source of healing for children who have experienced trauma. We often, unfortunately, become sources of harm. Rather than buffer children from the toxic stress of their childhood adversity, our relationships magnify it.

From Mis-Behavior to Trauma-Behavior

The signs of trauma often show up as challenging behaviors rather than cries for help. As trauma clinician and writer Mary Jo Barrett once told me, "What is inside of us has to come out." The pain always finds a way to escape. When children are carrying their trauma stories within them, what comes out is often not pretty. And our response can be equally ugly. Remember dysregulation is highly contagious. Instead of seeing their anger, avoidance, or shutting down as their response to their traumatic stress, we see it as disrespect, laziness, and defiance. Their behaviors push us away rather than compel us to help. Our dysregulation in response to a child's meltdown only adds fuel to the toxic flames of their trauma.

When we are dysregulated, the parts of the brain that we can't access are the parts we need most to help a child with trauma-based behavior. We lose empathy ("I don't care what they've gone through, they can't treat people this way!") and flexibility ("They need to learn that the world doesn't rotate around them!"). We then seek to regain control, most often through punishing them, shaming them, excluding them, or ignoring them. When we do this, we further activate their stress response, and, voilà, they act out more. Then, of course, we punish more, intensifying the impact of their traumatic histories. We are now in a downward spiral of co-dysregulation. Everyone loses.

This is the tragedy of how we address childhood trauma—well-meaning adults often do the opposite of what children need. Our go-to practices of punishment and exclusion for trauma-behavior only intensify the destructive power of their trauma. The research taught us this decades ago and yet we continue to engage in the same harmful practices. In 1958, Harry Harlow wrote, "the total social isolation of solitary incarceration is considered so drastic that Americans pride themselves on reserving it for the most pernicious prisoners." Sadly, the kids with the most trauma are often the ones who are punished and excluded the most. They are also the ones most likely to be incarcerated as adults.

We learned in Parts I and II that punishment and exclusion are not only ineffective, they can be destructive. Now we know that they are especially toxic for children who have experienced trauma. Rather than helping them heal through coregulated relationships, we further harm them through isolation. We do all of this with the misguided belief that being isolated and alone will convince them not to misbehave. But they already know not to hit their sister or swear at their teacher. Again, it isn't a matter of knowing. It is a matter of having access to the parts of the brain necessary to make our best decisions—and the only way we can help them regain access to that part of their brain is to help them regulate. The most powerful way to do this is through healthy and responsive relationships. These relationships buffer the impact of stress in the moment and also provide the foundation for long-term resilience.

Schools are uniquely positioned to buffer the impact of trauma in students and to help them regain their developmental footing after a traumatic event knocks their lives off balance. Schools are a captive audience for children for more than a decade—no one outside of the home can impact a child's life the way our schools can. Schools are filled with adults and other children wanting to connect and engage. It is the perfect recipe for reversing the impact of trauma. Place students in a safe and engaging learning environment, add caring students and teachers, then mix. The healing power of school communities is ready-made. Rarely do we take advantage of this power. Schools can either be a place of respite for a child from their trauma or they can accelerate the impact of trauma. Tragically, often, it is the latter.

Children with high ACEs come to school carrying their traumatic home life with them like another book bag. Their limbic system is vigilant as they get on the bus, walk into school, through the halls, and into their classroom. They are ready to fight, flee, or freeze at any indication of a potential threat. If they are not embedded in relationships that feel safe and in routines that are predictable and manageable, they will spend most of their day in lower brain. Their fight, flight, and freeze responses will be on full display. They will be less available for learning, more impulsive, and more guarded in their relationships with both their classmates and teachers. Their name will be the first to go up on the whiteboard, a message of shame and a public warning of impending punishment. They will misperceive relationships and be out of step with their peers and then struggle to form the friendships that could help them heal. Unable to develop meaningful relationships, many will become the bully or the bullied. Many will seem "out of it," or struggle to sit still and focus, impacting their ability to complete schoolwork. Many will struggle with their grades, then get labeled as lazy and disruptive.

Conversely, school could be a place where they are getting dose after dose of caring and connection from the staff and the students. When this happens, their stress response gets a break. Their breathing quiets, their heartbeat slows, their digestive system returns to baseline, and their brains open up for learning, enabling them to engage academically and socially. They are healthier physically and emotionally, and they are less impulsive and reactive behaviorally. As their relationships improve, as they connect more with others, they discover goodness in themselves that they rarely experience. School, then, not only buffers their stresses in the moment, it provides the foundation for greater resilience throughout their life.

The following diagram shows what happens in the brains of children who experience trauma as compared to children whose brains develop without the stress of high ACEs.

TRAUMA & BRAIN DEVELOPMENT

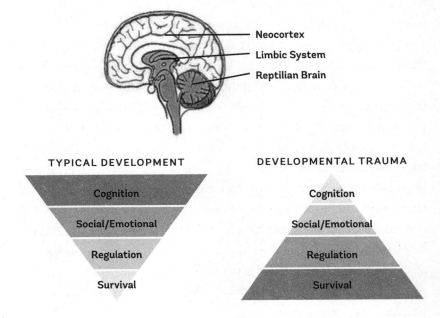

Children who are not experiencing trauma do not have to focus so much of their energy on their survival. As a result, they have a large bandwidth to fully engage academically and socially. They have more resources to devote to learning and navigating their social world. The brains of children who have experienced complex trauma are hypervigilant about threats to their safety. Their secret service is taking over, constantly scanning their environment for threats and managing their physical and emotional regulation to adapt to the ever-changing demands of school and home. They appear to be off track, they may be highly sensitive and reactive to the slights of others, they can be argumentative or simply shut down and put their heads on their desk. Because it is exhausting to have our limbic system so active, they hit their intolerable peak sooner, slamming on their limbic brake to regain a sense of control of a world that seems out of their control. As a result, they have very little bandwidth left to be available for learning or connecting with others.

When both school and home are places of adult hostility in response to trauma-behavior, children have nowhere to turn to feel safe, regulated, and connected. Their stress response system is constantly activated. But as any trauma expert will tell you, the way to reverse the impact of trauma is to take full advantage of the regulating power of healthy relationships. Relationships rewire the brain and quiet the limbic system. Schools, because they have an abundance of relationship potential, have the unique opportunity to do just that. And yet, our current educational practices of "zero tolerance," the shaming power of punishment, and the isolating power of exclusion in response to student trauma-behavior only serve to make things worse. Their mental health suffers rather than improves. Their physical health declines. And the seeds for devastating health, mental health, and behavioral health problems in adulthood are sown, fertilized, and watered.

We have been misunderstanding trauma and behavior for a long time, making children's lives worse instead of better. And yet, the path to healing trauma, and addressing trauma-based behavior, is clear and accessible for all of us. We just need to change direction and step onto a different path.

Quieting Our Stress Response

Jamal, a sixth grader, was new to NSA. He had the build of a tight end: tall and muscular. Although we only knew part of his story of trauma, it was clear that he was wounded. He guarded his feelings as a lineman would protect the quarterback—fiercely and aggressively. He seldom spoke and when he did, he tended to mumble, ambivalent about whether he wanted his words to be heard. He rarely smiled in groups but one on one he would allow a glimpse at his underlying warmth that was often accompanied by a wry smile and a full-bodied giggle. He was also quick to rage, his limbic system vigilant for any sign of threat. Often, that threat came in the form of adults asserting control. His phone, in particular, became the battlefield for many of his power struggles with staff. At the time we didn't know that Jamal's phone had a special meaning for him. We would discover that meaning the hard way.

We asked all of the students to hand their phones in to their teacher when they arrived at school. Jamal almost always refused. The battle that started during homeroom would continue to intensify throughout the day. One morning, Jamal was in the school gym when he put his phone on the floor to tie his shoes. In a moment of both opportunism and poor judgment, a teaching assistant snuck up behind Jamal and grabbed his phone. At that moment, the teaching assistant felt victorious. After hours of feeling rendered powerless by a sixth grader, he had regained control. Unfortunately, the battle had just begun. Jamal stood, spun, and ran at the teaching assistant, tackling him to the ground. Other staff jumped in and tried to restrain Jamal as he screamed and punched and grabbed at the teaching assistant in a fit of primal panic. Eventually, Jamal calmed down and was brought to Lara, the assistant principal.

Jamal, still in lower brain, had few words. "Give me my phone," he repeated in response to whatever Lara said. Lara knew that before she could talk to Jamal about his aggression, she first needed to help him become regulated by addressing the issue of the phone. "Your phone is really important to you," she reflected. "Help me understand why it is so hard to give it up."

Jamal's expression was impassive. "Give me my phone," he repeated.

Lara persisted, speaking quietly and calmly. Her tone exuded a caring that Jamal must not have expected given his aggression and defiance. "Is there a place that we could keep it so that it doesn't get in the way of your classwork? I could keep it locked in my desk so that you know it is safe."

"No. I don't trust any of you."

Then, Lara surprised Jamal, and everyone else in the room. "What if I gave you the key to my desk? That way only you could get it. You would know that it was safe, you could get it if you really needed it, and we could be sure that you didn't have it in class." He paused, and then relented. Lara handed him the key.

Throughout this interaction, Lara was coregulating. Her voice calm, her posture open, her expression caring. She listened to both his words and his body language. She was flexible and creative. She spoke with a tone and cadence that Jamal's lower brain could hear and understand. Lara was intentional, knowing that the more dysregulated Jamal was, the more regulated she needed to be. It took several minutes, but Jamal was slowly becoming more regulated and more flexible himself. He also felt seen—Lara understood that he needed to know that his phone would be safe. Sharing her key with Jamal meant that she trusted him and, as we know from Part I, trust goes a long way toward building relationships. It was a shortcut to connecting. Her limbic system was letting Jamal's limbic system know that he was safe. Lara knew, intuitively, that Jamal's phone had greater meaning to him than we knew. It was not just about Jamal wanting to watch YouTube videos in class. His intensity told her that there was more to the story. It turned out, her intuition was spot on. She found out the next day when Jamal's grandfather came in for a meeting to debrief what had happened.

We knew that Jamal was living with his grandfather because his mother had recently died of kidney failure, and his father was not able to care for him. When his mother died, everything in Jamal's life fell to pieces. Jamal was referred to NSA after struggling academically and behaviorally at his new school. "That phone is really important to Jamal," his grandfather explained. "When his mother was dying, she gave him that phone and told him that when things got hard for him, he could always call his favorite aunt in Indiana. I think that when you take away his phone, it feels like you are taking away both his mother and his aunt." The phone for Jamal was a lifeline—a connection to both a mother he had lost and an aunt who cared deeply about him but was miles away. Giving up his phone meant losing both of them all over again. When Lara gave him the key to her desk, he felt that his connection to his mother and aunt were protected. He felt a sense of control when so much of his life felt out of his control.

Once Lara and her team were able to partner with Jamal to create a plan about the phone, he was regulated enough to access the parts of his brain that he needed to address his aggression. He shared that his rage took over and that he felt badly that he responded the way that he did. Jamal met with the teaching assistant, who was upset but unhurt, and apologized. He also found the words he needed to explain why it was so hard for him to have his phone taken that way. When they were done, the teaching assistant, moved by his story and apology, gave Jamal a hug.

Jamal's connection to his phone was both unexpected and intense. Whenever we observe behaviors that seem irrationally reactive, we need to understand that there is likely an embedded memory that triggers the behavior. If we look and listen, we can get closer to understanding. Jamal's experience of loss and grief were upstream. His clinging to his phone, and subsequently his aggression, were downstream.

Jamal was lucky to have Lara work with him at that moment. Before we can help heal the trauma, we need to see the trauma, and Lara saw it. Most people would have made an assumption that he just wanted his phone to avoid work. They then would have confiscated the phone and punished him, through exclusion and isolation, for his aggression. Many would have called the police. This would have only intensified Jamal's rage, defiance, disconnection, and mistrust. Instead, Lara coregulated with him. She listened to Jamal and partnered with him to find a solution. She brought in his grandfather, a person Jamal trusted, to help us better understand his experience. She helped Jamal think through how to repair the damage that he had done when he was so aggressive. Together they found their way through a defining moment in Jamal's life. Within a few years, Jamal was back at his home school. Four years later, we received his high school graduation announcement. His smile in the photo was no longer hidden behind a scowl. It was radiant. He was heading off to college.

Buffering the Impact of Trauma

The devastating data about trauma can be both frightening and disheartening. However, we also know from so many stories of children, it is possible to learn to thrive in spite of childhoods that were filled with toxic stress. Most of us have experienced traumatic events and, while still impacted by them, many of us do not suffer from the profound health and mental health problems described in the ACEs study. The devastating impact of trauma is not etched in stone and there are many ways that adults can alter the course of trauma in ourselves and in our children. For children, we can not only buffer the impact of trauma in the immediate aftermath, we can also take an active role in helping them heal from the dysregulating effects of past traumas. Frequent and generous doses of healthy and regulating interactions heal trauma. The more doses, the greater the impact. For Jamal, it wasn't just Lara. It was an entire middle school team of staff and students. It was his grandfather. Then, it was the staff and students at his high school giving him dose after dose of feeling seen, cared about, and believed in.

Jamal is not alone. Research has found that the long-term impact of trauma is related less to the trauma itself and more to the community's response to the trauma. When the community acts as a buffer, rather than an accelerant, children learn to cope much more effectively. Simply stated, when children experience environments that are attuned and coregulating, the physical and emotional impact of the trauma is reduced. Relationships protect us. Trauma changes us and the nature of those changes depends on the quality of our relationships.

As I was learning more about trauma, I was asked to observe a student in a third grade classroom. The teacher, Colin, was tall—6'3" or 6'4"—and towered over the nine- and ten-year-olds in his class. I was there to observe one student, but I couldn't take my eyes off the magic Colin was creating. He was energetic, funny, and focused. The students laughed as he bounded around the room, their eyes tracking him as they would the Pied Piper. One boy, Blake, stood out, not just because of his bright blond hair but because of how he hung on every word Colin spoke. They shared laughs together and Colin made sure to stop by Blake's desk as he walked around the classroom, often placing a hand on his shoulder. They were attuned.

After school, Colin and I met to talk about the student I had observed. I commented on how much I enjoyed watching him teach. Colin shared that it had been a hard year in his class. "We have a lot of kids who are hurting," he said. "I'm not sure if you noticed the really blond kid, Blake. His father died suddenly six weeks ago." I was stunned. And then relieved. The tragic loss of Blake's father was being buffered by his relationship with Colin and the classroom community Colin had created. "He is off task a lot these days, but if I can stand closer to him he gets back on task. Just being near him seems to help." For thirty hours a week, Blake can feel connected to Colin and engaged in something outside of his personal tragedy. He can laugh and play and learn. He can feel seen. And during that time, his body's stress response can get a break. Those breaks, it turns out, allow his body to rest and recover. They can add years to his life.

The opposite is also true. A few months later, I was working with a fifth grade team that was meeting to discuss what to do about a student named Jimmy. Jimmy had been suspended a number of times due to disruptive and aggressive behavior. With the new state law encouraging schools to reduce suspensions, the team was required to develop a different behavior plan. They began by creating the typical menu of incentives and punishments that would compel Jimmy to behave differently when I asked, "What do you know about Jimmy's parents?"

"Oh!" the teacher responded. "That's a whole 'nother story. When we call the mom, she almost never picks up. She is a big part of the problem."

"What about the dad?" I asked. The psychologist looked at the file.

"Oh yes. I forgot to mention that his father died when he was in first grade." After digging deeper into Jimmy's history, we learned that after his father died, Jimmy's mother needed to pick up a second job to make ends meet. She worried that if she kept answering the phone or leaving work to attend meetings at school, she would lose her job and she and Jimmy would soon be homeless. Jimmy either spent his afternoons and early evenings at home alone or with his elderly grandparents in their one-bedroom apartment. The grandparents were the only adults at home, and one struggled to walk and the other was nearly deaf. No wonder Jimmy was struggling. No wonder his mother seemed so unresponsive.

Of course, the team was dealing with trauma-behavior, not misbehavior. The team, focusing on the mis-behavior, was trying to figure out what punishments would be effective enough to get Jimmy to comply. Trauma has a long tail. We experience traumas differently at different developmental stages in our lives. For the school, the death of Jimmy's father was a distant speck in their rearview mirror. For Jimmy and his mother, it was an issue they were still dealing with, directly and indirectly, every moment of every day. The school just couldn't see it.

Both Jimmy and Blake were at risk given the loss of their fathers. One school buffered the trauma, the other intensified it. Blake was seen and heard. Jimmy was excluded and punished.

This is the power of buffering relationships. As Nadine Burke

Harris states simply and clearly, "Adult relationships buffer the impact of adverse childhood experiences." Bessel van der Kolk agrees and explains it this way: "We are a very resilient species. So if we are around people who love us, trust us, take care of us, nurture us when we are down, most people do pretty well with even very horrendous events . . . the social context in which it occurs is fantastically important." How do we become buffers for children's trauma? Connect and regulate. Dose after dose after dose.

It turns out that the number of buffers in children's lives can be even more important to their health and well-being than the number of traumatic events that they experience. Just as the strength of our immune system is often more important to keeping us healthy than our exposure to a virus, the same is true for relationships and the impact of trauma. The more buffers we have, the healthier we are. Bruce Perry and his team researched the impact of healthy relationships on trauma and reported the following: "Our major finding is that your history of relational health—your connectedness to family, community, and culture—is more predictive of your mental health than your history of adversity." As a result, the lack of buffers—a lack of connected and responsive relationships—can put us at risk in the same way that trauma can. Without these buffers, we are more vulnerable to even low levels of stress. With these buffers, we can cope with even tragic events. As Maté writes, "Children can be harmed by bad things happening but also by good things not happening, such as their emotional needs for attunement not being met or the experiencing of not being seen and accepted, even by loving parents."

Small Doses Matter

Adults can change the course of the lives of traumatized children. We do so by creating caring and attuned relationships that buffer and reverse the impact of the trauma. Being embedded in schools and families that are filled with connected and regulated relationships gives a body's stress response a break. The greater the number of these relationships in a child's life, the longer the break, the bigger the short and long-term benefits. The repetition of experiencing caring, attuned, and calm connections with adults can rewire a child's brain, embedding new memories in the limbic system that, in time, can override memories of relational trauma with memories of relational safety. This can create a cascade of experiences that enhance health and well-being. A limbic system that feels safe rather than threatened around other people will approach others with greater openness, be more available to try new things, take risks, and tolerate failure—all of the qualities that allow us to engage in the world in healthy ways. People who have experienced trauma need this repetition to quiet and rewire their reactive limbic system.

This is hard work. So hard that many of us want to outsource it to individual therapists. As parents and teachers, we don't feel we have sufficient training to help children who have experienced trauma. We believe that, somehow, the forty-five minutes of therapy per week creates a magic that will help them overcome years of trauma. Interestingly, even trauma clinicians are moving further away from talk therapy, the primary intervention for trauma. The focus, they are learning, is to heal the body first. Rather than to try to help the child make sense of traumatic events, the more immediate goal is to quiet the stress response system and to rewire it to be less reactive. Healing from trauma requires many repetitions of helping a child regulate when they become dysregulated by embedded memories. It is about helping them feel seen. As poet Charles Finn wrote, they ask us to "please listen carefully and try to hear what I am not saying." The more significant the trauma, the more doses of coregulation they will need.

This is why our families and schools are so important to the well-being of our children. These are the places where children can get their most intense and repetitive doses of connection and regulation.

And these doses don't need to be long lasting or intense—often they need to be shorter and less intense so that we don't overwhelm a child who has been traumatized. A smile from a bus driver, a high five in the hallway from a former teacher, a laugh with the lunch room supervisor, a few additional minutes with a basketball coach after practice to improve their shooting form. These are all moments of feeling seen and heard and valued. As Bruce Perry wrote, "The neural networks involved in relational connection and regulation are very responsive to *moments*. This means that a meaningful dose of therapeutic interaction isn't forty-five minutes once a week. When you are dealing with an intense trauma, we've found that a 'tolerable' dose is only seconds long." It is Colin's hand on Blake's shoulder. It is a laugh that I share with Angelique. It is taking a short walk with Jamal when he is feeling restless. I saw a post on Facebook by an elementary school teacher, Lauren Boyd, that shows how important these doses are for children, even if you don't know the story of their trauma. "I have a boy in my class who comes in every morning with messy hair and every morning I comb his hair for him. This morning when I got done, he gave me the biggest hug and said, 'Thanks, Ms. Boyd. My mom is sick and can't brush my hair anymore, so I'm happy you do it.'" Such moments, often taken for granted, are the foundation of trauma-responsive care. The teacher saw that her student had a need. She addressed the need without even knowing its source. It is not always easy, but it is often that simple. The Mrs. Boyds of the world change the world of children who have experienced trauma.

Father Greg Boyle asks, "How can we seek a compassion that can stand in awe at what people have to carry, rather than stand in judgment at how they carry it?" Children who struggle behaviorally are carrying a heavy burden. We can choose to help them carry that burden or we can pile on.

Doses of relationships are a lot like a healthy diet. Many smaller meals are healthier than one big meal. We wouldn't expect one meal, once a week, to satisfy our nutritional needs. The same is true for therapy—we can't meet the trauma-based needs of a child with one forty-five-minute therapy session per week. It takes all of us, providing small doses of connection throughout a child's day, in addition to therapy, to help a child heal and to build their resilience for future stresses. As educators and parents, we need to be intentional about what "doses" our children will receive. Will they receive doses of connection and regulation that quiet their stress response and embed feelings of psychological safety within their limbic system, or will they experience the hostility of a punishing and shaming community that further triggers their stress response and embeds even more deeply into the limbic brain that relationships and communities are dangerous? In our schools, will we let their stress response get a break for thirty hours a week, leading to healing and adding years onto their lives or will we continue to trigger their stress response during those six hours a day, resulting in additional stresses that lead to breakdowns of their body systems a decade or two later? The stakes are high. For many students it is the difference between a longer life or an early death.

Creating Communities of Healing

Thankfully, we don't need to know everyone's ACEs in order to be helpful. What is good for kids who have experienced trauma is also what is best for all children. It's just more important for children with a history of ACEs because they need more doses. Everyone benefits from families and schools where the people in charge are emotionally regulated and attuned. In these communities, our brains open up, we collaborate, we connect, we learn from one another, and we grow.

A connected and regulated classroom community creates the opportunity for greater academic engagement and rigor for *everyone* in the classroom. When students feel safe and connected, they learn better. At home, when children feel safe and connected, they too embrace our values, grow, learn, and mature more quickly and in healthier ways. Growing up in emotionally regulated communities with healthy attachments is the tide that raises all ships. Everyone benefits.

Buffering and reversing the impact of trauma is not rocket science. It is as simple as giving the kids who need it the most the things we all want and need in our own lives. The experience of being seen and heard. Being treated with empathy in our hardest moments. Knowing that there will be a connected and regulated response when we struggle. Feeling connected to, and supported by, those around us. The problem is that we so often do just the opposite. We withhold these things from the kids who need it the most. How did we get it so backwards? We all have the resources we need to support children who are suffering. It is innate within us as humans. Our brains are built for empathy and connection. We became parents and teachers because we care about children. No one is more invested in their healthy growth and development. And yet, we are often the ones who undermine it.

One of the biggest barriers to our ability to help children cope with their trauma is the feeling that we are not doing enough. We cannot take away their experiences of abuse, we can't bring a parent back to life, we can't cure a parent's mental illness or addiction. If we can't fix these things, can we really be helpful? The answer is a resounding yes. It is also paradoxical. Helping children through trauma is often about doing less, not more. It is about being present and regulated with them rather than trying to fix them. It's about helping the child feel seen and heard rather than frightened, damaged, and punished. I am often reminded of a twist on an old phrase to guide me when I'm trying to support someone struggling with trauma.

"Don't just do something, stand there."

Regulate yourself. Be present. Coregulate. Listen. Soothe. Repeat.

PART IV

Community: The Road to Wellness

CHAPTER 9

Establishing the Roots of Community

After my parents' divorce, the fabric of my family began to unravel. Few memories exist from the year after the divorce. I don't remember the move from the expansive three-story parsonage to the first floor of a three-family house a few blocks away. I don't remember Mom looking for work or applying to graduate school. I don't remember anything about first grade and have retained only scattered fragments of memories from second grade. My mother went to work full time and to school at night. Life at home with my brother, ten, and sisters ages eight and four was chaotic. Our lives had turned upside down within a few months and we were all ill-equipped for the fallout. We played together occasionally but often fought or retreated to our own spaces. My father, following the norms of divorce at the time, saw us only on Sundays.

I attended Edward Smith Elementary School. At the time, kids were allowed to go home for lunch. I chose that option every day, enjoying the fluffernutter sandwich, Cheetos, and cookie that my mom left for me that morning. Inevitably, when it came time to go back to school, my stomach would start to ache and I would talk myself into staying home for the afternoon.

One day, my teacher, Ms. Doherty, pulled me aside before lunch. "You need to come back this afternoon. We are doing a group project and your group needs you." I assured her I would be back. I even believed it myself. When I got home that day, I was surprised to see my mother who was never home during the day. She told me that she and my father had just formalized the divorce that morning and she was taking the rest of the day off. She let me know that if I was upset, I could stay home, too. It was my first moral decision. And it was easy. I leapt at the chance to spend the afternoon with my mom.

When I walked into class the next morning, shame rained down on me. Ms. Doherty called me to the front of the class. She was a short and heavyset woman, but she seemed to tower over me. Finger wagging, she scolded me. "I'm disappointed at you." I remember those words so clearly. I remember wondering to myself, *Isn't it "disappointed in you"?* I blushed. Pressure formed behind my eyes and my lip shook as I walked back to my seat.

My mom, looking back on this time, said that I must have been depressed and that in the chaos of our lives she had missed it. But maybe she didn't miss it. After watching me struggle again through third grade, she enrolled me and my older sister, Betsy, into an alternative and experimental elementary school called Syracuse Institute for Enabling Education or SIEE. SIEE was located in the basement of my father's former church. In a strange way, it felt like coming home. SIEE had only a couple dozen students of all ages and had nontraditional instruction and curriculum. It felt like a one-room schoolhouse. My teacher, David Knapp, was right out of central casting for a 1970s era hippie—long red hair pulled back in a ponytail, torn jeans, and lime green van. We had self-directed assignments where we were encouraged to leave school and explore the city in pairs or small groups. Our art teacher owned a farm where we spent days lashing logs together to build a two-story platform. I walked to school with a group of friends, exploring a different part of the Syracuse University campus each day. I was cast as Christopher Robin in *The House at Pooh Corner*. I thrived. I felt seen, trusted, and appreciated by the adults and students around me. Instead of feeling scared and shamed in school, I was engaged and connected. My nervous system began to quiet. The experience was transformative. Although my life at home was as chaotic as ever, my school community not only kept me afloat, it helped me learn to sail.

Then it all came crashing down.

My mother met a man named Bill Murphy who was full of energy, creativity, and big dreams. He swept my mother off her feet. She bought a house in nearby Skaneateles—a beautiful, wealthy Syracuse suburb with a picturesque downtown overlooking Skaneateles Lake. We lived just outside of town, three houses up from the cemetery and across from a service station and trailer park, just down the hill from the bowling alley. I was happy that my mother found someone and was hopeful for their marriage. My brother, Jim, didn't share my optimism and I didn't share his foresight. Angry battles between Jim and Bill became common. After the wedding and before we moved, Jim decided to move in with my father, unwilling to live under the same roof as his new stepfather.

As a budding seventh grader I was excited about moving into a new and preppy town. I was earnest and loyal to the people who helped me through my hardest times at home and at SIEE. My art teacher gave me a gift of a silver wire knot ring to remember how much I was cared for at SIEE. My mother and Bill gave Jim and me silver bracelets engraved with our names as gifts at their wedding. To prepare me for school, my mother spent money she didn't have to buy me a beautiful leather backpack from the hippest store in Syracuse. Equipped with all of the symbols of support from the people who cared about me, I was excited to begin my new future life at Skaneateles Middle School.

It couldn't have gone worse. I showed up in the 1976 suburban middle school uniform—corduroy pants and Izod polo shirt, collar up. What everyone saw, however, was the new kid with a ring, a bracelet, and a leather purse. Everywhere I turned I heard "fag" or "homo." Anyone who spoke to me would also be called gay. I was socially radioactive before I could say my first "hello."

Things weren't better at home. Shortly after the wedding, Bill Murphy's colors began to show. As it turned out, he left a trail of broken dreams and empty Rolling Rock bottles wherever he went. Unemployed and drinking more and more, he was always ready to unleash his anger. I could smell the beer on his breath as he greeted me from school by grabbing my shoulders and calling me a "fag" and a "fem."

Ashamed, I told no one. Even as an adult, I have a hard time talking about it. I wonder if my mother knew and whether my sisters witnessed my humiliation and alienation from a distance. Within a year, my sister Betsy decided to leave, too. She joined my brother and lived with my father and our stepfamily in a town about thirty miles away. My mother, having realized the magnitude of her mistake, told Bill that he needed to move out. My younger sister, Kristin, and I stayed with her, each looking for a path of acceptance in this new community. I started to play sports, trying out for the eighth-grade soccer team. I had never played on a team before, and the first practice quickly revealed that I was the least skilled player on the field. Because I was tall and they were desperate, the coaches made me a goalie. I loved it. The following season I tried out for basketball, just barely making the team. Slowly, through these teams, I started to get to know people. I began making friends, developing skills, and moving my way up the roster in both sports. Finally, in the spring of my eighth grade year, I was invited to a friend's house. I remember being so nervous, worried that I would lose the one person willing to take a risk on me.

In my high school years, the community of sports opened up a door that changed my life. As I got better at sports, I also got better at friendships. I felt valued, important, cared about, included. In soccer we went to the state semifinals my junior year and state finals my senior year. I was voted prom king, mostly due to my ballot-stuffing soccer teammates. My mother was there when I was crowned. Unable to share my years of shame, I was glad that she was there to share a moment of pride. I had found my place in the community.

When I graduated, I had a confidence in myself that I had never had as a young child. My mother often said, "You were such an unfortunate-looking child—your pants were always falling down and your nose was always running. Now look at you!" I had been shy and withdrawn and now I felt ready, as a young adult, to head off on my own to a new community—at Bates College. College sports and dorm life suited me well and quickly I became a part of a new community where, again, I felt fully engaged and alive with new friends and professors who saw me, challenged me, and believed in me. As with any skill, the more practice we get being in a healthy community, the better we get at it, and the more we get out of it.

My junior year in college, I felt ready for another challenge. I traveled to Scotland to spend a year at St. Andrews University. I can remember the initial loneliness I felt, friendless and missing my family. Again, it was soccer (football) that was my path to connection. I never imagined I could be good enough to play for the university team but, as it turns out, within a few months, I was starting for their first team. The soccer was wonderful, but even more impactful was the way that the team embraced me. They included me in everything they did, each person making sure that I never felt alone and that I would experience everything that Scotland had to offer: Angus lent me his kilt so I could go to a formal dance and took me to an international rugby championship game. Paul took me home to visit his family in northern England. Judith made sure that I didn't miss a party and would sit with me over tea and scones, listening patiently as I told her about my many failed attempts to find a Scottish girlfriend. A few years later, I would return to Scotland to deliver the best man's toast at Paul and Judith's wedding. Thirty years after that, I attended their oldest child's wedding. When my junior year in Scotland finished, I returned to Bates for my senior year, reconnecting with friends that I still see regularly, forty years after we met.

These communities transformed me from the "unfortunate-looking child" of my early life to a confident young adult. Able to rely on past relationships for support and equipped with the belief that I could form new relationships wherever I went, I felt ready for the world that was awaiting me. These communities that embraced me helped rewire my attachment system. I knew what it was like to be seen and heard and cared for. My communities regulated me and supported me during stressful times, which allowed me to be more fully present. I was so present in the moment in college that I didn't really plan ahead. By the time I received my college diploma, I had friendships that spanned continents. What I didn't have was a vision for what I would do with my life.

Then, just weeks after graduation, I crossed the rustic, single-lane bridge and entered Wediko, a community that would forever change me and the course of my life.

I was twenty-one when I walked into the musty cafeteria and found my place on the floor with the other camp counselors. A light breeze was blowing off of the lake, carrying the scents of the New England forest into the screened dining hall. I took it all in. The building was rustic, showing both its durability and cracks from decades of hard use by children and the adults in charge of their care. We sat shoulder to shoulder in shorts and T-shirts, the returning counselors reuniting and the new counselors just trying to find their bearings. We were there to work with 150 children and teenagers, mostly from Boston, whose behavior was creating problems both at home and at school.

Harry Parad, the clinical director, quieted us. A journalist who wrote a story about Wediko once described Harry as a mix of Groucho Marx and Albert Einstein. The description was apt, not just because of his appearance, but for the depth of his wisdom, his authenticity, and his wry sense of humor. He gave the same talk at the start of every summer, and over the years each time I heard it, I gained a greater depth of understanding. His message was simple: "The program is the primary intervention." If the program is strong, everyone grows and gets healthier. It doesn't matter which cabin you are in, what challenges you are facing, or who your supervisor is. Change happens through the community we create. Our focus, first and foremost, is to build and maintain that community. If we can do that, we all thrive.

After that first year, I couldn't stay away. I returned to Wediko for the next three summers and parts of the following four years. As a young adult, I thrived in that community where I felt such a strong sense of belonging. I was also part of creating a community of belonging for children who, like me when I was their age, so desperately needed it. There was a powerful synergy—children and adults both creating and benefitting from a community of connection. After getting my Ph.D. in clinical psychology, I realized that a fifty-minute weekly therapy session wouldn't be enough for the students I most wanted to work with—those whose struggles left them on the fringes of their communities. These students needed the kind of community I experienced at Wediko. And where better to experience a healing community than in schools? I wanted to be a part of creating communities for children who lived at the margins. After a few years in other schools, I found my professional home, North Shore Academy, where I experienced the power of community for myself and watched as that community transformed the lives of children and families. Soon, it would be my turn to lead that community as principal. That's when my learning really began.

Lessons Learned from Forests

Creating connected communities—in families and schools in particular—where children are surrounded by people who care deeply and model the most adaptive skills is our best tool for supporting healthy childhood development. Being connected to others in a community is an inherent part of our humanness. It turns out, nature has long known this, using these strong bonds to create a diverse, complex, and self-sufficient world.

Think about the atom. It is the smallest particle known to exist and yet, it still has a group of neutrons, protons, and electrons, working together, balancing one another, merging to become the building block for everything in our world. Molecules, too, create their magic through connection. They gather together, in groups of two or more atoms to form compounds of increasing complexity to eventually become a countertop, a coffee mug, or a computer. Without these bonds, our world would not exist. And, without the bonds of community, neither would we.

There is a term in the design world called "biomimicry." The theory behind the concept is that nature has already figured out answers to many of our world's most complex problems. If we are struggling with a problem, we just need to find the solution in nature. I first became aware of biomimicry during the 2008 Beijing Olympics. World records continued to fall at astounding rates during swimming competitions. Twenty-five world records and sixty-five Olympic records were set in the two weeks of competition. How did these swimmers achieve times so much faster than the swimmers before them? There were two answers. The remarkable talent of Michael Phelps. And biomimicry.

In the years leading up to the Beijing Olympics, Speedo, NASA, and a number of universities were researching aqua dynamics in an effort to produce the most effective swimsuit. Human skin is not built for speed in the water and the scientists were interested in finding a fabric that would reduce drag and support the muscles without constraining motion. Rather than invent new technologies, they instead looked to nature, which had answered this problem 450 million years earlier. Sharkskin. After applying nature's technology to swimsuits, records fell like dominos.

I wondered if biomimicry could provide design ideas for building resilience in children. In nature, every species of plant and animal is a testament to the idea of resilience. Otherwise, they would have been wiped out in the grueling gauntlet of evolution. Charlotte Gill, in her memoir about planting trees in British Columbia, introduced me to the power of community in forests. As I read, my mind kept returning to our students. A forest community buffers and supports each individual tree. "Trees are community beings," she wrote. "They shelter one another from wind and weather. Underground, they hang on to each other with intertwined roots. A lone tree is almost certainly toppled in a big storm, but when a stiff wind blows through a clustered grove, they sway and bend together." Botanists call the underground network or roots and fungus the "wood-wide-web" (who knew botanists could be so clever?) and through it they nurture their own offspring, send warning signals about injury or disease, and donate resources to conserve the forest. Trees share nutrients and water; these resources are "optimally divided among them so that each tree can grow into the best tree it can be." When a tree dies, the nearby trees tend to the stump, trying to keep it alive. I realized that the same thing happens in our healthiest families and classrooms.

When we look into a forest, it looks like a chaotic struggle for space and light, but it is actually a graceful dance, each tree moving toward light and making space so that other trees can find their path to the sky. Our work then, in our families and schools, is to create communities where every child finds their path and helps others to reach for their light.

Forests are also essential to our planet. Together, they engage in a dynamic process of absorbing carbon dioxide and using it for photosynthesis, helping to maintain the carbon balance in our world. Tragically, we are cutting down our forests at alarming rates, choosing short-term solutions that endanger the long-term health of our planet. We are doing the same with our communities for children—as we will discover, our urgency to promote the happiness and success of our own children often comes at the cost of what they most need to be happy and successful—communities that are connected and regulated.

How Our Communities Shape Us

Although we often think of ourselves as consistent in our behavior across situations, most of us show up very differently depending on the community that we are a part of. Adults are generally more empowered to choose the communities where we live and work and play. For children, however, their community is a roll of the dice. As Robert Sapolsky wrote, "Your life will be unrecognizably different, depending on which culture the stork deposited you into."

Within each broader society, we become embedded within smaller communities—a family, a classroom, a school, a neighborhood, a workplace—and we are highly sensitive to the culture within those communities. Although we may not notice, our body responds to the environment it enters. Depending on our sense of internal safety, our blood vessels either constrict or dilate, our immune system relaxes or activates, our body releases either cortisol or oxytocin. In a community we may feel hopeful and engaged or cynical and resigned. We may feel like we are in it together and share our resources with one another or we may "circle the wagons" to protect ourselves from threats within the community. Our community is the lathe that shapes our experience of the world.

The sociologist and physician Nicholas Christakis has researched the impact of social connections and describes how we behave differently in different communities this way:

> People often think that personality traits such as kindness are fixed. But our research with groups suggests something quite different: the tendency to be altruistic or exploitative may depend heavily on how the social world is organized. So if we took the same population of

people and assigned them to one social world, we could make them really generous to one another, and if we put them in another sort of world, we could make them really mean or indifferent to one another. Crucially, this indicates that the tendency to cooperate is a property not only of individuals but of groups.

Before reading this, I believed that I lived my core values in every setting with consistency. When I looked closer I was startled and disheartened to realize how vulnerable I am to the community in which I happen to be. As a principal, I tried to bring a positive energy, always eager to partner with my colleagues on the district administrative team. We had hard discussions when we disagreed, and our commitment to the kids and families always manifested in our willingness to go above and beyond, regardless of the task. I would arrive to meetings early and stay late to talk more with my colleagues. I would share my thoughts in the meetings (perhaps too often) and I often volunteered for projects that would help our work outside of the meetings.

A new administrator was hired and our administrative culture changed quickly. As I experienced the culture transform from collaborative to directive, from trusting to insecure, from empowering to micromanaging, from transparent to suspicious, from supportive to self-interested, my participation changed. I talked less and when I did, there was a cynical edge to my comments. I started talking behind the backs of people who upset me rather than speaking with them directly. I rushed in late to meetings and left as soon as they ended, cringing as the administrator closed every meeting with, "For the good of the team we go!" Within three years our core team of eight had all left. After twenty-one years at NSA, it was clear that I needed to leave.

Fortunately, we were able to find new communities where we began to thrive. But new communities aren't always available on demand to people in toxic cultures. Powerful barriers to choosing a community include, among other things, racism, poverty, disabilities, gender inequities, and age discrimination. Children are uniquely powerless to choose their community. They do not get to choose their families or leave if the culture feels toxic. They don't get to choose their schools, classrooms, their coaches, or their neighborhoods. Different families and classrooms and neighborhoods have very different opportunities and risks. This is where support from adults is so important. If we want to create the foundation for our children to lead a life that is healthy and resilient, we need to do everything we can to create connected and regulated families, schools, teams, and neighborhoods for all children.

Our Slow and Steady Drift Away from Community

The challenge for contemporary society is that our social bonds are becoming more frayed than ever before. The statistics are convincing and alarming. Self-reports of loneliness are increasing every year. While we may instinctively seek the protection of belonging to a social group that meets consistently, the trends in recent decades have shown that active involvement in these group activities has decreased significantly over the past several decades, as poignantly captured in Robert Putnam's landmark book, *Bowling Alone: The Collapse and Revival of American Community*. Since 2000, when the book was originally published, the trend has continued to accelerate, leading to what is now being commonly described as a loneliness epidemic. Social media, our political divisions, and, more recently, the isolation caused by COVID, are all factors in causing significant tears in our social fabric. As a society we embrace our independence and credit our nation's success to our independent spirit, but our biology desperately needs us to be interdependent and interconnected.

Over the last several generations, our choice of independence over community is one reason that many scientists believe that we are seeing our current spike in mental health issues. Hunter and gatherer communities, where there are no reports of suicide, anxiety, or depression, chose connection over productivity, working only as much as they needed to provide the food for the tribe. Our ancestors lived in communities of 40–150 people, sharing living spaces and collaborating on all of the tasks that were needed for the community to survive and thrive. Our ancestors' success is a testament that our survival as a species is due to our interdependence, not our independence.

Things have changed. Dramatically. In our modern society, a marker of success is often defined by our ability to create distance from others. The wealthiest in our society seek more space and privacy. They often live in gated communities, some on exclusive islands, or on expansive ranches miles away from the nearest neighbor. Success is also measured by our individual achievements—our salaries, the square footage of our homes, the quality of our schools and neighborhoods, our professional stature, and the selectivity of the colleges our children attend. Houses of the wealthy are often so big that parents need to call or text their child to communicate with them. Financial success, paradoxically, often leads to greater alienation from our family and from our neighbors. The more isolated we become, the more vulnerable we are to the tragic consequences of this disconnection. Despite all of the wealth on the north shore of Chicago, where I work, the psychiatric supports for children continue to expand to meet the ever-increasing need. Wealth, clearly, doesn't protect us from mental health problems and, in many cases, it can exacerbate them. Ironically, as we continue to define success as wealth, and use wealth to isolate ourselves from one another, we risk losing the powerful benefits of a connected community.

Our loss of community has come to define a generation. Young people are expressing alarming rates of loneliness. A 2019 you.gov report described millennials as the "loneliest generation" after finding that 30 percent of them said that they have no close friends, significantly higher than Gen Xers (20 percent) and twice the percentage of Baby Boomers (15 percent). Great Britain was so alarmed by these trends that they appointed a Minister for Loneliness. Our children's distress is the most frightening symptom of a society that is slipping away from its biological and evolutionary foundation of connection and community.

As we drift further away from living in interconnected communities, we also are losing the primary source of our strength as a species. Our success as a species was not based on our ability to accumulate scarce resources and isolate ourselves from one another. In fact, our resilience has been based on the opposite: our willingness to pool our resources, to cooperate, and to collaborate. Jamil Zaki, in his book, *The War for Kindness*, writes, "Humans are world champion collaborators, helping each other far more than any other species. This became our secret weapon. As individuals, we were not much to behold, but together, we were magnificent—unbeatable super-organisms who hunted woolly mammoths, built suspension bridges, and took over the planet."

Christakis explains how our reliance on one another extends beyond our immediate survival and has been crucial to our development as a species by allowing us to learn from one another. "Cooperation is a crucial predicate for social learning, one of our species' most powerful inventions. No human has to learn everything on his or her own; we can all rely on others to teach us, a hugely efficient practice present in all cultures." This learning takes place through proximity and interaction. When we are separated from one another, we have more freedom but we lose the power of partnership and the opportunity to learn essential social and life skills. We place a lot of emphasis on formal education, but most of our life skills are developed by observing and then mimicking others inside and outside of the classroom. This type of social learning is happening constantly. School districts invest in rigorous curriculum and teachers exhaustively invest in their lesson planning, but very little focus is put on all of the lessons children are learning by simply being part of the classroom and school community. What are we modeling? If we really want to nurture happy, healthy, and successful children, our primary focus should be on embedding them within connected and regulated communities.

I saw an advertisement for a preschool on the back of a bus that read, "The classroom is a child's first community." I believe that the family is a child's first community, but the classroom is really the place where children learn about who they are outside of the family. Until they are eighteen, during the prime years of development, our families and our schools are the communities that shape the lives of our children and create the building blocks for their future. How do we make strong and healthy communities that, in so many ways, define how children experience the world and shape who they will become? That is the focus of the next three chapters.

CHAPTER 10

Feeling Seen and Heard

At North Shore Academy each classroom had group therapy meetings twice a week, led by the therapist and teacher. In 2004, our classroom had an interesting mix of students. We had Edgar, the heavyset and perpetually irritable and threatening young gang member. Nathan, on the autism spectrum, was bright, wide-eyed, naïve, and always annoying to his streetwise peers. There was Amy, who was sassy and opinionated. Travis, the Eeyore of the group, was younger and quieter than the others but when encouraged to talk was negative and stubborn. Mark, struggling with drug use as a seventh grader, had trouble focusing and, like Edgar, had a quick temper. It was hard to figure out why Cameron was with us at first. He was affable and cooperative. Then we asked him to do some work. Quickly he became defiant. Stacy, having lost a sibling in a car accident followed shortly by her parents' divorce, seemed perpetually angry and oppositional.

We knew that the real group work was beginning when the students stopped complaining about Dan, the teacher, and me and started talking to one another. The less Dan and I talked, the stronger the group became. In one meeting, Edgar was the first to speak. "I've got an issue," he stated authoritatively. He looked menacingly across the room, directly at Nathan. "I want him out of this classroom." Nathan looked surprised and hurt. He began to fidget nervously. With a voice that was both innocent and pleading, he asked, "Why me?" It was the opening Edgar needed, the invitation to unload on the scapegoat of the classroom. It was clear he had been rehearsing this moment and now he was on the main stage. He could assert his high status by getting everyone else in the group to pile on Nathan. "You never leave us the hell alone! You are always in our business! We can't have a conversation without you butting in, and you are always snitching on us. Nobody likes you!" Other students were nodding, occasionally adding their own, "Yup!" More fuel for the bonfire that Edgar had lit.

Dan and I stopped Edgar there. He had done his work to establish the hierarchy. He was on top, Nathan was on the bottom. The world of the classroom could rotate on its axis for another week. "That must have been hard for Nathan to hear," I said. "Does anyone feel differently?" The room was quiet. Any dissenting voice could help disrupt this hierarchy and could also doom the speaker to lowered status. Was the group safe enough to take that risk? Cameron took the leap. He looked at Nathan. "I think you are a cool kid, Nathan." Nathan had an awkward smile, appreciating the lifeline that Cameron was throwing at him. "But Edgar is right that you tend to butt into people's business a lot." Cameron had bridged the gap, and now Nathan could more safely step across.

He looked down, gathered himself, and then spoke in his slightly formal, slightly scientific way. "This happens to me wherever I go. I never know how to make friends. I have Asperger's. It's a condition where you don't have good social skills and people always find you annoying. I've never really had friends. I keep trying to learn how to make friends, but I can't even do it in a school like this." With each word, gravity pulled on his head until he was looking straight down. A tear dropped onto the carpet. The room was silent. The air felt heavy.

Edgar was the first to talk. I was nervous, afraid that in Nathan's moment of vulnerability, Edgar would strike again. He didn't. "Why didn't you tell us this before?"

Nathan gathered himself. "I thought that you guys already knew. I thought it was obvious."

Nathan had opened up a door, and Edgar, of all people, walked through. "It was way different for me, but nobody wanted me at my old school. I never fit in with the rich white kids. They were always scared of me. When something happened, it was always my fault. I always got in trouble." There was silence, then the reach. "Nathan, you can hang with us. But if you get annoying, we are going to tell your ass to shut up."

Nathan, his voice cracking, said, "Thank you, Edgar. Are we friends now?"

"Yup," Edgar responded. "You're my new homie." Nathan's smile, big and awkward, filled the room.

Nathan, through his story, then Edgar, through his story, began breaking down the walls of shame that kept people from sharing the most important things in their lives. They could more clearly see one another. They each were finding their voice. In the coming weeks, the other students began sharing stories about their vulnerability. It isn't through asserting our power that we connect in community. It is through our vulnerability. Taking the risk of being vulnerable is the key that unlocks the power of psychological safety.

Psychological Safety

Amy Edmondson, a psychologist by training and currently a Professor of Leadership at the Harvard Business School, coined the term "psychological safety" and identified three factors that are essential for creating psychologically safe communities. First, people need to be safe enough to take a risk in the group. Second, if someone takes a risk, they need to feel confident that others won't embarrass them, punish them, or reject them. And finally, she describes a team climate that is trusting and respectful enough that people can feel comfortable being themselves.

On a team, can I share an idea that goes against the grain and feel confident that others won't talk about me in the parking lot? As a student, can I take the risk of trying a challenging reading passage without hearing classmates snicker when I trip over a word? If I failed a test, can I tell my parents without feeling a sense of shame and the expectation of punishment?

The research all points in the same direction—whether we are talking about attachment, emotional regulation, trauma, or getting the best out of our teams, the two things that matter the most are whether we feel seen (people are attuned to us) and heard (our voice matters). As journalist Charles Duhigg wrote, "The behaviors that create psychological safety—conversational turn-taking and empathy—are part of the same unwritten rules we often turn to, as individuals, when we need to establish a bond." These are the unwritten rules that create psychological safety in our classrooms and dining rooms as well. Our focus then, as parents, as teachers, and anyone else lucky enough to be an important person in a child's life, is to embed them in communities where they feel seen and heard. Communities of psychological safety.

There are many ways that we can establish families and classrooms that are psychologically safe for children. This chapter focuses on four elements to consider when creating communities for children: the power of the pecking order, our use of rules to maintain order, the benefits of giving children responsibility, and the importance of predictability.

The Power of the Pecking Order

In preschool, Matthew loved going to the park. He would run around with other kids, full of joy, sliding, swinging, and climbing. Yet he was smaller and thinner than most of the other children. He was also slower, and often not as strong or as daring. He could outtalk any of them but struggled to keep up physically.

One day, Matthew sat down next to a boy his age sitting on a bench.

It was only when they stood up that I noticed how his new friend towered over him. "Let's race!" the other boy said. Matthew's face lit up. "Yes! Dad, you tell us when to start." They lined up and set the fence on the other side of the field as the finish line.

"Ready. Set. Go!" And they were off.

Matthew never made it to the fence. Less than a quarter of the way across the field, the other boy had a big lead that was growing with each stride. Suddenly, Matthew went down as if tackled by an invisible linebacker. He grabbed his leg. "Ow ow ow!" he cried. I ran to him and quickly realized that he hadn't popped his hamstring or blown out his ACL. His pride was broken.

"Are you ok?" I asked.

"I just want to go home," he said, holding back a sob. He fake-limped most of the way back to our house. As we walked, I found myself feeling sad and somewhat defeated myself. I realized that the race was about more than speed. It was a test of status. I wished that I could have protected Matthew from the stresses of the social pecking order. Kids who develop slower are often the ones that find themselves on the bottom. I remembered how hard that was for me. I could imagine how hard the next several years would be for Matthew as he waited for his body to catch up with the other kids in his class. Low social status, more than just about anything else, can undermine our sense of psychological safety.

From cradle to grave our culture is inundated with messages of status. Outside of conscious awareness, we are constantly scanning our environment to determine where we are in the pecking order of any room we walk into. We can perceive social status differences within the blink of an eye. We unconsciously note where people are sitting, their posture, who is talking, and their tone of voice and volume. Our brain is always assessing who is submissive, who is dominant, and where we fit in.

In his research on resilience in children, Tom Boyce, a pediatrician and researcher, identified social status as a significant risk factor for children. Boyce studies resilience in children through intensive observations, interviews, and tracking of biological markers of stress—the stress hormones found in saliva. He followed children from preschool through high school and discovered that the lowest status children in classrooms had the highest levels of cortisol in their saliva. Their lower status was triggering their stress response—their bodies were experiencing the threat of alienation. Low status was also triggering a number of other problems including increased levels of depression and inattention and greater academic and social challenges.

As we saw with Matthew and his friend, awareness of status begins early. Boyce found that children of all ages organized themselves into pecking orders. Children as young as kindergarten organized their social world in a way that relegated some students to lower social status, which "resulted in more frequent and more severe disorders of health and development."

If pecking orders develop organically in any social group, and they can be so toxic to lower status children, what can we do as parents and teachers to create healthy communities for them? The first thing we need to do is to be aware of these pecking orders and how we contribute to them. Do we compare our children with one another or to other, more successful kids outside of the family? "Billy is the athlete in the family. Maddie was born with the brains." We often support these pecking orders unwittingly. "Billy, if you studied like Maddie, we wouldn't get so many calls from your teacher." "Maddie, you need to take more risks like your brother." Although it may be true that Billy needs to improve his study skills and Maddie needs to take more risks, comparing classmates or siblings establishes or reinforces status differences that are not only unhealthy but likely also interfere with, rather than encourage, the development of study skills or appropriate risk taking. These comparisons also can keep children from feeling seen—one child casting a shadow over the other.

Other signals of status may be hard for us to notice. Do we praise children with the same frequency? Who do we trust with responsibilities? Who lights up our face when they walk into the room? Who do we make the most eye contact with? How is our tone of voice different when talking to one child versus another?

The children most likely to experience subtle and nuanced negative messages from parents and teachers are the children with executive functioning problems. They are consistently late and disorganized. They struggle to follow through on commitments or don't follow directions. They are more impulsive and are more often dysregulated. As adults, we roll our eyes. We scoff in frustration. We lose our temper with them more often. As isolated occurrences, these signals may have only momentary impact. However, after years of feeling, consistently, like a burden to the family or classroom, the current of shame embedded in these messages can erode a child's sense of self, making them feel less safe in the communities where they are supposed to feel the safest. And, even more concerning, it constantly triggers the activation of their stress response and all of the subsequent physical, behavioral, and mental health issues that follow.

The antidote to the pecking order is the creation of egalitarian communities. Egalitarian communities believe that all people are equal and deserve equal rights and opportunities. As the adults in these communities (in our families, our schools, and on our sports teams, theater troupes, camps, and orchestra pits) our work is to find ways to make sure that everyone feels valued despite their academic ability, athleticism, acting skill, or their tendency to be helpful. The core principle is that children may have different skills, but they all have the same value. Their voices are all equal. They are all worthy of feeling seen. This is not to say that everyone should receive a trophy. It is to say that the secret sauce of an egalitarian community is that everyone consistently experiences the feeling of being valued for who they are.

Every community is somewhere on the spectrum between being

highly hierarchical and highly egalitarian. Boyce's research indicates that, in schools, teacher behavior can reinforce or undermine classroom hierarchies. "The experiences of subordinated students were highly dependent on the teacher's use of child-centered, egalitarian teaching practices. In classes where teachers ignored or fostered dominance relationships, the links were strong. When teachers had classrooms that undermined the hierarchies, the symptoms went away." In other words, when we are aware of these pecking orders, we can undo them. In doing so, parent and teacher behaviors can keep children feeling psychologically safe, keeping their stress response dormant. Early egalitarian communities create road maps for children's limbic systems, forming a template that allows them to feel psychologically safe within communities in general, opening up their brains for learning and relationships as they enter new communities as they get older.

How can we create psychological safety at home? A great place to start is with family dinners. Whenever we come together as a family, parents are creating and modeling the family culture. Psychological safety in families is based on whether everyone feels like their voice matters and whether everyone is attuned to one another. Dinnertime is the perfect time to do this. As parents, we hope that our children will discuss their challenges with us and yet, how often do we share details about our conflict with a colleague, a mistake we made with a friend, or times when we are feeling down or discouraged? The way that our kids learn that it is safe to talk about hard things is by watching us do it first and often. It is similar to teaching them how to swim. If a child is scared to jump in the water, we jump in first to let them know that it is safe. Then we wait to catch them when they jump. Children need the same modeling and support to know that it is safe to take emotional risks as well. When others talk, do we listen? Can we tolerate other opinions at the table? Do we model how to manage conflicts? How are we emotionally present for them and for one another? Our children are watching and constantly learning from our example.

Research on the impact of family dinners on children's healthy development is powerful. In families that regularly have dinner together, children have a broader vocabulary, greater academic achievement, and greater resilience. They also have lower rates of suicide, depression, aggression, sexual behavior, and substance abuse. It is important to note that the magic isn't in the broccoli. For many families, parents may be working different shifts in order to make ends meet and may not be home during dinner. Dinner, here, is a metaphor for any time that you are together, consistently, as a family. If you can't have dinner together, find other times in the day or week when everyone can be together, talk about one another's lives, find one another's voices, and experience attunement. The magic is in the modeling.

From Rules to Values

From very early on in children's lives, we establish rules to gain control. Unfortunately, rules can often undermine psychological safety and lead to unexpected problems.

I've experienced this firsthand. At NSA, whenever there was a problem behavior, we would create a new rule. We learned slowly that our rules could never outpace our students' ability to create new problems. As our student handbooks grew in size, so did the stacks of incident reports.

This was particularly true around an issue that threatened the physical and psychological safety of our school—gang violence. It began with a few random gang signs on a desk and in a bathroom stall. Soon, students were flashing signs in the hallway at one another. As more and more students from different gangs came to our school, the physical and emotional safety of staff and students was suddenly at risk. Fights began to break out. Threats of more extreme violence filled the hallways. It quickly became scary for everyone.

We felt like we needed to gain control. We responded by creating new rules to eliminate gang representation. No gang colors. The gang representation continued. The kids just became sneakier. They would roll up one of their pant legs to represent their gang. So, we created a rule for pant legs. Then they took the laces out of one shoe, leaving the laces in their other shoe. We established a new shoelace rule. They would shave a notch out of one eyebrow. Hello, "eyebrow rule." If you shaved a notch in your eyebrow, we covered it with a Band-Aid—ironically making it even more obvious. We were caught in a game of cat and mouse—and we were never going to catch the mouse. The more energy we put into catching students and punishing them, the more toxic our community became. Our relationships suffered. Student and staff morale started to plummet. Most concerning, the gang activity continued to escalate. Rather than being part of the solution, we had become a big part of the problem.

One day, it reached a boiling point. Three students arrived at the bathroom just as a rival student was leaving. The four students fell to the ground, staff jumping in to stop them. It was unnerving for everyone. Our school had never felt less safe. Rules hadn't worked, and we were at a loss about what to do next.

Ron Strong, one of our social workers, finally came up with a solution. Ron had been at NSA longer than I had and knew more about gangs than I ever would. He was also aptly named. At 6'4" in height, and muscular, if anyone could gain compliance from students through sheer intimidation, it was Ron. But that wasn't Ron's way. I asked him what he thought we should do. His wisdom that day was counterintuitive to me. It also forever changed how I understood the power of clear values within a community. He leaned forward, gesturing with both big hands to make his point. "We have to understand that it's not the adults who make this community safe. It's the students. Each student needs to understand their responsibility to the safety of our school and take that responsibility seriously." He was right. As adults, we had been unable to manage the safety of the school on our own. School safety is a partnership between staff and students. Rather than try to take the students' power away, we needed to empower them to embrace values that strengthen the community.

Our conversations with students began to change. We met with each gang-involved student and let them know that our school could only be as safe as they were. We told them that we wanted them to feel safe at school and also shared that they were responsible for the safety of others. We asked them, "Can you share responsibility for the safety of our school community?"

Although some conversations took longer than others, all of the students eventually agreed. Gang-related threats and violence dropped quickly. There were still issues between the gang members, but the nature of our conversations changed significantly. We were no longer having discussions about shoelaces and eyebrows. We were no longer arguing about the fairness or consistency of our punishments. We were having discussions about personal responsibility. And students, feeling respected and empowered with responsibility, responded.

When we shifted to a culture of responsibility based on the shared value of safety, the culture changed. We needed to have high expectations for our students in order to trust that they would embrace this responsibility. We believed they could do it, and they did.

Framing issues as values instead of rules also changes the culture of a family. Rigid adherence to rules leads to power struggles and dysregulation for both parents and children, plunging everyone into lower brain. Values are more flexible and encourage us to reflect, teach, and talk, keeping the child's brain open to make more thoughtful decisions and to learn lessons they can apply in the future.

This is the paradox of rules. The more we rely on rules, the less we expect people to take personal responsibility. Rules are implemented to gain compliance when we don't trust people to act appropriately. What is the active ingredient in rules? Fear of punishment for breaking that rule. What does fear do? It shuts our brains down. In order for children to learn and take responsibility, we need their brains to be engaged, not fearful. We need them to take responsibility, not take our punishment. This is not to say that we should abandon rules altogether. However, it's important to reflect on the rules that we have and to see if we can encourage responsibility rather than compliance.

The threat of punishment creates a culture of fear, and fear, of course, undermines psychological safety. Conversely, teaching values within a community empowers a sense of belonging, enhancing psychological safety. Rather than being threatening, values are connecting. We all share a common vision. We are all valued. When we make a mistake in a values-focused community, we can trust that there will be a lesson, not a lashing. When we belong, we take responsibility rather than rebel.

It is important to mention that focusing on values instead of rules in your family does not come at the cost of having healthy limits and boundaries. Ideally, it helps to better create those expectations. When children struggle with limits we have set, our conversation focuses on the values that drive the limits rather than just the expectation of compliance and the threat of subsequent punishment. When we share that we expect our teenager to be home by eleven, we also explain that we cannot fall asleep until we know that they are home safely. If they think that they will be late, we would expect them to call to let us know. Good communication and good sleep are both family values. When they inevitably show up late without calling, we can discuss the impact of their staying out late has on our sleep and ability to work the next day. We can be curious about why it was difficult for them to call or be home on time, and we can figure out a better solution for next time. We have the conversation, we reassert our values, and we problem solve together.

Often, a child's mis-behavior is a result of conflicting values. Your teenager's loyalty to a tearful friend who asked them to stay at a party because they are upset conflicts with the family values of sleep and communication. This leads to an important discussion and reflection for everyone. Working together to come up with a solution creates a partnership for solving problems as they arise. When your teenager walks through the front door late, they already know that they made a mistake. The threat of punishment doesn't teach them anything new. It only further dysregulates them and makes them less open to talking, reflecting, partnering, and learning. Even more problematic, they are more likely to avoid punishment in the future by lying.

Finally, we tend to develop rules at the worst time—when we are dysregulated. When we are feeling powerless, rules are often irresistible because, in the moment, they help us regain a sense of control. However, they also shoot us in the foot by plunging everyone else into lower brain. My brother, Jim, told the story of having dinner with his two daughters when they were seven and four. He was late getting the pasta on the table and their evening routine of bathing, changing, and bedtime reading was already thrown off. As they sat down to eat, the girls' favorite song came through the speakers and they leapt from their seats and started dancing together, singing and giggling. My brother checked his watch and then yelled a brand-new rule: "There is no dancing at dinner!" He turned off the music; his youngest daughter beginning to cry as they both returned slowly to their seats. They had also lost their appetites. Jim composed himself. Did those words really come out of his mouth? Did he really undermine one of the greatest joys of parenting—watching your children dance and laugh and sing? He looked at his girls and said, "I think that's the dumbest rule I've ever made. Let's turn the music back on and dance!" They didn't get a bath that night but knew that they could dance at dinner whenever they wanted.

Encourage Responsibility

When I was at university in Scotland, I visited my friend Paul's family in the town of Sunderland, in the north of England. Paul was the oldest of eight children and the first person from both his mother's and father's families to attend university. His family owned a service station, and they worked hard to make ends meet. I had no idea how hard until I visited.

The first morning, Paul woke me abruptly. "Let's go, Doogie—we have work to do!" He had been up and showered and already at work at the garage. I wiped the sleep from my eyes and stumbled downstairs to see his mother and sisters in the kitchen. They were an assembly line, making lunches for the family. I looked outside and there was his six-year-old brother, cleaning the windshield of a car as another brother pumped gas. Paul and his father were in the garage, trying to fix a piece of hydraulic equipment that had stopped working the day before. They were a well-oiled machine (pun intended).

I would have been no help with the hydraulic lift, so I helped the brothers who were pumping gas. After breakfast, Paul's siblings went off to school. That's when our real work began. We went up into the space above the garage and spent the day cleaning and reorganizing. By dinnertime, I was exhausted. And I loved every minute of it. Although I could have traveled to Loch Ness or climbed Ben Nevis that weekend, as we drove back to St. Andrews, I felt fulfilled. I had contributed to the family that was kind enough to invite me to stay with them. I felt like I was a part of something bigger. I have no doubt that Paul and his family felt that, too. Every day.

When I became a parent, our kids struggled to do simple chores. We weren't alone. Lots of parents were struggling with this. Not only were the chores we were asking our kids to do much easier and much less time consuming than what Paul and his siblings had to do, but we were actually paying them to do it. Why were we struggling so much?

It turns out that we were quickly experiencing how incentives do, in fact, undermine intrinsic motivation. Paul and his brothers and sisters saw their roles in the family as a responsibility connected to something bigger than themselves, not a chore. It turns out that being responsible feels very different than doing a chore.

In many families, parents identify chores for children and pay them an allowance in exchange for doing those chores. The allowance system is very common in the US, and Kathy and I jumped in without considering some important drawbacks. Once we established that the reason that Matthew and Anna were doing their chores was for the money, if they didn't need the money, they wouldn't do the chore. Why would they? They could simply say, "No thanks, I don't need the money this week. You can do my chores." Further, as with most incentive programs, you often need bigger and bigger incentives over time to get people to do the same task. In allowance-for-chores systems, money becomes the currency of compliance. In Paul's family, the focus wasn't on money or compliance. It was a responsibility and a shared value, and everyone stepped up. Paying their kids to do the work wasn't an option anyway—they didn't have the money to pay their children to do work that needed to be done.

I wondered, "What if we did it differently?" What if we focused on the values that we want our kids to learn? In our home, we realized that in urging our children's participation in chores for allowance, we were really trying to teach two different values. The first value was that we are all responsible for managing the needs of our home. The second value was that everyone in the family is responsible for their own money.

When Matthew and Anna were in middle school, we shared with them that managing a house was everyone's responsibility and that our value was that everyone contributes in whatever way we can. We divided the household responsibilities—cleaning up after dinner, taking out the garbage and recycling, putting away the groceries, etc., between all of us. We also emphasized that if any one of us saw something that needed to be done, that we should do it. With this system, it was nice not to have salary negotiations every time we asked them to do something above and beyond their usual chores. It wasn't always pretty, but the conversations about values felt more productive than haggling over money.

We also decided to give them a monthly allowance that was generous enough to take care of all of their basic needs—clothing, entertainment, toys, and games. We set up bank accounts so that we could help them monitor their spending. How they spent their money became *their* decision. At first, they spent all of their money in the first ten days of the month. There were some painful moments when they realized that they didn't have money to go to the movies with friends. We coached them to think ahead about what they might need. In June we let them know that if they wanted to go school shopping in August, they might want to save a little more for the next few months. Each had their own style with money, but both became more and more independent. It was also a relief to not have daily conversations about what we would buy for them. That new pair of Jordans? That was *their* hard decision. They quickly learned that if they wanted an expensive pair of shoes, they couldn't afford that new pair of jeans.

Encouraging children to take responsibility can be surprisingly difficult because it means that, as adults, we lose some control. Amid Matthew's school challenges and his increasing isolation from us as a family, we were getting ready for a trip to Florida. The night before our departure Matthew surprised us by asking if he could pack the car. This should have been a welcome light in the darkness of our relationship. At that moment, for me, it wasn't. *Packing the car is my job!* I know where things need to go to avoid blind spots. I know how long it will take to pack. I know what we need to have available during the drive and what can be buried more deeply. Besides, I reasoned, Matthew struggled to keep track of time, so we would surely leave late and then get stuck in rush hour traffic. Obviously he couldn't be trusted to pack the car.

It goes without saying that this incident is now a source of embarrassment for me. The process of leaving on vacation was always stressful for me and I became uptight until we merged onto the highway, free of rush hour congestion. Matthew wanted to take on a responsibility, and my lack of flexibility kept him from experiencing something more important than whether the car was packed the way I wanted it packed or whether we left on time. He would have learned that I trusted him with something I valued. He would have felt the power of being generous when he so frequently felt like a burden. And I lost the opportunity to teach him how to pack a car and to connect with him in a shared project together.

When we give kids responsibility, they grow. And it's always a risk. We may have arrived thirty minutes later if Matthew packed the car, but he would have begun to redefine his role in our family and would have felt the positive power of contributing. When children struggle with responsibility, we then can teach rather than scold. When we ask our toddler to bring the milk to the table and they spill it, we teach them how to hold it differently and how to clean up after we make a mess.

Giving responsibility to another person is a way of saying, "I trust you with something important." When given this responsibility, children tend to see themselves differently. Because others see them as competent, they begin to see themselves as competent. When others see them as dependable, they begin to see themselves as dependable. The opposite is also true—when we don't trust children with developmentally appropriate tasks, we are sending the message that they are unable to manage the responsibility. Unfortunately, the children who struggle the most often are given the least responsibility. We are afraid that they will screw it up. Yet, they are also the ones who most need to see themselves differently—as valued, as competent, as independent.

213

They are also the ones who need practice. Instead, they hear the message that they are unworthy of our trust loud and clear.

As a society, we are giving children less and less responsibility. When extended families lived near one another, children helped more with the care of their elderly grandparents and in raising their younger siblings. That kind of responsibility is less common today, and Urie Bronfenbrenner, a Russian-American psychologist, had this warning for us decades ago:

> *In the United States, it is now possible for a person to graduate from high school without ever having cared for, or even held, a baby; without ever having looked after someone who was old, ill, or lonely; or without ever having comforted or assisted another human being who really needed help. No society can long sustain itself unless its members have learned how to care for other human beings.*

Providing children with responsibility can support their healthy development in a number of ways. Responsibility gives them status, whether it is in our family or in a classroom. It tells them and those around them that they are trusted and competent. Children who exhibit challenging behaviors seldom see themselves as trustworthy, competent, and as having purpose and value. Responsibility gives them a sense of purpose and lets them know that they are valued and needed.

Unfortunately, as adults we can create a self-fulfilling prophecy. A parent doesn't trust their child with basic responsibilities. The child gets fewer opportunities to learn how to manage responsibility. When they are given a responsibility later, they are less competent at it, so they make mistakes, reinforcing for both the parent and the child that they are unable to rise to the occasion. However, knowing that some children will struggle more with responsibility does not mean that we shouldn't give it to them. It just means that they may need more coaching than a sibling or a classmate. If we can predict how they may struggle, we can give them additional support to be successful. In doing so, we help them develop the skills and belief in themselves to better manage responsibility in the future.

◆

One of our seventh graders, Kenny, would enter school with a big smile every day, wearing a Boston Red Sox jersey, ready to mock my beloved Yankees. His parents were soft spoken and exuded kindness. They always found the balance between communicating to Kenny how much they love him while also fully supporting the school when Kenny struggled. We needed every bit of that support because Kenny struggled in really unique and challenging ways.

Seemingly unprovoked, Kenny often became disruptive in class and disrespectful to others. Because it seemed to happen out of the blue, we worried about taking him off campus for activities in the community. These worries came to a head when Chuck, our service learning coordinator, Kenny's school counselor, and teacher arrived in my office one afternoon. Each week, a different classroom from NSA would travel to Chicago to tutor a classroom of second graders. Kenny's class was scheduled for the next day. The three of them were there to tell me that Kenny had completely fallen apart in class that day. He was as disruptive and disrespectful as he had ever been. Chuck was a former Peace Corps member and semiretired tennis pro. He searched our community for opportunities for children and always believed in giving students a chance to be generous. "I've been doing these trips for twenty years and I've never had a problem. I think Kenny should go. It will be good for him."

Two things were clear. First, it was a big risk for Kenny to go on this trip. If he was disrespectful and disruptive, it would not only be a problem for that classroom that day—it could jeopardize the tutoring for future classes. And, second, no one needed to go on this trip more than Kenny. Could we keep Kenny regulated so that he could benefit from the experience of serving others? We realized that there was never going to be a time that we could feel sure that Kenny would not be disruptive on the trip. We decided to talk with Kenny about it.

Before he left school that afternoon, we spoke with Kenny and several things became clear to all of us. Kenny wanted to go. He wanted to help. And he would need a lot of support on the trip. With Kenny and his parents, we created a plan. He would ride down next to his favorite staff member and that same staff member would shadow him in the classroom. A parent would be working in a nearby Starbucks in case Kenny needed to leave. We also engaged the classroom. They all had struggles of their own that brought them to NSA and had been excluded from many activities in their lives because of their behavior. They, too, agreed that Kenny should go, and Kenny's best friends in the class agreed to sit next to him and partner with him at the school. We felt as ready as we would ever be. We took the leap.

I waited anxiously for the vans to return from the trip. I didn't have to wait long to know how it was going. Chuck sent me a photo of Kenny, his big smile barely visible amid the hugs of four or five of the students he tutored. The text message below the photo was brief. "He thrived!" Kenny asked if he could join other classes to do the tutoring. Chuck was all for it. We wanted him to have even more time with this classroom in Chicago that seemed to love him as much as he loved them.

Kenny had discovered his sense of goodness. I don't believe that it is a coincidence that, upon discovering that goodness within himself, he began to show up differently in school. His disruptions declined, his academic engagement increased, and within two years, he was attending his freshman year in his home school. He never looked back.

Aligning our values with the culture we want for our family or classroom while removing controls doesn't remove all conflict and result in uniform compliance. Often, like with Kenny, it feels like a leap of faith. There will always be times when children act in ways that are not consistent with our values or our expectations. The question is, What kind of conversations do we want to have with them in those moments? Do we want to be talking about values and responsibility or rules and the conditions of their punishment? For me, that answer is easy.

The Benefits of Predictability

Predictability is regulating. When we know what is coming, we feel a sense of control within our environment. When life is unpredictable, we need to constantly be on our toes to manage whatever is coming next. That naturally activates our limbic system, which is always assessing novel situations to make sure that we are safe. The more time we spend in a world that is unpredictable, the more our limbic system is activated, the more likely we are to become dysregulated. Predictability and routine soothe us, creating an environment of psychological safety.

Knowing what is coming next not only gives us a sense of control over our lives, it also helps buffer against unpleasant events. Dan Gilbert, in his book, *Stumbling on Happiness*, describes a study conducted in the early 1990s by a team of psychologists who sought to understand the emotional and physical impact of being able to predict a very unpleasant experience. Participants volunteered to get twenty electric shocks, three seconds apart, on their right ankle. One group got twenty high intensity shocks. The other group got only three random high intensity shocks and seventeen less painful shocks. Despite receiving a majority of less painful shocks, the low intensity group showed more signs of both physiological stress (sweating, increased heart rate) and reported that they found the experience more frightening as compared to the high shock participants. As Gilbert summarizes, "Apparently, three big jolts that one cannot foresee are more painful than twenty big jolts that one can." Predictability is soothing.

Predictability also opens up our brain for more abstract and reflective thinking. When we have a routine, the brain doesn't have to focus on a specific task or weigh multiple options about what to do next, opening it up to broader and more creative thinking. Morning routines, for example, are universal because they help us, immediately after waking, get ready for the day while our brain is gearing up to be more fully online. We take the same route to work each morning, so we don't have to figure out which turns to make before the coffee has kicked in. These routines help us to go on autopilot, allowing our brain more flexibility for other kinds of thinking. This is why some of our best insights are sparked in the most mundane moments. Some of my best ideas come at times when I least expect them—in the shower and on my commute to work. The opposite is also true—when my routine is disrupted, I often have to focus so much of my energy on the moment that I struggle to see the bigger picture and creative thinking goes out the window. If there is construction and I have to follow that blue dot on my map app, I struggle to carry on a conversation, listen to a news story, or mentally prepare for a challenging meeting that morning.

The same is true for our children. The more predictable the environment is, the easier it is for them to navigate it. At home, morning routines can help our children get to school with less chaos, and evening routines offer cues that help children settle into bed. The same is true in classrooms. Teachers love routines because they make everyone's life easier. The more routines there are in our life, the more we know what to expect, the more regulated we are, and the safer the environment feels for everyone.

It is inevitable, however, that at times our routine is thrown off. This is when adult flexibility is essential to coregulate our children. If I forgot to set my alarm and this makes everyone late in the morning, it is a great opportunity for me to model how to manage unpredictability. Instead of those pancakes I was going to make for breakfast, it may be quicker and easier to give my children a couple of granola bars and some juice boxes as I send them out the door. In school, if there is a fire drill in the middle of my lesson, a teacher gets to model how to adapt on the fly.

Unfortunately, whenever we, as adults, are dysregulated, we are much more prone to impulsive and unpredictable behaviors. We may suddenly yell. Or take something away. Or leave. Or argue with our spouse. You name it, I've done it all. Our unpredictability magnifies the impact of our dysregulation. We are upset, and our child or student doesn't know what will happen next. This shoots everyone deeper into lower brain.

There is an alternative. Like having fire drills, it is always helpful to have a plan for our meltdowns and theirs. This way, children and adults know what to expect when the other is melting down. This is a perfect time for the adult to engage in a regulation strategy or for the child to implement their own regulation plan. This way, we can add predictability into the chaos when everyone knows what the next step is—engaging in regulating strategies as soon as we can. When I'm upset, I'll take a walk. When my child is upset, they will go to their room and play with their LEGOs.

We often melt down in predictable ways. As a result, if we notice a pattern in when we or our child or student become dysregulated, a change in pattern or routine can eliminate many of our most challenging moments. If our child frequently falls apart when doing homework right after school, it may be helpful first to add a break and a snack before they open their assignment notebook. We can also add homework time after dinner—when they are fed and have had a longer break from the school day—to complete any unfinished work. I worked with a family whose fifth grader, Cody, struggled with school refusal. They created morning routines to help him stay regulated as he became anxious about attending, which improved his attendance. However, on the days that he did stay home, it was reassuring for him and both parents to know what to expect during the day. They decided to tell Cody that since he would not have access to technology if he'd gone to school, he would not have access to it when he stayed home. Because Cody and both parents knew what to expect, they didn't have the added stress of the battle over the iPad every time he spent the day at home.

Many schools and families believe that in order to have predictability, every adult needs to have the same language and the same response to misbehavior. Having the same response is helpful, but not essential. What is essential is that children can predict that when they struggle, there will be a regulated and connected response from the adults in their lives. When children know that when they melt down, the adults will be regulated, that they will have empathy for the stress the child is experiencing, and will problem solve to address the child's concern, the child will be much more likely to experience psychological safety rather than an intensifying of their dysregulation.

Psychological safety is the foundation for everyone's mental health. We experience psychological safety in a community when we feel seen and heard, when we don't feel the constant need to fight for our place in a pecking order, when values rather than compliance to rules provide the guardrails for our behavior, when we are given responsibility, and when that community is predictably connected and regulated. These methods help us to get in front of meltdowns, preventing them before they happen. Meltdowns, however, are inevitable. When they happen, we have some important tools to help us make the hardest moments into moments of growth and change. The next chapter shows how.

CHAPTER 11

The Importance of Repair

Carlos and Monique, both juniors in high school, were destined to collide. I didn't see it at the time—they were in different classes and rarely interacted. In hindsight, however, how could they not? Monique grew up in violent and impoverished neighborhoods in Memphis. Carlos had grown up thousands of miles away in a rural and violent neighborhood in Colombia. As products of these traumatized communities, they also experienced overwhelming personal trauma. They came to NSA wary and guarded with histories of rejection and failure. Both were prone to violent outbursts, reactive to even the smallest social slights. Monique, tall and strong, had required physical restraint in the past to keep her safe from hurting others. Carlos, shorter and muscle-bound, often ripped off his shirt when he was angry, challenging staff to fight whenever he felt disrespected by a limit they set—which was often.

Their conflict began innocently enough. Carlos had left class and was lying on the floor in a common area, head on his arms. The staff person with Carlos took the opportunity to make a quick run to the bathroom. Monique then arrived in the common area and began intentionally scuffing her shoes to bother Carlos. Carlos leapt to his feet. "Shut the fuck up, bitch!" he yelled in his thick accent. Feeling threatened, Monique yelled, "Get away from me, bitch!" and pulled out a switchblade. Sue, a longtime teaching assistant, heard the yelling and rushed to help. Calmly and bravely, she stepped between them. They were both screaming, threatening one another. Monique, knife out, stared at Carlos with unnerving intensity. Sue interrupted her gaze. Their eye contact reconnected Monique to herself and others. "I need the knife." Monique hesitated for a moment, then closed it and gave it to her. The pressure left the room. Everyone was able to breathe again. Staff were able to separate Carlos and Monique and move them to different parts of the school. You could hear Carlos yelling that he wasn't safe in "this fucking school." Monique, too, was yelling, "Ain't nobody going to step up on me like that!" With time she calmed and explained that she carried the knife because she wasn't safe in the neighborhood she had to walk through to get to her bus to school. She had also scared herself. What if she had really hurt Carlos? As she waited for the police to show up, she worried about the legal implications she was facing.

Monique was released to her mother with charges pending. We met with Carlos and his parents and, later, with Monique and her mother to figure out how we could make sure that everyone could feel safe in school. Both families felt upset, worried about their child's safety in school. Both Monique and Carlos were still our students, and both wanted to stay at NSA. And, neither wanted to ever see the other again.

In separate meetings Monique agreed not to bring a knife to school and to submit to searches. Carlos shared his commitment to try to manage his feelings without becoming violent. In order for this to work, however, we knew that they needed to work this out with one another. This was the problem. Monique had written a letter of apology but refused to talk to Carlos. Carlos didn't ever want Monique back in the school. Their battle lines were clear. It was trench warfare.

Time is often healing. We kept them in school but separated, continuing to let them know that they were responsible to one another and to the community. Eventually we got them into the same room. Carlos listened intently while Yolanda, his teaching assistant and translator, started to read Monique's letter to him. "She's only saying that—

she doesn't mean it!" he yelled at Yolanda. "This doesn't come from her heart!" he said, pounding his chest. As Yolanda finished the first few sentences of the letter, Monique stopped her and looked at Carlos. "I didn't mean to scare you." Carlos shot back, "I wasn't afraid! I didn't care if you were a girl, I will do what I have to do to take care of myself!"

"I was scared," Monique responded. "You looked like you were going to come at me. I've seen you go at people before. I needed to protect myself. I was never going to use it. I just wanted to keep you away." She was looking down, nearly mumbling now. "I've had a lot of trauma in my life. I need to protect myself. I have to face charges for this." Her voice began to break. "I'm really sorry." She was sobbing.

Carlos was also looking down. In his best English, he said, "I know that you have pain in your life. I do, too. Don't ever bring a knife to school. It makes people feel unsafe. But I don't want you going to jail for this, either." Monique nodded. Carlos turned to me and asked if Monique would be back in classes. I nodded. "Good," he said.

Monique left and Carlos stood up and gave me a hug, then sat back down, exhausted. He looked at me and said, "No one has ever apologized to me before." It was his turn to cry. A lifetime of hurt and pain and trauma and no one had ever told him they were sorry, that they had made a mistake. No one had acknowledged his pain. Monique, through her apology, found her way back to our community, and Carlos discovered a window into forgiveness.

We didn't say to Monique that she needed to apologize but we did share the value that when we hurt others or the community, our work is to own our behavior and make it right. Monique found her unique way of making it right.

Interpersonal Accountability

We learned in Part I that punishments aren't effective at changing behavior. They also aren't effective at finding resolution or repairing communal or interpersonal relationships after a conflict. If we had Monique serve a ten-day suspension, the school may feel safer for those ten days, but it would do nothing to help improve the safety for the other 170 days. In fact, after experiencing exclusion from the community, missing ten days of instruction, and returning to school without resolution with Carlos, she would likely be more dysregulated than ever. After ten days, without resolution, would Carlos have felt any safer seeing Monique walk through the hallway? Punishments don't repair. And when there are meltdowns, there is almost always a need for repair. In the process of repair, we often not only restore relationships but also strengthen them.

One of the things that I feel like I did right as a parent was to help my kids when they melted down with one another. When Matthew and Anna were in preschool and elementary school, like most siblings, they would fight. I would separate them, usually in their rooms. I would let them play with their toys or read their books—these, after all, are regulation strategies. I would offer to stay with them but more often than not, they wanted to be alone. I would tell them to let me know when they were ready to work it out with the other, and once one was ready, we would check in with the other. When they were both ready, I would ask how they would make it right with the other, and they would often apologize while also letting the other know, with words rather than fists, why they were upset. Sometimes they would need coaching, but eventually, they could do this process on their own. Now, as adults in their twenties, they are far better at managing their conflicts than Kathy and I ever have been.

When someone melts down, there is a strong emphasis in our culture of *holding them accountable* for their actions through punishment.

This punishment, I assume, is meant to teach them to treat others better. However, Matthew and Anna had learned not to hit or say mean things to one another at very early ages. Punishment wasn't going to teach them anything that they didn't already know, even in preschool.

I completely agree, however, that we should hold children accountable. What I don't agree with is how accountability is typically defined. We often conflate accepting a punishment with being held accountable. *Merriam-Webster*, however, defines accountability differently, as "an obligation or willingness to accept responsibility or account for one's actions." There is no mention of punishment, but of taking responsibility and explaining, with transparency, why the behavior happened. When we punish, we are not asking them to right their wrongs. We are not, actually, holding them accountable.

In fact, it is often easier to "do the time" rather than take responsibility for a shameful meltdown. Remember how Matthew was always late to class, accumulating a record number of detentions? He was happier to take his detention than to have to talk to his teacher about why he missed class—his avoidance of talking to his teacher was what caused him to miss class in the first place. Yet, talking with his teacher would have helped them build their relationship and to address the upstream problem—his shame at not being able to complete his assignments.

When I talk with parents and educators about the difference between "accountability" and "punishment" they often express the concern that they need to prepare children for "the real world." Often, they are referring to the world of consequences and punishment. But the reality is the world is less punishing for adults than it is for children. When I come home later than expected from my favorite brew pub, Kathy doesn't ground me. If I show up unprepared for a meeting at school, I don't get detention. If I am disrespectful toward a colleague, I don't get two periods in the Quiet Room. I would, however, be expected to fix the problems that I have caused. I would need to take responsibility for the impact of my behavior on others and do my best to make it right.

The inevitable question is, "What about discipline?" I was surprised to discover the original meaning of discipline and how it dovetails so perfectly with this newer model of supporting child development. The word "discipline" comes from the Latin word "disciplina" meaning "instruction and training." It's derived from the root word "discere" which means, "to learn." Discipline, originally, referred to teaching and learning. The modern definition of discipline from the *Oxford Learner's Dictionary* is also telling. It is "the practice of training people to obey rules or a code of behavior, using punishment to correct disobedience." Our definition of discipline has moved from learning to punishment. I think we had it right to begin with.

One of our values at NSA was that students needed to be accountable to one another when their behavior impacted others, rather than be accountable to a punishment. They needed to own the hurt they have caused and repair the relational damage. I think of this as *interpersonal accountability*. When we don't expect interpersonal accountability when children melt down, we lose two important opportunities. We undermine the opportunity to enhance psychological safety for others, and we lose the opportunity to teach our child the essential relationship skill of repair. Interpersonal accountability is essential. Children need to own their behavior and take steps to repair the relationship damage they have done to an individual or to the community.

Interpersonal accountability is at the core of restorative practices. When we don't live up to the values of a community, we are required to repair our relationships, to right our wrongs. This is a lesson that is best learned early in life. While the active ingredients in punishment are fear, isolation, and shame, the active ingredients in repair are responsibility, connection, and empowerment. The power of these practices lies in not only correcting the specific problem they caused in that moment, but also in helping them gain greater insight, improved relationships, and enhanced problem solving skills that they can use to better manage problems and relationships in the future.

Rethinking Our Toolbox

I'm not suggesting we take punishments out of our toolbox—yet. Taking away our most relied upon tools without having mastered new tools will just make it harder to feel competent and, as a result, everyone will be more dysregulated. However, if we are going to hang on to punishments, I would recommend a few changes to how we typically apply them.

First, as we have discussed already, only employ a punishment when you are regulated—as frustrated as you might be in the moment, it's never a good idea to implement a punishment when you are in lower brain. You have time. You don't need to use your hammer to swat at a mosquito. Regulate yourself first, wait until your full brain is available, then share the punishment in a way that is reasoned rather than reactive.

Second, make sure that after the punishment, there is still an expectation for the child to repair any harm they have caused (more on this below). A repair done well will be more impactful than any punishment we could employ.

As we hang on to those tools, let's consider adding some more tools that will support their ability to take "interpersonal accountability." I think of these as the 5 R's of managing meltdowns:

1. Regulation
2. Reflection
3. Responsibility
4. Repair
5. Return

Each of these steps is essential and the sequence matters. We can't access the parts of our brain necessary for reflection if we aren't regulated. We can't take responsibility without reflecting on our role in what happened. We can't repair until we are able to take responsibility. Finally, we shouldn't return until we have sufficiently repaired. Although hitting all of these steps each time is ideal, life can get in the way. We can be forgiving of ourselves and our child if this doesn't go smoothly. It is the accumulation of these moments, not any one specific event that leads to change.

Let's take a look at how to use each of these tools.

Regulation

Regulation is the gateway to the process of managing meltdowns. Nothing good happens until everyone is regulated. As discussed at length in Part II, we all have our own unique menu of strategies that regulate us. The sooner children can recognize their dysregulation and employ their most effective regulation strategies, the smaller the meltdown. As adults, our job is to be partners in this process. We will know that a child is regulated by observing, among other things, their more relaxed body language, the tone of their voice, and their ability to use words. Indications of empathy and flexibility are also important.

Reflection

Once a child is regulated, we have the opportunity to help them reflect on the meltdown to help them think through why they think it happened and how they will take responsibility for it. As mentioned in Chapter 5, it is essential for the adults to help them through a spirit of curiosity rather than blame or shame. It is our job to help them be curious about their behavior. There are three basic steps to this process:

1. First, we want them to identify the stresses that sent them into lower brain.

2. Second, we want them to learn how to better assess their states of regulation. This involves thinking about how their body felt, the feelings they experienced, and the thoughts they had when they were dysregulated. This helps them learn to identify the physical, emotional, and thinking patterns that catalyze their dysregulated behavior.

3. Third, we want them to identify strategies that would have helped them avoid the meltdown. What could they do differently in the future to assess and then manage their dysregulation?

Responsibility

We help them take responsibility, first, by normalizing meltdowns. Feelings of shame can lead to defensiveness, which is the biggest barrier to taking responsibility. Everyone gets dysregulated at times. Everyone melts down in their own way. We can describe moments that we were dysregulated to help the child understand that they are not alone in these struggles. It is important to note that shame is different from guilt. Guilt is feeling badly that we did something wrong. Shame is feeling that there is something wrong with us. If we have hurt others in our meltdown, guilt can be a healthy and helpful response. It can push us to right our wrongs. Shame, on the other hand, is a destructive emotion that not only undermines our sense of self ("something is wrong with me—I'm damaged") but is also more likely to push us toward withdrawal or defiance. You want children to hold two truths—that you see their goodness and that they did something that was hurtful to others.

Whereas the reflection stage is focused on the child, the responsibility stage is focused on others. Taking responsibility requires us to take the perspective of others so that we can understand the impact of our meltdown. It requires empathy. This can be particularly hard for some children on the autism spectrum and for younger children.

Empathy develops over time and if taking the perspective of others is a challenge for a child, we push as far as we can, knowing that it will continue to develop if we have these conversations in a thoughtful and regulated way. These are our teachable moments. Like any skill, some children will be farther along than others.

Finally, they need to develop a plan for talking about the meltdown with the person or people most impacted. Unfortunately, we either skip this step or we let them off the hook by accepting a quick and insincere "sorry." Genuine repair is more thoughtful, more impactful, and more difficult than a quick apology. It requires them to think about how they want to repair the damage that they did to the relationship and find a way to communicate that to the people they harmed.

Repair

The repair is the most important step in this process because it reestablishes psychological safety and gives the opportunity to strengthen relationships. Without repair, the opposite happens. Psychological safety is compromised, and relationships are further damaged. Because we often struggle with repair the most, I will spend more time on this step than the other steps.

We avoid and omit the repair part of the process for a number of reasons. First, many believe that the punishment we deliver holds the child accountable and nothing more needs to be done. Second, it takes time—often time that we don't think we have. Finally, it requires everyone involved to step into the discomfort of directly addressing interpersonal conflict—something that is often more difficult for adults to do gracefully than it is for children. Hopefully, the following guidelines will make the repair process feel more manageable.

In order for a repair to be successful, we need to set the stage for both the adult and the child to feel as safe and regulated as possible. This involves being intentional about the when, the where, and the who of the repair. When does the repair happen? Where does the repair happen? And who is part of the repair conversation? The answer to each of these questions needs to be considered through the lens of regulation. When will everyone be most likely to be regulated? Where will everyone be most likely to be regulated? And, if the relationship between the people in the repair is dysregulating for one or both people, who is someone who can be there to coregulate?

WHEN

We need to have enough time to ensure that everyone can both listen and feel listened to. Usually, we need to set aside ten to fifteen minutes for a good repair. Also, the time of day is important. Both the child and the adult need to be regulated and, as we know, time of day can impact emotional regulation. At home, after a meal is generally better than before a meal when either parent or child could be hangry. For younger kids, their morning brain may be more likely to be regulated than right before bed. For teenagers, morning may be the worst time to try to access their full brain. You also need to consider when you, as a parent, will be most regulated. Personally, right before dinner and late in the evening are times I need to avoid if I want to access my best listening and flexibility.

In a school setting, it is important to find a time of day when both the teacher and the student are most regulated. It is hard to find the time for repair without interfering with the instruction for the other students or taking away important planning or lunch time from the teacher. Although we worry about the impact of taking the time to repair, what is often lost in this discussion is the cost of doing nothing. A child with challenging behaviors often disrupts instruction several times a week and also takes time away from a teacher's planning period as they need to instead write incident reports, email parents, or work with the principal or dean to think through punishments. If done well, a good repair process is an investment in the future of the class, a team, and a school. The short-term investment of time saves much more time in the long run. To help, teachers can enlist others on their team to watch their class while they step away with the student.

WHERE

Next you want to consider the best location for the repair. Repair requires vulnerability from everyone—does the space allow for that vulnerability to happen? Is the space private enough so that the participants can speak candidly? Is it a space that is regulating for both the educator and the student? Is your child too distracted by the LEGOs in their room to focus on the conversation? Or, does fidgeting with LEGOs and being in their room make them feel more comfortable? Do they feel intimidated in the principal's office? Are they easily distracted by the windows that are looking out on children at recess? It is important to think through the best location so that you can access their best brains (and yours).

WHO

Finally, the relationship that you have established with the student is an essential cog in the wheel of repair. We can only repair what is broken. If there is no relationship, there is nothing to repair. This is why creating strong attachments with children is so important. This is the payoff for all of the hard work of connecting that we talked about in Part I. If we have yet to develop a strong relationship with a child and our mere presence is dysregulating (or theirs is dysregulating for us), it would be helpful to include a person who you and the child both trust to help build a relational bridge that, hopefully, you both can begin to cross. At home, this might be the other parent or even a sibling or aunt or uncle. At school, it could be a social worker, a trusted teacher, an assistant principal, a coach, or, in some cases, even another student.

Repair is a two-way street. Both parties need to be invested in the repair. This investment then can allow adults to model how to repair, not just be a passive recipient of a child's work to repair. Like any skill, kids learn best through modeling. One of the reasons we have survived as a species is our social modeling—let's take full use of its power. Modeling how to repair is one of the most difficult and important things we can do for children as caring adults. Typically, when a child or student has behaved in a way that has hurt others, we expect them to carry the load for the repair. We don't stop to think about how hard this is for them. If I did something to anger my boss, it would be very hard to go to their office and "face the music." I'm approaching sixty years old. Imagine how hard this is for a six- or sixteen-year-old.

These conversations make everyone anxious, and we often avoid them if possible, which, of course, creates more problems down the road. We can help them learn how to do this—by going first. Given that "mis-behavior is stress-behavior," one of the ways that I prepare for a student's repair is to imagine that, in some way, I was part of creating a stressful moment for them. At NSA, I realized that whenever a child was hurtful to me, there was almost always something that I did that was dysregulating for them. The same is true at home. If I can identify my role in the issue, I can go first and model how to repair.

> "As I look back on it, I knew that you were hungry and stressed about homework when I asked you to take out the garbage. I could have waited until after dinner to ask you."

> "I should have noticed that others could overhear us when I told you that you had failed the test. That must have felt terrible. I'll be more careful if I need to share something like that with you again."

This does not excuse their behavior, but it shows empathy, which is both regulating and connecting. It also models what I am looking for in the repair. Then, almost always, the child is ready to jump right in with their effort to repair.

"I know that I was hungry and stressed, but I should have done it anyway. Sorry that you had to do it yourself."

"Thanks for saying that, but I still didn't have any right to swear at you. I'm sorry I didn't handle that better."

Repair doesn't necessarily mean an apology. Often, we think that an apology is how we repair, but even that can get tricky. If all we require is an apology, we may very well get a perfunctory, "I'm sorry. Are we done here?" They have done what we have asked, and yet it feels terrible to the person on the receiving end, and it is a roadblock to the learning opportunity for the child. An insincere apology breeds cynicism about the intentions of the child and the process and, thus, undermines rather than reestablishes psychological safety.

When I'm preparing a child for a repair, I always let them know that they should only say that they are sorry if they really are sorry. Many times, kids will say, "I'm not sorry—they deserved it!" What I will then ask is, "Do you think you could have handled the situation better?" Almost always, the answer is yes. Then I'll ask, "Can you try not to do it again in the future?" Again, almost always, they will say yes. I'll then suggest that they say something like, "I shouldn't have [insert behavior here], and I'll try not to do it again in the future." These words often have even more meaning than a pre-rehearsed, get-out-of-jail-free "I'm sorry." And, almost always, once they are face-to-face with the person who is ready to repair, they quickly, impulsively, and sincerely apologize. If the incident is public and witnessed by others in the family or in the classroom, it is important for the others to know that repair has happened. If they struggle the first time, we can always learn from the initial struggle and try again later.

As with teaching our children how to engage in healthy relationships and teaching them how to manage dysregulation, adult modeling is the best teaching tool for repair. And, given the number of times that I melt down, I have found that there is plenty of opportunity for this kind of modeling. If I lose my temper on a road trip, I can model repair by offering a sincere and thoughtful apology when we get to the hotel. If a teacher becomes impatient and uses a tone of voice they regret with a student, they can, at the beginning of the next class, let the student know that they should have handled things differently and will try to be more sensitive in the future. Believe me, this modeling is easier said than done. As I reflect on my struggles to take responsibility and to initiate a repair, to own it and make it right, I have newfound compassion for my children and students when I ask them to do it.

Return

And then, when they have completed the repair, it is time to return to the classroom, living room, or locker room. It is important that they are welcomed back, free to reengage in the classroom, family, or sporting activity. The key is, in these moments, to reestablish belonging. The prodigal child is returning.

As with any skill, if we model and repeat this process enough, children begin to manage this more independently. When they begin to trust that there is no shame in dysregulation, it becomes easier to take responsibility for what they have done. They now have a history of healthy repair; they trust the process and they continue to develop the skills to resolve conflicts with others. And they know that they can then return to the group, feeling wanted and welcomed back. Each dysregulated moment is a teaching moment. With each meltdown, the child has the opportunity to learn more about how to regulate, how to repair, and, in the process, develop stronger relationships, and experience a greater sense of belonging.

These tools don't need to be used for every moment of misbehavior. If the behavior is low in impact and the relationship is high in trust, you may only need to have the child regulate and return. If a repair is needed, the child may be ready right away to say, authentically, "I'm really sorry—it won't happen again, I promise." Because there is high trust, you believe that they have learned from the moment, and if it is an isolated incident, that may be enough.

However, for major incidents that threaten the physical or psychological safety of others or that significantly disrupt the lives of others, we want to be sure that we address the concern directly and immediately. If they need to be removed from the classroom or from the living room due to their meltdown, it is important to take full advantage of this learning experience to repair relationships and reduce the likelihood of similar meltdowns in the future. If a student is not ready to talk to a teacher, it is ok to keep them out of class until they are ready. If a child needs to be separated from a sibling until they are regulated and able to resolve the issue, they can stay in their room. It is essential, though, that this time away is not framed as a punishment. We often need to wait for things that we want. If they want to go back to class or to the living room, they need to go through a process first. In order to have dinner, we need to prepare it. In order to return after a major incident, we need to repair it.

Adults, too, may need time to regulate. How do we know if we are ready? Internally, we can check. Do I have empathy for whatever stress was dysregulating for the child? Am I curious about why they are struggling? Can I be flexible in thinking about this problem and possible solutions? It's ok for us, as adults, to let the child know that we are glad that they are regulated, but that we aren't ready yet. We can then give them a timeline for when to expect the conversation. It is important, however, to make sure that we are not using this as a passive-aggressive way to assert our control and make it feel like a punishment by prolonging their time away from us and others.

In order to take full advantage of this process, the child may need to stay in their room or be kept out of class until they can complete this process. This may seem inconsistent with previous chapters about the evils of isolation. This is a nuanced and important point. Children may need a time to regulate—we all do. The difference is that in this process, we are not using isolation as a punishment, but rather as an essential tool. When we use time-out as a punishment, children have no control over the location or duration of their time in isolation. The goal is compliance. In this process, children monitor their own regulation and determine when they are ready to return. They are choosing the place and the activity—ideally in advance as part of their regulation plan—that will be most regulating for them. Schools have started creating spaces they call "cool down corners" or "zen dens" to reframe for children how to use their time. It is a partnership between the child and adult. If a child uses these strategies proactively, to calm down to avoid a meltdown, they can just return to their desk or to the family activity.

However, when meltdowns happen we need to have high expectations for children—and similar expectations for ourselves when we melt down. The child is expected to wait until others are ready for the repair. There is an expectation that they will reflect on what happened, take responsibility for their role in what happened, and repair with the people who felt harmed by what happened. Finally, if the child is regulated and ready for repair but it's time for lunch followed by their baseball game, we can check with our child to see if they are regulated enough to manage lunch and the game with a plan to repair later in the afternoon. This is no different from having a problem with my boss at work. I still need to do my job until I meet with her later in the week to discuss my performance issue. *This* is preparing kids for the "real world."

This is not a one-and-done process. This is a process that fosters development of skills, not a sudden acquisition of skills. Steph Curry, arguably the best shooter in the history of basketball, still has a shooting coach. Shooting a basketball effectively takes a ton of repetition—

as does this process. If Curry struggles with free throws one night, you can bet he will be practicing free throws with more intention for the next several days. If children continue to struggle with a behavior after they have repaired, it is not because the repair was not successful. It just means that they have yet to gain mastery over the behavior they are struggling with. Children will repeat problem behavior. Then again, so do I. It takes time and repetition for behaviors to change. All of this is to say that we should do our best to refrain from the comment that will inevitably come to mind when the behavior recurs: "You repaired before, and it clearly didn't mean anything because you did it again." We are all just a work in progress.

The children who struggle the most, need this process the most. Because their behavior will impact others more often, they will need to repair with others more often. They will need more doses of the repair process in order to learn how to be interpersonally accountable when their dysregulation impacts others. Every child develops these skills at their own pace, and we need to adapt our expectations for the students who have the least developed skills. A younger child may struggle at first to face the person who they hurt and, instead, the best they can do is draw a picture, or make a LEGO car as a gift of apology. A teenager may struggle to have empathy for others but may still be able to commit to trying not to engage in the behavior again. The Goldilocks rule applies here: it shouldn't be too hard or too easy. We want them to stretch their skills, but not beyond what they are capable of. They will be developing skills through the practice of this process, even if they struggle with it. Isn't that how all learning works?

My guess is that as you use these new tools more often, the tool of punishment will naturally find its way to the bottom of your toolbox, gaining dust and rust, as you find it both unnecessary and unhelpful in these hard moments. In your dysregulation, you may be tempted to reach for it—in order to gain control—but like using a sledgehammer to install a window, the hope is that you, or others, will recognize that you have better tools in your workshop. If you do, you will discover the power of encouraging responsibility rather than fighting for compliance, teaching skills of repair instead of shaming, and engaging with students in their hardest moments as opposed to rejecting and isolating them. The more that we embed children in communities that support this way of understanding and intervening when they struggle, the healthier we all become. Although this may feel novel, it is less about creating something new, and more about returning to our ancestral roots. As we will discover in the next chapter, indigenous communities have been supporting children this way for centuries.

CHAPTER 12

The Circle of Courage

History is full of examples of how the right people, meeting at the right time in the right place, discover and uncover new and essential truths about the world. I imagine that's what happened in the 1980s at Augustana College (now, Augustana University) in Sioux Falls, South Dakota, when three psychologists—Larry Brendtro, Martin Brokenleg, and Steve Van Bockern—came together to better understand the mystery behind childhood resilience. They wondered why some children were able to thrive despite their brutal childhoods while other children, who seemingly had little stress, struggled. What they learned was that it had to do less with the child, and more with the community that surrounded that child.

As they began their research, Martin Brokenleg knew where to look to find practices that support healthy child development. He is a member of the Lakota tribe and found striking similarities between the tenets of Lakota tradition that were based on ancient tribal knowledge and what he was learning in his own research on childhood development. The trio of psychologists then integrated these themes and created a model of resilience they called the Circle of Courage. In 1990, they described this model in a transformative book, *Reclaiming Youth at Risk*. Since then, the model has been applied in therapeutic programs for children across the globe. However, I think that their model has broader application—their framework can be a model of resilience for all of us.

The Circle of Courage is not so much revolutionary as instructive, giving us a road map for building community that combines the practices of our indigenous ancestors with the knowledge of modern science. This map leads us to look, first and foremost, to the power of community when we seek to enhance the resilience and well-being of our children. According to this model, there are four universal human needs: belonging, independence, mastery, and generosity. Early on in my career, I would refer to these four qualities as values. In a conversation with Larry Brendtro, he gently but clearly corrected my language. He let me know that they are not values—they are needs. They are required for our survival. One of the more remarkable elements of the Circle of Courage is that it was developed a decade before brain science would confirm their conclusions. Research continues to uncover the biological bases for our needs for belonging, mastery, independence, and generosity. When our community feeds these needs, we grow, develop, and thrive. When these needs are not met in a community, the consequences can be devastating.

I have seen the principles at work in my personal experience as well as in a school setting. Here are a few examples of how the Circle of Courage can apply to our lives as parents and educators.

Belonging

On Father's Day, 2019, I opened a gift from Anna. It was a small painting— I didn't even know that she could paint. It was a beautiful picture of the sun setting over a mountain lake, the silhouette of pine trees and soaring birds, the water wavy. Even more beautiful, I thought, was what the painting said. She had a sentence written across the painting, words of different sizes and fonts cut out from newspapers and magazines, like a ransom note, spread out across the small canvas. The sentence was her definition of "community." At nineteen, she had seen how passionate I was about the power of community. She, too, was experiencing this power herself, becoming more and more active in our city of Evanston, helping to create far-reaching support systems for those with the fewest resources. Here is her definition:

"Community is the complicated, messy, beautiful fight to simply see each other."

I love this definition for two main reasons. First, the definition puts belonging at the heart of community. We experience belonging when we can see one another and be seen.

The other reason I loved it is that it so clearly describes the hard work that must go into building community and creating belonging. Whenever you bring people together, it is complicated and messy, like trying to create a jigsaw puzzle with pieces from different puzzles. A belonging community doesn't just happen—it takes work; it requires us to lean into discomfort. It is always a work in progress. And yet, when we experience that community, there is nothing quite as beautiful.

Or impactful. Stanford psychologist Geoffrey Cohen defines belonging as "the feeling that we're part of a larger group that values, respects, and cares for us—and to which we feel we have something to contribute." In his thoughtful and important book, *Belonging*, he summarizes the research on the power of belonging. As I read his data, I realized that belonging addresses virtually all of the concerns we have about our children. "Students with a strong sense of belonging," he wrote, "are more motivated to learn, perform better academically, have better attendance, engage in less misconduct, they are healthier, have higher self-esteem and better mental health." He cited a study of twelve thousand teenagers that found that "the most powerful protective factors for every form of adolescent risk behavior—emotional distress, drug abuse, violence, and suicidality—*is their sense of belonging at school and at home.*" (Italics mine.) As parents, we do everything we can to make sure that our children will be ok. For many of us, as parents and educators, our lives revolve around ensuring children achieve in school, in sports, and any other activities that they participate in. We believe that this is what drives healthy adjustment and success. And yet, the most powerful elixir for all forms of childhood distress and the answer to the biggest problems our schools face (academic progress, attendance, misconduct, mental health) is a sense of belonging.

The Circle of Courage road map begins with belonging. Belonging is attachment on steroids. Although the data for attachment and belonging are both powerful and, in many ways, may be measuring similar qualities, they are different. Attachment is our connection to a person and belonging is our connection to a community. Both have powerful physical health, behavioral health, and mental health benefits. Both quiet our stress response and flood our brain with oxytocin, the self-generated opiate that soothes us, connects us, and heals us. Both enhance our resilience. Both improve our success in the classroom and at work. Whereas attachment is isolated to a single person, belonging is an interconnected network of relationships.

Attachment, in isolation, has its limitations. A child who comes out as gay to one parent but not to the rest of the family will find comfort in that relationship but will likely not feel safe around the dinner table or holiday gathering with the rest of the family. A child who has high ACEs may feel understood and cared for by their teacher, but if they feel alienated from classmates, their stress response will continue to get triggered the moment they think about stepping into their classroom. A 2020 study found that we feel more support from a friend group than from individual friends. As journalist Eric Barker writes in his book *Plays Well with Others*, "Friends are great. Communities can be even better." Attachment is necessary. It is not sufficient. We all need to feel like we belong within a broader community.

Belonging is upstream, but unfortunately as parents and schools, we often find ourselves looking downstream. We become anxious about children's grades, their friendships, their ability to concentrate, their motivation, their behavior (you name it), and we work to solve any and all of these isolated problems. However, in doing so, we can undermine our child's greatest resources for resilience—our families and our classrooms. When our children walk to the table for dinner, do they feel connected and safe or do they feel guarded, knowing that the missing homework conversation is always right around the corner? When a student walks into class, are they greeted with a smile or are they warned about their missing assignment? Does their guard go up or go down? As Brené Brown says, "learning can only happen in spaces where armor is neither necessary nor rewarded."

◆

My father spoke on our wedding day. Speaking came naturally to him, and when he was a minister he was admired for his thoughtful and moving sermons. He stood on the altar, a step above Kathy and me, close enough to touch. The irony of my father—whose failure as a husband caused my greatest childhood distress—sharing marital advice at my wedding didn't register then.

After using humor to break the tension, he became more serious. He said that in every marriage there needs to be "grace." He defined grace as the "*in spite of* love." It is easy to love others when they make it easy to love them. But in marriages, we will see the ugliest sides of one another. Grace is our ability to love the other *in spite of* their worst moments. Though he had hurt us when he left our mother, there he was, a part of our community of family and friends celebrating our marriage. We had given him grace and he enriched our wedding day.

Belonging is full of grace. It is not conditional. We feel belonging *in spite of* our differences within a group. In a belonging community we know that others will struggle. We assume that each one of us will become dysregulated and, at times, do things that hurt others. These challenges are what make being in a community so messy and also so beautiful. In a belonging community, we don't threaten others with exclusion and rejection when things get hard. Knowing that we belong gives us the foundation for feeling safe enough, and motivated enough, to repair the hurt that we have caused when we struggle. It also gives us the strength to be forgiving with others, knowing that, at some point, there will be a time that we will need the community to be grace-full with us.

A sense of belonging is not all or nothing. It is constantly a work in progress. Our "belonging security" ebbs and flows. A smile from a colleague when we walk into a meeting makes us feel connected. Then, minutes later, a sideways glance from another colleague quickly shames us. That is why we have to be vigilant about our commitment to belonging and constantly be willing to fight for it. Effectively managing and responding to all of the moving parts is the work of a community of belonging.

There will always be crises of belonging within any community. There are moments when it is not physically or emotionally safe to have someone in the community. The key to belonging is not whether or not there are moments when people have to leave. The key is whether or not they know that they are welcomed back. Do we circle our wagons, becoming more insular, making them feel like an outsider even if they are allowed to return? It is easier to reject someone than to give them grace. (Note: we need to be careful not to take this to the extreme. There are some people or events that are so abusive that psychological safety can never be reestablished and the perpetrator needs not have contact with a victim.)

There are also different developmental stages of belonging. For younger children, the family is the core of their sense of belonging. Then comes middle and high school, when belonging within their peer groups eclipses their pull to seek belonging within their family. In these moments, young adolescents, together, try to figure out how to create community, often by rejecting the adults in their lives. Because teenagers are new at belonging, they may struggle to create communities that feel safe to everyone in the group. Belonging distress is perhaps most poignant at this time. There is no childhood angst quite like the teenager rejected by their peer group. As parents, we need to give them grace when they reject the family and be opportunistic when they discover that they need us after all.

Because NSA serves children whose struggles with their relationships is often a primary reason for their referral, it is a school filled with students who have been chronically alienated from schools, friendship groups, teams, and, sometimes, their families. For many students, it was initially hard for them to trust that they belonged within the NSA community. And, at times, they had good reason not to trust us. They had a history of being rejected by schools in the past and although we embraced the value of belonging, for years many of our practices betrayed a belonging culture, doubling down on the threat of alienation to gain compliance. We had a rule, for instance, that if a student left the building, they would have an in-school suspension when they returned. This rule made sense to us—it was a deterrent that helped kids stay in school. Then, we began to wonder, "If we punish them when they return, do we really want them to come back?" As we looked closer, our practice seemed even more counterproductive. What would we say to someone who is really upset? "Take a break. Get outside. Take a walk." Walking outside is a great regulation tool. We were trying to teach regulation. And yet, we were punishing students for using the very regulation tool that we, ourselves, would use.

We changed our practice. Rather than greeting a returning student at the door with news of an in-school suspension, we began to welcome them back. We let students know that if they left the building, we needed them to stay on school grounds and, for the most part, they did. Students would push the door open in anger and furiously pace around campus. Sometimes they would sit on the curb. Other times they would walk in loops on the sidewalk that circled our campus with a staff person following behind them. Predictably, their pace would slow. Their dysregulated brain would slowly come back online.

They would let us catch up and begin to walk with us. Then they would begin to talk about what upset them. They would make a plan with the staff person about what they needed when they returned.

◆

Josh's road to belonging at NSA would end up changing his life. Josh struggled with drug use and he came to us because substance use intervention had become one of our strengths as a school. Knowing that our students were at higher risk for substance use and abuse, we worked hard to create supports that helped them cope with life's stresses without using drugs or alcohol. We conducted assessments, did random drug testing, led support groups, and engaged them in innovative outdoor experiential education. All of these research-based interventions tried to stem the tide of the devastating impact of addiction on so many of our teenagers. School districts and parents were requesting placement with us specifically to provide these supports for their children.

Josh was fun. He was disruptive but respectful. Athletic. Good-looking. Smart. Charismatic. Muscular. Tattooed. And, at fifteen, he had already failed to complete two drug treatment programs. In addition to his substance use, he was constantly getting into fights in and out of school and failing classes. I wasn't a part of his intake meeting, but Adam, our assistant principal, told me that Josh's parents chose our school to help with his addiction. Three weeks later Josh went to Chicago with friends to buy heroin and overdosed. His friends left him in a gas station parking lot. He was revived, and his parents immediately took him to a treatment center in Minnesota.

His father, Ken, called me after dropping Josh off. His voice was clearly passing through gritted teeth. He was measured. Clear. Serious.

"Josh's choices are Josh's choices. We understand that and Josh understands that. But when we came to your school, we believed that you would help Josh with his addiction. Rather than help, things have gotten worse. We are devastated."

I realized that he was right. As much as we were doing, it wasn't enough. Our substance abuse team began meeting with a new sense of urgency. It wasn't a problem we could solve completely, but we also knew that we had to do better.

Four months later, the phone rang again. It was a call that I never expected to receive. It was Ken.

"Josh is coming out of treatment in a few weeks. We want him to return to NSA."

I paused to let the shock pass through me. "I'd love to have Josh back, but I want you to know that we have worked hard, but we haven't changed that much. Why would you choose to have him come back?"

"Josh told us that in all of the programs he has been in, he has never felt as cared for as he did in his three weeks at NSA. If he is going to kick this addiction, he is going to need to be in a place where he knows people care about him."

Upon his return, we doubled down on our efforts to create a community of belonging for Josh. We knew that belonging is not passive—it is active and engaged. It is reciprocal—to feel a sense of belonging, we also need to create belonging for others. We had Josh, a tattooed, drug-addicted, and occasionally violent teenager, mentor middle school students, spending several afternoons a week with them. Whenever Josh entered the classroom, he was the main event. Students would celebrate whenever he showed up and would cling to him when it was time for him to leave. He also invested in other students who were struggling with their own substance use. He sat with them. He listened. He connected. He was attuned to them in a way that I had only seen in the most talented therapists. Josh had a unique and wonderful way of helping others feel seen and heard.

He stayed sober and eventually graduated, relieved to leave the frustrations of schoolwork behind. At graduation, he raised his arms in an expression of both victory and relief. As I handed him his diploma, he leaned in and said, "I'm so glad I graduated. I never have to read another book for the rest of my life!"

After graduation, he began an apprenticeship in electrical engineering, living in Chicago. He had Friday afternoons off and in his free time, he returned to NSA to continue to mentor his middle school classroom and to meet with students who were struggling with their substance use. After one of his visits to NSA, I found this note on my desk addressed to both me and his NSA therapist, Sue Smith. Sitting on top of it was a black and gold medallion.

Ms. Smith and Dr. Bolton!

I was blessed to have 5 years sober May 1st. Here is my chip I promised you. NSA has had a strong influence on my sobriety. You guys showed me what it's like to be kind and help others. I am forever grateful. Show this chip to any student struggling, because it's possible to live a good life and get out of the misery of addiction. If I can do it, anyone can! Thank you for your help, and I hope to continue one day at a time.

—Josh

After a few years, he began to share that he was unhappy with electrical engineering. His passion, he had discovered, is people. He let us know that he had enrolled in a social work program. He began the coursework and found that as he got older, his brain could focus better. He loved his classes. Rather than dreading reading, he began to devour the books that he was assigned. He needed to do an internship in a school as part of his degree. He interviewed at NSA and, guess what? We hired him. In his interview, we saw how his natural gifts, his personal experience, and his training created an alchemy of talent that was unique and powerful. Sue, his former therapist, became his supervisor. She retired at the end of his internship, and hiring Josh to take her place was an easy decision for the interview team. In observing his work, I realized that I had never seen anyone as naturally talented as Josh.

When Josh returned from treatment his sophomore year, it would have been easy to protect the younger children from this teenager who struggled with drugs, fighting, and whose tattoos seemed to tell the world to stay away. Instead, it was his connection to others—students and staff throughout the building—that made all of the difference.

Belonging, it turns out, is contagious. And powerful. In Josh's case, more powerful than addiction.

Mastery

In the years following 9/11, Stephen, a middle school student on the autism spectrum, was fascinated by computer technology and obsessed with the images of the planes crashing into the World Trade Center. In a moment of impulsivity, he figured out how to use the school computer to email the White House using the name Osama bin Laden. Clearly this did not go over well with the Secret Service, and after federal authorities contacted the school, Stephen was on his way to NSA. Although we did not have a robust STEM class in those years, Stephen continued to teach himself about computers. We helped him sort out his social emotional world and he returned to his home high school where he excelled and eventually went on to college, where he majored in computer science. In college, he was chosen for a highly selective internship at, you guessed it, the White House. He went on to start his own software consulting company. This is the power of mastery.

Mastery is our drive to get better at things that are meaningful to us. When we are engaged in mastery, we feel a drive to dive deeper, to understand more. When we are away from our mastery activity, we are thinking about it and feel a gravitational pull to return to it. This is why the fifty-year-old garage band continues to try to perfect "Stairway to Heaven." Or why someone trains for their first marathon at age fifty. It is not for the money, or the trophy—they won't get either. It is for the thrill of mastery.

We often confuse achievement with mastery. Mastery describes the process. Achievement describes a possible outcome. Mastery describes our engagement in an activity. Achievement describes our success at meeting specific standards of proficiency. Mastery is our personal journey of learning. Achievement is rooted in social comparison—how we do in relationship to others. Mastery is our passion for playing the violin. Achievement is becoming the first chair in the orchestra.

Unfortunately, our focus on our children's achievement undermines the very spirit of mastery. When we see ourselves in competition with others for the highest grade, for enrollment in a highly selective college, or making the travel team, we become focused on winning and losing. The Lakota culture inverts this formula. When we focus on mastery rather than achievement, someone else's success does not undermine our sense of ourselves. We can celebrate, rather than feel threatened by, the achievements of others. As Brendtro, Brokenleg, and Van Bockern write, "The simple wisdom of Native culture was that since all need to feel competent, all must be encouraged in their competency. Striving was for attainment of a personal goal, not being superior to one's opponent . . . Success became a possession of the many, not of the privileged few."

Psychologist Mihaly Csikszentmihalyi used the word "flow" to describe our engagement in activities we are passionate about. Interestingly, "flow," not achievement, is associated with happiness. According to Csikszentmihalyi, happiness is achieved by pursuing a challenging goal that matches our skills. In order to be in a state of flow, the activity must be voluntary, require skills, and be enjoyable and challenging.

Video game designers have figured out how to help children find the sweet spot of mastery, triggering obsessive levels of engagement by making the next level barely, yet ultimately, achievable. Taking our skills to the next level takes effort and risk of failure. Mastery experiences aren't without stress—managing the stress is actually an essential part of mastery. As psychologist and Holocaust survivor, Viktor Frankl wrote, "What man actually needs is not a tensionless state but rather the striving and struggling for some goal worthy of him."

There are two ways to help our children engage in mastery. The first is to indulge them in the activities that they are naturally drawn to. Their "unique genius." What do they like to do when they are left alone? Do they play with LEGOs? Do they draw or color? Climb trees? Read? Spend hours in the street learning a new skateboard trick? If we watch, we can see the unique ways that they are engaged. Ideally, we create "Goldilocks" experiences. In his book *Drive*, Dan Pink describes these experiences as "challenges that are not too hot and not too cold, neither overly difficult nor overly simple." He explains that when tasks far exceed our capabilities, we become anxious. In the words of Stuart Shanker, the stress we feel when the challenge far exceeds our skill leads us to slam on our "limbic brake." The opposite, however, is also true when it comes to the stress/mastery dance. When the expectations are too easy to meet, children become bored and disengage. Our brain engages when there is a manageable challenge.

The second way to create mastery is to indulge the "curiosity gap." Curiosity creates the conditions for children to engage in things that they may not otherwise be interested in. The curiosity gap is the space between what we know now and what we could know if we dig just a little further. This sparks our desire to engage just a little more. I can remember hearing former educator and public speaker Richard Curwin say that he once started a Shakespeare lesson for his middle school classroom by saying, "We are going to learn how Romeo and Juliet is much sexier than a Janet Jackson music video." Dated reference, yes.

But you can bet that his students' brains lit up more than if he had asked them to open their books to Act II and start reading. Advertisers are experts at using "clickbait" to create a curiosity gap. They get us to click on a story or product by giving us a teaser. Just enough information to make us want to engage to close the gap. When our children are not interested or motivated to dive into tasks at home or in school, can we trigger curiosity rather than try to force compliance? When a teacher puts a learning goal on the board to start a lesson, can there also be a teaser? Can we help our kids engage in raking leaves by wondering how big a pile of leaves we can make? How soft will that pile be to jump into? (Answer: not very soft.) Kathy still gets our kids to clean the kitchen more quickly by having each person guess how long it will take to finish the job.

The problem is that as a society, out of our anxiety for our children's future, we focus on achievement at the expense of engagement. We see success as a score on a standardized test, rather than the excitement of learning a new concept or skill. As we continue to define success in narrower and narrower ways and increase the pressure to achieve, more and more uniquely talented students will experience themselves as failures and feel like failures in their school, family, and community. For many NSA students, it took time for them to discover their areas of mastery. It is essential for us to be patient and, when they are ready, to help our children discover their passion and to fuel that passion with curiosity.

◆

Discovering our passion for an activity through mastery can completely alter the course of our lives. I discovered this passion for working with children during my first week at Wediko, and my drive to master how to understand and support children has persisted for the last thirty-five years. Remember Ryan from Chapter 3? From the moment he picked up a guitar, he was hooked and made a career in music.

Independence

What we most look forward to as parents can also make us sick with fear. Watching our child take their first steps. Teaching them to ride a bike. Sending them off to camp. Sitting in the passenger seat as they practice driving, then, license in hand, watching them drive away. Leaving their dorm room after dropping them off at college. As we encourage their independence, we are also losing control.

Of all the needs described in the Circle of Courage, I think that independence is the hardest to nurture in our children. To embrace a child's independence, we need to overcome two formidable inner obstacles: accept the risks inherent in giving our child autonomy and tolerate their distress when they struggle. Like any developmental skill, children are clumsy as they practice independence. And when they fail, there is always a cost. If it was just up to us as parents, we may never let them out of the nest. Whether it is an eight-year-old walking four blocks across a busy intersection to a friend's house or letting a teenager drive to homecoming, we could avoid the anxiety of these moments by never letting our children try new things. We, and they, would not be vulnerable to the potential costs of their lack of experience, lack of skill, and lack of judgment.

Evolution, however, has a different plan. We couldn't survive as a species if every child took up residence in their parents' basement after high school. So it provides a cascade of neurotransmitter activity that peaks in adolescence, when teenagers explore the world beyond the comforts of their home. Adolescents, through the power of dopamine, are pushed to explore people and experiences outside of their family. This is meant to ensure that our children begin families of their own and keep our species growing. Thankfully, when our children are finally ready to leave the nest, as parents, we are often equally eager to see them off.

It was in my conversations with Larry Brendtro that I began to grasp the nuances of independence. I shared with Larry that I defined independence essentially as assertiveness—the ability to find the balance between being defiant and deferential. He didn't disagree, but he offered another definition. "I think that it is about children finding ways to get their needs met. To identify a goal and be able to do what it takes to achieve that goal."

I was reminded of a story from his book, *Reclaiming Youth at Risk*. Psychologist Abraham Maslow, father of the "hierarchy of needs," was visiting a Native American community and recalled this interaction.

I can remember . . . a toddler trying to open a door to a cabin. He could not make it. This was a big, heavy door, and he was shoving and shoving. Well Americans would get up and open the door for him. The Blackfoot Indians sat for half an hour while that boy struggled with that door until he was able to get it open himself. He had to grunt and sweat, and then everyone praised him because he was able to do it himself.

The elders, through their patience and wisdom, showed Maslow how to foster the development of independence.

In Western cultures, our ambivalence about children's autonomy often leads to distress for children, parents, and teachers. In most of our educational and parenting practices, we limit autonomy by expecting compliance to rules and expectations. Violations of these rules result in punishment, which asserts our control and, consequently, limits their autonomy. These systems foster either a spirit of dependence in our children as they come to rely on adults to help them navigate their world or push them to become more defiant as they assert their autonomy in a rule-governed world.

In indigenous communities, children are given responsibilities at early ages. They are coached when they struggle and given more responsibility when they succeed. As parents and educators in Western culture, we often don't know when to give support and when to let children struggle. The answer most often lies in our own ability to tolerate our loss of control or our feelings of distress when our children fail. It is uncomfortable to watch them struggle. It is frustrating when they are slow to develop a skill. Then, we open the door for them in one of two ways. We either open it quickly at their first whimper of discouragement or we become frustrated that they haven't learned the skill yet and open it angrily, our frustration translated by their young brains into shame. Either way, we are robbing them of the opportunity to learn both about how to open a heavy door and about persistence. Then, if they do master the ability to open the door, we worry that they will now be able to wander off and we quickly put a child lock on it.

Failure and frustration are essential for the development of the skills we need to independently navigate the world. Children can't learn to walk without falling. We don't learn to shoot a basketball without missing. Development requires both exposure to new experiences and large doses of failure. Our anxiety about our child falling doesn't mean that we don't help them learn to walk. It simply means that their new mobility will cause brand-new stresses for us as parents. Stairs and streets, in particular, become more frightening than ever before. Safety gates get installed, and we put padding on the sharp corners.

When children fall as they are learning to walk, we don't call them clumsy. However, when children are older and struggle with independence—when they show up after curfew, when they lie about something they've done wrong, when they sneak their phone into their bedroom to text their friends—we call them irresponsible, liars, manipulative, immature, and selfish. And yet, figuring out how to leave a party when it is still going strong, taking responsibility after screwing up, and managing the impulse to be on social media at night are all rungs on the ladder to independence. They are all challenges that I often still struggle with in my own life.

When we fight the development of independence, our children

often respond in one of two ways. They either become so fearful of the distress of failure that they become increasingly dependent or they break away, asserting their autonomy in equally destructive ways. Dependence can often show up as being overly clingy in younger years and as avoidance in adolescence. Feeling unable to navigate the stresses of school independently, children will retreat to their bedrooms where they feel safe and better equipped to manage life with fewer stresses. Just thinking about attending school slams on their limbic brakes.

Some children assert their autonomy through defiance, often expressed by engaging in power struggles. At NSA, Trevor, for instance, saw every limit we placed on him as an opportunity for defiance. After a rule infraction, he would be told that he had two periods in the quiet room. "You can give me two periods if you want," he challenged, "but I'm staying for four." He constantly reminded us that we could not control him. Sadly, the other thing that he was telling us was that our punishments could not hurt him any more than he was already hurting. Unhappy with his teacher, he organized a slow but insidious act of civil disobedience within the classroom. He convinced all of the students in the classroom to stop washing their feet and changing their socks. Every day when class began, students would quietly remove their shoes, releasing the powerful and pungent odor of adolescent feet. It became intolerable. Gandhi would have been proud.

Defiance and dependence are really opposite sides of the same coin. Both happen when we struggle with independence. And both happen when we are dysregulated and seeking control. Avoidance can quickly become defiance when you push a child to do the thing they are avoiding.

When a child is defiant, it is often helpful, if not counterintuitive, to respond to their inflexibility with our own flexibility. I know, easier said than done. But if we are curious, then listen, then work together to find a solution, we are modeling for them how to solve problems as they get older. For Trevor, I might begin by trying to understand the nature of his stress. "You seem really unhappy in class lately. What is most frustrating for you?"

I can imagine his response. "Let's start with being in a class with little kids. Only Bill and I are eighth graders—everyone else is in sixth or seventh grade. I feel like I'm a babysitter."

This makes sense. At NSA, because we were so small, we combined grades within our classes. I could understand his frustration now. And, because we were so small, we could also be flexible. For instance, we could offer him and Bill to have lunch and PE with a high school class.

Giving Trevor a choice in his schedule may be challenging in some ways, but the time we would spend dealing with his defiance was significantly more than any time we would spend figuring out his new schedule. It also would show him that when he asserts himself in ways that we can hear, we are more likely to be responsive.

If we can stay regulated and see their defiance as a clumsy way to gain independence, we can partner with them to find a solution. Unfortunately, though, there is no way to get through this process without discomfort. Whenever we empower a child, there is always a risk that they will struggle with managing that power. It will make us (and often the child) anxious. If Trevor spends more time with the high schoolers, will his drug use increase? Will they be bad role models? For Trevor, he may wonder if he will fit in or, if he fits in well, it may be harder for him to tolerate the rest of the day with his middle school classmates. A good solution will necessarily make everyone a little (or a lot) anxious. Can our families, schools, and classrooms tolerate the short-term discomfort enough to help our children take the next step toward greater independence?

Andrew had struggled as an elementary school student at NSA for years. As his parents' divorce got messier, Andrew continued to shut down at home and at school. Constantly asked to choose sides in his parents' conflict, he withdrew more and more, knowing that there was no place to hide in this constant battle. In school, he expressed his struggles through defiance. Although bright and capable, he refused to engage in any work and his biting humor came at the expense of both staff and students. He made it clear in sixth grade that he did not want to be at NSA and he was going to hunker down for a long war of attrition. When he was in the classroom, he would disrupt the class. He could be incredibly mean to staff and students until having him leave was the only option. He would then refuse all directions until eventually he would lie down at the end of the hall on the cold tile floor and sleep until the end of the school day. Eventually, when he arrived at school, he detoured the classroom and went straight to his spot at the end of the hall. Multiple elaborate plans to help Andrew be successful came and went with no success. Finally, after two years of intensive interventions, including meetings with Andrew and his parents, partial hospital programs, medication changes, family therapy, and multiple collaborative problem solving sessions, his therapist, Lauren, came to me and said, "The only thing he wants is to be at his home school. What if we just tried him for a couple of periods a day. If it goes poorly, we can discontinue it. What do we have to lose?"

This idea required flexibility from everyone. Just thinking about it made us uncomfortable. Our school was based on the idea that in order to be able to return to your home school, you needed to be able to show that you are independent enough to manage the demands of school effectively. Andrew was as far away from meeting any of those expectations as any student in our building at that time. We would need to completely disregard our long-established criteria for him. How could this be fair to other students who were working their way through the system? His home school would need to be prepared if he became disruptive in their classes and disrespectful to students and staff. Andrew needed to be more flexible, altering his demand from wanting to transfer all day to his home school to only attending for two periods. His parents didn't see eye to eye on this decision and both needed to agree. Andrew had not been engaged in a classroom in nearly three years and frequently disrupted NSA where we had many people to support him. He would need to participate appropriately and independently in a classroom in one of the highest performing districts in the country without any additional supports. After reviewing all of these challenges with the team, I joked, "What could possibly go wrong?" We decided to give it a go.

He thrived. He was quickly able to move from taking two classes to attending for a full day. The following year, his father sent pictures of Andrew as a freshman with his classmates. Andrew, on tiptoe in the back, his arm around a classmate, showed a smile that we never saw when he was at NSA. He had made the honor roll. He was more independent and capable than we realized. Luckily, he had a creative therapist who convinced us to give it a try. I am learning slowly that partnering with our children to help them stretch to new levels of independence is always healthier than trying to keep enforcing compliance. When we take that risk, the students will almost surely struggle, and when they do, we can be there for them, ready to teach, comfort, support, and then encourage them to try again. Not every student was ready to jump back into their home school. Andrew was unique. Then again, every child is unique and we need to develop a unique approach to address their unique needs.

As adults, when things get hard with children, we often develop the solutions and impose them unilaterally. Fostering independence requires engaging our children in the spirit of "doing with them," rather than "doing to them." When they struggle, it involves being curious, rather than accusing. Asking children to reflect on why they struggled and collaborate with them about solutions for the future helps engage and develop that prefrontal cortex. Investing in the development of independence is perhaps the most important and difficult task of both parenting and teaching. And it can pay off years later.

I hadn't seen or heard about Andrew in six or seven years, which was not a surprise—when he was at NSA, he seemed to harbor an anger toward me for representing everything that was keeping him from his home school. As I was completing this book, I wanted to be sure that Andrew was ok with me including his story. I emailed him, now a student at Northeastern University, but I didn't expect to hear back. He responded within a day and asked to see what I had written about him. I sent it on, worried that he would be upset with how I portrayed him and his journey. I was sure, now, that he wouldn't approve. Again, I heard back within a day. I couldn't have been more wrong.

> *I think it's a very accurate, insightful, and respectful account of my time at NSA. I'd be honored if I was included in your book. Initially, I was worried you'd give me too much credit; when I think about how I was in middle school, most of what I remember is how hateful I was, and how I prided myself on how difficult I was and how good I was at pushing others away. So when I read that it was the story of how I knew my needs better than anybody else, I was a bit confused. Did I really, and was I really able to communicate them?*

> *I realize that most of your memories of me are from that time period, and I know it must have been at least a little bit difficult to reach out to me in light of that. I'd like to apologize for how I acted back then. Defense mechanism or not, I don't think it's fair how I treated everybody at NSA during that time. It took me far too long to realize that there were adults in my life who actually wanted to support me, not torment me. To this day, still I have no idea how you and some others at NSA were able to see through everything and support me nonetheless, but thank you. Please know that it made a world of difference. So much has changed since then; middle school feels like a completely different life, lived by an entirely different person.*

Our investment in Andrew's independence reaped dividends we never could have imagined years earlier when we watched him walk into school feeling hopeless and defeated, and lie down on the cold tile floor at the end of the hallway.

Generosity

Bennett would bounce off walls—literally. As a fifth grader, he was into parkour—the niche sport of getting from one place to another on foot in the quickest way possible, using obstacles as opportunities to leap or flip over or around. I think of it as watching a gymnast navigate city streets and stairways. He was active and daring, always wanting to climb, or run, or jump. Sitting still was not easy for him. As a result, school was really challenging. His body's race car engine did not do well in the rush hour traffic of the school day.

Bennett was a square peg that was always getting pushed into round holes. He was funny and gentle and kind by nature. Yet, his struggles to sit and focus on his academic work made his skin crawl. This was followed by academic failure and all of the shame that comes with not achieving. At first the battle was internal—he would become angry at himself for his struggles. By sixth grade, his struggles became external—he began to blame others for asking him to do things that he wasn't able to do. He became disrespectful, disruptive, and mean to other students. And after he had sufficiently disrupted his own class-room, he would wander the hallways, looking for other classrooms to disrupt.

There was one student in his classroom Bennett wouldn't mess with. Evan was bigger and older than Bennett. And Evan had autism. When others became frustrated with Evan, Bennett defended him. When Evan struggled academically or behaviorally, Bennett was by his side, helping him calm down or complete his assignment. As vola-tile as Bennett could be, he never wavered in his support of Evan.

Because of Bennett's struggles in school, we had developed a close relationship with his parents who were consistently supportive and equally at a loss for how to help him. When we are stuck with how to help a student, it is always helpful to get back to the basics: Where do they feel a sense of belonging? What activities give them a sense of mastery? How can we promote independence? Rather than focus on when they do poorly, we need to think about when they do really well. In one of our meetings, as we were scratching our heads, wondering what else we could try, Bennett's teacher, Ann, shared that Bennett was great with Evan. On our campus, just one hundred yards away, was Arbor Academy, a school for kids with autism. Maybe Bennett could spend some time there each day.

Even after we shared Bennett's behavior profile, Kim, the principal of Arbor, was eager to give it a try. Kim told us that Bennett would need to be trained and that the work he would be doing would be highly structured. We asked Bennett if he was interested. He looked both surprised and excited. I'm sure that he was wondering the same thing: Why would we put him in the care of vulnerable children when he struggled so much to care for himself? We gave it a go. And the results shocked all of us.

Regardless of how Bennett's day was at NSA, for two hours, three times a week, Bennett would leave NSA and walk to Arbor. The moment Bennett stepped into Arbor, everything changed. He was focused and polite and engaged. He was his best self. He learned the teaching strategies, observed how they are done in practice, and then, did them himself. The Arbor Academy staff was in awe. Kim told me that the work that Bennett was doing with her students was as good as other staff in the program. Bennett was patient, consistent, and disciplined as he mastered the complex and nuanced teaching strategies they were implementing. I thought perhaps this was hyperbole—I knew that he was doing well, but to be as strong a support as other staff? I was doubtful.

Then they showed me a video of him working with a student. Bennett was sitting, facing the student he was working with. He was calm and patient as he nonverbally went through a series of teaching exercises, manipulating objects of different sizes and shapes and colors, reinforcing the right answers and gently correcting the wrong answers. He would sit there for hours, in service of the learning of children whose struggles to navigate the world were much more profound than his. His commitment to the students drove him to show up nearly every time and his empathy anchored him to his chair, helping him to sit still when his body was wanting to move. He was beloved by the staff who would light up when he walked into the school or classroom.

This was the Circle of Courage in action. Because he was so welcomed and appreciated, he felt a sense of belonging every time he went to Arbor. Because the work was so meaningful to him, he was engaged at mastering the skills of teaching. He had discovered his "unique genius." Because the staff trusted Bennett to work with the students, he experienced independence. And, because he was able to share his "unique genius" for a purpose greater than himself, he was experiencing generosity.

At the core of generosity is the belief that we have gifts to share with the world. As a result, our lives have purpose. We are an active part of an interconnected community in which we take care of one another. Evolution has tipped the scales in favor of generosity by flooding our brains with "feel-good neuropeptides and endorphins" when we help others. Unfortunately, many children who struggle the most experience the opposite. People don't recognize their "unique genius," and only see the trouble they cause. Children internalize the constant messages they receive that they make the lives of others worse, not better. They hear that they are lazy, mean, disruptive, needy, and manipulative. What could they possibly have to give to others?

Children who struggle the most also get the fewest opportunities to give to others. As parents and teachers, we don't trust them to manage the responsibility to care for themselves, much less other people.

We are missing an important opportunity when we think this way. It may seem paradoxical, but the children who struggle the most are often the most generous. They know and understand pain and often this magnifies their empathy for others. They show up in ways that we would never imagine. But first, they need to know that they have unique gifts that can make the world a better place. Once they believe that they have these gifts, they can be unrelenting in their desire to share those gifts with others. And, in the process, they gain perhaps the greatest tool in their own resilience toolbox: a sense of purpose.

Our service learning coordinator, Chuck, took students all over the Chicagoland area, into homes to settle refugees, into shelters to support the homeless or victims of abuse, into food pantries to stock the shelves. They cleaned our roads, held fundraisers, played games with the elderly, lobbied the Illinois congress on behalf of foster children, and brought joy to everyone they met. No matter what the students were dealing with in their personal lives, no matter what conflict they may have had with one another, they always rose to the occasion. They recognized that they were needed, that others were hurting, and that they could be agents of healing. On these trips, they were defined by their ability to give, not by the problems that they caused. They were reminded of their goodness. And it was transformative. For everyone.

Research has found that the link between generosity and happiness is strong. If we want our kids to be happy, we need to give them opportunities to be generous. Martin Seligman, founder of the Positive Psychology movement, tells the story of a friend who, whenever he was in a bad mood, his friend's mother would say, "Stephen, you are looking piqued. Why don't you go out and help someone?" The mother's parenting strategy was supported by strong research. Seligman writes that "Scientists have found that doing an act of kindness produces the single most reliable momentary increase in well-being of any exercise we have tested." It seems counterintuitive. In order to be happy, we should focus on ourselves. But the research tells a different story. In one example, psychologists from the University of British Columbia conducted a study in which they gave participants twenty dollars and asked them if they thought they would prefer to spend it on themselves or someone else. A vast majority said that they would rather spend it on themselves. The team, led by Elizabeth Dunn, then told them how to spend the money. Some were told to give it away as a donation or a gift. Others were told to spend it on themselves. Those who gave away the money were happier at the end of the day than those who indulged themselves. Shawn Achor, in his book *The Happiness Advantage*, summarizes the outcome this way. "A long line of empirical research, including one study of over 2,000 people, has shown that acts of altruism—giving to friends and strangers alike—decreases stress and strongly contributes to enhanced mental health." If we want our children to be healthy and well adjusted, one essential tool in our toolbox is encouraging generosity.

Becoming aware of our interconnectedness to others, realizing that we have gifts that can improve the world, and having the opportunity to share those gifts, can provide not only a momentary boost of happiness. When embedded in our lives, it can provide a foundation for a life of mental health and wellness.

Where Is the Circle Broken?

Our first step in building the resilience of our children is to believe in the power of community. We need to believe that a healthy community is much more powerful than any one of us. Then, we need to create Circle of Courage cultures for them—in our homes, in our classrooms, on our teams, in our orchestra, Dungeons and Dragons club, Quiz Bowl team, or on our stage crew. The more places our children can experience the alchemy of belonging, mastery, independence, and generosity, the healthier they will be.

Even within healthy communities, children will struggle and melt down—we all do. In these moments, the Circle of Courage can be a tool to help us identify how to be most helpful. When any of us is struggling, you can bet that one (or more) of these needs is not being met. Rather than think about these struggles as issues of "defiance," "manipulation," "laziness," "avoidance," or "selfishness," we can think about where their circle is broken. In their book, Brendtro, Brokenleg, and Van Bockern list what happens when each of the needs from the Circle of Courage isn't met.

When children do not experience a sense of belonging, they present as guarded, detached, lonely, aloof, and distrustful. Or, they may be attention craving, clingy, or overly dependent.

When they are not experiencing mastery, children appear unmotivated, risk-avoidant, and inadequate. Or, they may be an overachiever, a perfectionist, a workaholic. Cheating is often an indication that a person is struggling with mastery.

When children struggle with independence, they can appear submissive, lacking in confidence, or helpless. Conversely, they may become defiant, dictatorial, manipulative, bullying, or rebellious.

When they are not experiencing generosity within a community, they can appear selfish, narcissistic, indulgent, overinvolved, or disloyal.

When we see children behave in these ways, rather than try to change them through incentives and punishments, can we look upstream and change their community? If we see a child who is attention seeking as having issues related to belonging, can we give them more doses of connection throughout the day so that they can feel less anxious about needing to have adult attention constantly? If a child is not completing schoolwork, can we be curious about why they are struggling to effectively engage, rather than punish them for laziness? When they become defiant, can we see their dysregulation as stemming from their struggles to feel a sense of independence within the family rather than as a failure of character? Finally, when a child seems to lack direction, can we help them find purpose through sharing their unique gifts with others?

We experience children's behaviors differently when we see them as trying to address unmet needs. When Angelique seemed aloof, I was more patient and gentle when I saw it as a crisis of belonging rather than her not caring. When I was able to see Matthew's academic challenges in high school as resulting from crises of mastery and his occasional defiance as resulting from his quest to gain independence, I was able to partner with him to address these needs. When students at NSA were disruptive and mean-spirited, instead of wondering what I could take away from them to get them to behave better, I would ask, "I wonder what gifts they have that could help others?" Looking upstream in this way helps me see the bigger picture. It also helps me feel more regulated, allowing me to access the empathy, flexibility, creativity, and curiosity that I need in order to help them.

Making things trickier, children's needs change as they develop. The goalposts are always moving. Independence looks different for a five-year-old, for instance, than it does for a fifteen-year-old. What we know is that when children are thriving, the four needs of the Circle of Courage are being met. When kids struggle and we don't know where to turn, we can find direction by identifying which of these needs is not being met. In my family and in my work, the Circle of Courage has been a steady beacon, a North Star, for both creating community and understanding what to do when a person or a community begins to unravel. Myself included.

This model, reinforced by experience, helped me through many crises at home and at school. That does not mean that I didn't feel lost. I felt lost, a lot. I, however, slowly began to realize that feeling lost is different from being lost. I was holding a map—the Circle of Courage—and I learned to trust that map in the hardest moments.

As I reflect on the most engaged and productive times in my life, I realize that they each occurred within communities where these four needs were being met. At Wediko, I felt a strong sense of connection with both the staff and the children. I was learning, mentored by supervisors committed to my growth and development. I was trusted to work independently with children and, when I made mistakes, I was coached, not punished. Finally, I felt a strong sense of purpose. We worked sixteen- to eighteen-hour days for eight weeks with only five days off. We made eight hundred dollars for the entire summer. We were giving everything of ourselves for the children. And it was worth every moment. My experience at NSA was similar. And the same is true in my own family.

A Circle of Courage community is never static. It requires constant attention and maintenance. In each of these communities where I found so much comfort, the circle would break. I may feel excluded from a social outing or feel shame about a decision that I made. I may begin to feel stagnant in my learning or find myself anxious about the work of someone I supervise and begin to micromanage them. I often wonder if my work has meaning when a child I'm working with falls apart. It is inevitable. Once we have created this community, we need to maintain it. We need to repair it when it is broken. We need to lean in rather than check out. We need to reestablish psychological safety when it has been threatened. It is not a matter of if the community will struggle, it is a matter of when. And when it happens, we need to return to our map, and repair the circle.

O ur children are in pain like never before. As parents and educators, this is happening on our watch. Our children are failing to grow in the gardens we have created for them, unable to find sustenance in the soil we have tilled. It is time to change the soil. Over the course of the book I have shown that creating connected and regulated communities for our children is the loam that nourishes their garden. Like the magical soil on the forest floor that protects and enriches the lives of trees, the communities in which we plant our children can foster interconnections that rewire their brains and cultivate resilience.

The richest I have ever felt is when I was in vibrant communities. When, as a child, I was wilting, my mother transplanted me into a new garden. As I got older, I bloomed on sports teams, at camps, and places of work. In these Circle of Courage communities, I could grow and develop more fully. The same thing was true for Anna, Matthew, and Angelique. Watching them, as adults, I bask in the moments that reside in the liminal space between the memories of their past challenges, and how their futures, eventually, unfolded. As I was finishing the writing of this book, I thought of two of these moments. One moment was ceremonial. The other, a fleeting epiphany.

The first moment was in the field house at St. Lawrence University. Matthew was moments away from graduating. As I waited, I looked at the pamphlet with the list of graduates. I couldn't find his name among the students, listed in alphabetical order. *Is he not graduating after all?* I wondered, panic beginning to settle in. Did he not complete a final paper? Did we owe money to the registrar? How could he not tell us? I scoured the dozens of columns of names and then, toward the very end, I saw his. The graduates who had achieved summa cum laude appeared last in the pamphlet. Not only was Matthew graduating, he was doing so with the highest honors.

I thought about all his challenges but also the communities that enabled him to grow along the way. The teachers who saw his goodness and offered support, who cared less about his grades than his presence in the classroom. Instead of being frustrated with him, these teachers saw his struggles, believed in his future, and wouldn't let his difficulty getting things in on time get in the way of their relationship with him.

While he didn't have the communities of sports teams or social groups, he always had his family. Anna became a best friend to him. Angelique, the thoughtful older sister. Kathy, ever positive, was fully present with him, providing moments of respite when I was anxious and more distant. His grandparents adored him. When he looked into their eyes, he could see his own goodness. And me, in my own clumsy way, pushing too hard at times but also continuing to repair, to love, and to care. These relationships sustained him through his toughest challenges.

With Angelique, the moment came in a flash, electric, though easy to miss. After she graduated from DePaul, Angelique moved to Paris where she completed her MBA and met the man who she would marry. Shortly after they were married, they visited us and as they sat on the couch, I watched Angelique's hand rubbing Thomas's bald head as we talked. It wasn't the gentle and intimate gesture that struck me—it was how natural and instinctive it was for Angelique to reach out and connect through touch. I had never seen her so physically comfortable with anyone. It reminded me of the familiar intimacy of crawling into my mother's lap, when, as a three-year-old, I watched her talk to a friend on the couch, not even pausing as I settled into her body like a missing piece to a puzzle.

With all of the loss and trauma in her life, Angelique was able to create a community—through us, her adopted family, through her mentors in high school and college, and through a group of friends from different African nations who came together in college to create their own home away from home. The cadence of their language, the familiarity of their humor, the scents of the food emanating from the kitchen, the spontaneous laughter that erupts when you are surrounded by people who see and hear you must have soothed her limbic system, helping her to heal and grow. She surrounded herself with new communities that helped her heal from old wounds.

This is the power of a healthy community. It is the salve that calms the pain and the vaccine that protects us from injury. It is the medicine that heals us when we become sick. It is the vitamin that makes us stronger. It buffers us from stress. It heals our bodies after trauma. And it is essential to help us thrive. This is what happened for me, for Matthew, for Angelique. My guess is that it has happened for you, too. In these communities, our needs for belonging, mastery, independence, and generosity are met. Connected and regulated communities are the secret sauce of our resilience as a species.

Tragically, we often engage in practices that undermine rather than enhance community. We use methods of control rather than partnership. We focus on compliance rather than engagement. Instead of embracing the abundance of community, we have created systems of exclusion and scarcity.

But we can change all that. Bryan Stevenson—an American lawyer, social justice activist, law professor, and bestselling author of *Just Mercy*—spoke at an event at our local high school one evening in March of 2015. I sat transfixed as he spoke about the four things we can each do to change the world.

1. Get Closer to the Problem. No one is closer to the problem of children's mental health and wellness than us. We are parents, teachers, grandparents, aunts, uncles, neighbors, coaches, and mentors. No one has the time or the access to the lives of children like we do. We each have the resources (ourselves) to help children learn to attach, to develop the ability to stay regulated when stressed, and to reverse the impact of trauma through their connection with us.

2. Change the Narrative. Is it mis-behavior or stress-behavior? Should we stand in awe at the burdens that children have to carry or in judgment at how they carry them? When they struggle, is it an issue of development or compliance? Seeing children through a different lens helps us engage with them differently. It helps us to see and hear them in new ways.

3. Choose to Do Uncomfortable Things in the Service of Justice. This, I think, is the most difficult. It is hard to stay connected to a child who, because of insecure attachment, pushes you away. It is uncomfortable to stay regulated in the face of a child's rage or self-harm. It feels wrong to invite children back into communities when they have hurt others. And yet, having people in our lives who stand by our side through our hardest moments has been the key to our survival as a species. It is also the key to the survival of our children.

4. Protect Our Hopefulness. We don't need to look far to find stories of hope. The pages of this book are full of children who created joyful and meaningful lives after early years of intense struggle. These stories are not unique—each of us is surrounded by people who, because of their communities, overcame remarkable challenges. We just need to look.

Planting a bulb in a garden always begins with the belief that, if we create the right environment, it will grow into a flower. It spends months hidden in the earth. Then, on its own timeline and in its own unique way, it breaks through the soil, reaching for the sky, unfolding its beauty for all of us to see. And the wonderful thing about healthy communities? They are abundant, available any time two or more people are together. They cost no money. From classrooms to orchestras, from boardrooms to living rooms, a connected and regulated community is the tide that raises all ships.

Now that we know, what will we do?

ACKNOWLEDGMENTS

I knew that I needed to write this book, I just didn't know whether it would ever be read. The stories of children and families I worked with captured my heart, and to memorialize them, I began to journal. The journey from that collection of stories to this book was made possible by many thoughtful and brilliant people. I am so grateful.

This book would never have been published without Teresa Barker. Teresa was the first person to read my long and rambling draft. She believed in this book, in me as a writer, and was committed to helping me find my footing in the publishing world. She introduced me to Heather Jackson, my magician agent, who took the time to understand me and my manuscript. Heather's vast understanding of the publishing landscape, deep care for her authors, and fiery passion for supporting books that help people and improve our world made her a perfect partner for this project. It was Heather who, within days of taking me on as a client, brought me to Lucia Watson and her team at Avery/Penguin. From the moment I met her, it was clear that Lucia cared deeply about this topic. Her thoughtful, responsive, and insightful engagement helped me find the book that was hidden behind so many words. Isabel McCarthy held my hand through this new world of publishing with patience and positivity. When it came to the work of rewriting and editing, Julia Serebrinsky was with me word-for-word, coparenting this book into adulthood. Her wisdom, patience, and partnership are infused in every page.

I also had a support team whose belief in this book continued to inform and energize me. Dan Cates and Cammie McGovern's thoughtful reading of the manuscript and subsequent feedback energized and encouraged me when I needed it the most. John Frampton invited me to join Formative Psychological Services, giving me a soft landing after leaving NSA and the perfect springboard for writing. My thirst for learning was constantly quenched by the amazing authors and thinkers who spoke at the Family Action Network (FAN) and who are referenced in this book. Executive Director Lonnie Stonitsch is a friend with a powerful vision for galvanizing a community through collective learning. And Dan Chamberlin, I will take you up on your offer to "sell the back of the room" anytime.

At NSA, our administrative team of Leslie Amezquita, Adam Berkson, Lara Buti, Ann Bystedt, and Scott Dever was devoted and courageous as we stepped into the unknown process of tackling age-old ideas and practices with new approaches. The care they took with one another, their commitment to children and families, and their ability to lead engaged teams created the magic that so many NSA staff, students, and parents experienced. That spirit did not end with the administrative team. Everywhere—in every classroom and hallway—NSA was filled with staff who embodied the Circle of Courage, who enriched not only the lives of children but one another. I learned as much about supporting children from watching the teaching assistants, teachers, and therapists at NSA do their work as I did in any book or workshop. What a gift to work with such talented and caring people. Lara Buti joined me in consulting after leaving NSA, and her passion and wisdom continue to guide, inform, and energize my work.

I have learned that writing is a journey that begins long before any words hit the page. I was just out of college when I met Harry Parad, who, as the Clinical Director of Wediko Children's Services, invested in me in a way that would forever change my life. His vision for this work has been my guiding light, and his four decades of friendship have been a blessing to me and my family. Bob Gottlieb was the first principal of North Shore Academy and introduced all of us to the Circle of Courage. Bighearted, wise, and generous, he let every child and family know that they were welcome, that they belong, that they are valued. He did that for me, too. And still does. I was lucky to have had over twenty years of learning from Mary Jo Barrett, who, through her deep understanding of trauma, showed me how to stay grounded and present in the most painful moments with families and how to help teams improve their work by taking the risk of being present with one another. Bill Levin was officially a consultant to NSA, but he was so much more. He became a trusted therapist to all of us who knew him. He was insightful and funny, challenging and humble. His death left a hole in my life and the lives of so many others.

The voices of both of my parents, in very different ways, are embedded in my work and within this book. My father was the thinker and writer; my mother was the compassionate doer. They both, in their own wonderful and imperfect ways, showed up for me throughout my life, and my memories of them continue to guide me. My siblings—Jim, Betsy, and Kristin—all writers and avid readers, helped me believe that I, too, could write. Their love for me helped me love this book all the more.

When I began writing, I didn't expect to share so much of my own life. It is one thing to share my story, but it also meant sharing the story of our family. Angelique, Matthew, and Anna allowed me to tell their stories as I experienced them. As my children, they couldn't be protected with a pseudonym. I'm grateful for their vulnerability, for allowing their stories to be told, and for their ongoing forgiveness as I stumble through my parenting with each of them. My wife, Kathy, has been steadfast in her love and support for me for over thirty years. Those years included many moments when I struggled to navigate the demands of work, marriage, parenting, and writing. My partner in life, she continues to show up for me with enduring grace. These words just scratch the surface for how lucky I am to spend my life with all of them.

Finally, this book is full of stories of the students and families that I have been lucky enough to work with, laugh with, cry with, struggle with, and learn from. I hope that this book honors those stories. The beauty of places like NSA and Wediko is that they are so full of humanity—the hurts and the joys, the fear and the overcoming, the loss and the intimacy. Our collective journeys have changed me forever. It is because of them that I continue to believe in the power to transcend our hardest moments within the flawed beauty and power of a loving community.

NOTES

4 In the decade before COVID: Burstein, Brett, Holly Agostino, and Brian Greenfield. 2019. "Suicidal Attempts and Ideation among Children and Adolescents in US Emergency Departments, 2007–2015." *JAMA Pediatrics*, April. https://doi.org/10.1001/jamapediatrics.2019.0464.

4 when school is in session: Black, Tyler. 2022. "Children's Risk of Suicide Increases on School Days." *Scientific American*. August 22.

5 environmental conditions harming adolescent wellness: Breheny Wallace, Jennifer. 2019. "Students in High-Achieving Schools Are Now Named an 'At-Risk' Group, Study Says." *The Washington Post*, September 26.

9 "but not simpler": While this quote is frequently associated with Einstein, it's difficult to pinpoint a single, verifiable source for it in his writings or speeches. It's more of a paraphrase that captures his perspective on simplicity in science and problem-solving.

9 "everything that was not David": This is widely attributed to Michelangelo but may also be a paraphrase of his statement that "I saw the angel in the marble and carved until I set it free."

20 a public health parable: Heath, Dan. 2020. *Upstream*. New York: Simon & Schuster, p. 1.

22 defines *behaviorism* this way: APA Dictionary of Psychology. 2014. "APA Dictionary of Psychology." Apa.org. https://dictionary.apa.org/behaviorism.

23 showing any kind of affection: Watson, John B. 1928. *Psychological Care of Infant and Child*. New York: W. W. Norton.

24 Two-thirds of the monkeys: Pink, Daniel H. (2009) 2018. *Drive: The Surprising Truth about What Motivates Us*. Edinburgh: Canongate Books, pp. 1–4.

25 "Introduction of reward": Pink, Daniel H. (2009) 2018. *Drive: The Surprising Truth about What Motivates Us*. Edinburgh: Canongate Books, p. 4.

25 They define *intrinsic motivation:* Ryan, Richard M., and Edward L. Deci. 2000. "Intrinsic and Extrinsic Motivations: Classic Definitions and New Directions." *Contemporary Educational Psychology* 25 (1): 54–67. https://doi .org/10.1006/ceps.1999.1020.

26 "considerable long-term damage": From Pink, Daniel H. (2009) 2018. *Drive: The Surprising Truth about What Motivates Us*. Edinburgh: Canongate Books, p. 4. Original source: Deci, Edward L., Richard Koestner, and Richard M. Ryan. 1999. "A Meta-Analytic Review of Experiments Examining the Effects of Extrinsic Rewards on Intrinsic Motivation." *Psychological Bulletin* 125 (6): 627–68.

26 psychologist Barry Schwartz: Schwartz, Barry. 1982. "Reinforcement-Induced Behavioral Stereotypy: How Not to Teach People to Discover Rules." *Journal of Experimental Psychology: General* 111 (1): 23–59. Page 53, note 5. https://doi.org/10.1037/0096-3445.111.1.23.

28 "what is otherwise a moral act": Schwartz, Barry. From a May 1, 2012, speech at the Winnetka Community Center, Winnetka, IL.

28 Israeli day care organization: From Pink, Daniel H. (2009) 2018. *Drive: The Surprising Truth about What Motivates Us*. Edinburgh: Canongate Books, pp. 51–53. Original source: Gneezy, Uri, and Aldo Rustichini. 2000. "A Fine Is a Price." *The Journal of Legal Studies* 29 (1): 1–17. https://doi.org/10.1086/468061.

30 business incentives at work: Kohn, Alfie. 1993. "Why Incentive Plans Cannot Work." *Harvard Business Review*. September 1993. https://hbr.org /1993/09/why-incentive-plans-cannot-work.

31 financial incentives in business: Grant, Adam, Jitendra Singh, Harbir Singh, Maurice Schweitzer, Michael Useem, and Peter Cappelli. 2011. "The Problem with Financial Incentives—and What to Do about It." Knowledge@Wharton. 2011. https://knowledge.wharton.upenn.edu /article/the-problem-with-financial-incentives-and-what-to-do-about-it/.

34 "A person who has been punished": Skinner, B. F. 2002. *Beyond Freedom and Dignity*. Cambridge, MA: Hackett, p. 81.

Notes

36 shamed in school: Brown, Brené. 2017. "Embrace the Uncool: Brené Brown on Overcoming Shame." *Next Big Idea Club.*

44 "handling a baby": Karen, Robert. 1994. *Becoming Attached: First Relationships and How They Shape Our Capacity to Love.* New York: Oxford University Press, p. 19.

44 A 1915 review: Karen, Robert. 1994. *Becoming Attached: First Relationships and How They Shape Our Capacity to Love.* New York: Oxford University Press, pp. 18–19.

45 "the infant and young child": Bowlby, John. 1951. "Maternal Care and Mental Health." *Bulletin of the World Health Organization Monograph Series* 2, 179. Geneva, Switzerland.

45 Eighty-five percent of children: Karen, Robert. 1994. *Becoming Attached: First Relationships and How They Shape Our Capacity to Love.* New York: Oxford University Press, p. 52.

45 a sense of comfort and soothing: Blum, Deborah. 2011. *Love at Goon Park: Harry Harlow and the Science of Affection.* New York: Basic Books, pp. 145–149.

46 "cuddly contact proved much more important": Karen, Robert. 1994. *Becoming Attached: First Relationships and How They Shape Our Capacity to Love.* New York: Oxford University Press, p. 121.

46 every aspect of the children's development: Weir, Kirsten. 2014a. "The Lasting Impact of Neglect." American Psychological Association. June 2014. https://www.apa.org/monitor/2014/06/neglect.

49 the "Strange Situation": Lehrer, Jonah. 2017. *A Book about Love.* New York: Simon & Schuster Paperbacks, pp. 20–33.

49 The children who were identified: Lehrer, Jonah. 2017. *A Book about Love.* New York: Simon & Schuster Paperbacks, p. 29.

50 mean, antisocial, and immature: Tough, Paul. 2014. *How Children Succeed: Confidence, Curiosity and the Hidden Power of Character.* London: Arrow Books, p. 36.

49 attachment status at age three: Lehrer, Jonah. 2017. *A Book about Love.* New York: Simon & Schuster Paperbacks, p. 31.

50 four scales of maternal behavior: Karen, Robert. 1994. *Becoming Attached: First Relationships and How They Shape Our Capacity to Love.* New York: Oxford University Press, p. 155.

51 **"Happiness is love":** Vaillant, George E. 2015. *Triumphs of Experience: The Men of the Harvard Grant Study.* Cambridge, MA: Belknap Press of Harvard University Press, p. 52.

51 **"Loneliness is far more":** Murthy, Vivek. 2023.
Our Epidemic of Loneliness and Isolation: The U.S. Surgeon General's Advisory on the Healing Effects of Social Connection and Community. Office of the U.S. Surgeon General, p. 4. https://www.hhs.gov/sites/default/files /surgeon-general-social-connection-advisory.pdf.

52 **their physical and mental health:** From Lehrer, Jonah. 2017. *A Book about Love.* New York: Simon & Schuster Paperbacks, pp. 45–46. Original sources: Vaillant, George E. 2012. *Adaptation to Life.* Harvard University Press, pp. 304–306 and Vaillant, George E. 2015. *Triumphs of Experience: The Men of the Harvard Grant Study.* Cambridge, MA: Belknap Press of Harvard University Press, pp. 14, 113, 123, 134.

52 **"does not push love away":** Vaillant, George E. 2015. *Triumphs of Experience: The Men of the Harvard Grant Study.* Cambridge, MA: Belknap Press of Harvard University Press, p. 50.

52 **"the ultimate source of resilience":** Vaillant, George E. 2015. *Triumphs of Experience: The Men of the Harvard Grant Study.* Cambridge, MA: Belknap Press of Harvard University Press, p. 52.

52 **"a kind of protection":** Lehrer, Jonah. 2017. *A Book about Love.* New York: Simon & Schuster Paperbacks, p. 37.

54 **"the human attachment system":** Lehrer, Jonah. 2017. *A Book about Love.* New York: Simon & Schuster Paperbacks, pp. 34–35.

55 **"Love never loses the capacity":** Lehrer, Jonah. 2017. *A Book about Love.* New York: Simon & Schuster Paperbacks, p. 51.

55 **"teachers change students' brains":** "Richard Davidson—a Neuroscientist on Love and Learning." n.d. The On Being Project. https://onbeing.org /programs/richard-davidson-a-neuroscientist-on-love-and-learning -feb2019/.

56 **"create the possibilities of learning":** Cozolino, Louis J. 2013. *The Social Neuroscience of Education: Optimizing Attachment and Learning in the Classroom.* New York: W. W. Norton, p. xvii.

60 **Father Greg Boyle:** Boyle, Gregory. 2011. *Tattoos on the Heart: The Power of Boundless Compassion.* New York: Free Press, chapter 9.

60 **"reminded of their goodness":** Boyle, Gregory. 2018. *Barking to the Choir: The Power of Radical Kinship.* New York: Simon & Schuster Paperbacks, p. 116.

60 **"goodness is our preexisting condition":** Boyle, Gregory. 2021. *The Whole Language.* s.l. New York: Avid Reader Press / Simon & Schuster, p. 40.

60 **"is the task":** Boyle, Gregory. 2021. *The Whole Language.* s.l. New York: Avid Reader Press / Simon & Schuster, p. 26.

61 **"When we attune with others":** Siegel, Daniel J. 2012. *Mindsight: Change Your Brain and Your Life.* Melbourne, Australia: Scribe Publications, p. 27.

62 **tiny treasure hunters:** Blum, Deborah. 2011. *Love at Goon Park: Harry Harlow and the Science of Affection.* New York: Basic Books, p. 259.

62 **living life on the "narrow ridge":** Buber, Martin, and Ronald Gregor Smith. 2002. *Between Man and Man.* New York: Routledge, p. 218.

63 **"an intense psychological involvement":** Bolton, Robert. 1979. *People Skills.* New York: Simon & Schuster, p. 32.

63 **"listening with the whole body":** Bolton, Robert. 1986. *People Skills.* New York: Simon & Schuster, p. 33.

63 **"providing a mirror to the speaker":** Bolton, Robert. 1986. *People Skills.* New York: Simon & Schuster, p. 50.

64 **In his now-famous video:** "Tronick's Still Face Experiment." YouTube. https://www.youtube.com/watch?v=f1Jw0-LExyc.

65 **"an active participant in relationships":** Tronick, Ed, and Claudia Gold. 2020. *The Power of Discord: Why the Ups and Downs of Relationships Are the Secret to Building . . . Intimacy, Resilience, and Trust.* New York: Routledge, p. 26.

65 **"successfully repairing them":** Blum, Deborah. 2011. *Love at Goon Park: Harry Harlow and the Science of Affection.* New York: Basic Books, p. 289.

66 **"interactive error and interactive repair":** Blum, Deborah. 2011. *Love at Goon Park: Harry Harlow and the Science of Affection.* New York: Basic Books, p. 289.

66 **to make it better:** Tronick, Ed, and Claudia Gold. 2020. *The Power of Discord: Why the Ups and Downs of Relationships Are the Secret to Building . . . Intimacy, Resilience, and Trust.* Melbourne, Australia: Scribe Publications, p. 29.

66 **reconnect with their parent:** Tronick, Ed, and Claudia Gold. 2020. *The Power of Discord: Why the Ups and Downs of Relationships Are the Secret to Building . . . Intimacy, Resilience, and Trust.* Melbourne, Australia: Scribe Publications, p. 40.

67 **"never failed to imitate them":** Baldwin, James. 1993. *Nobody Knows My Name: More Notes of a Native Son.* New York: Vintage Books, p. 187.

67 **"when their mothers fail them":** Attributed to D. W. Winnicott, first mentioned in Winnicott, D. W. 1971. *Playing and Reality.* London: Routledge.

67 **"inevitable but essential":** Tronick, Ed, and Claudia Gold. 2020. *The Power of Discord: Why the Ups and Downs of Relationships Are the Secret to Building . . . Intimacy, Resilience, and Trust.* Melbourne, Australia: Scribe Publications, p. 70.

68 **"the fundamental unit of connection":** The Gottman Institute. 2021. "3 Ways to Make a Better Bid for Connection." The Gottman Institute. May 11. https://www.gottman.com/blog/3-ways-to-make-a-better-bid -for-connection/#:~:text=Dr.

69 **only 33 percent of the time:** Ury, Logan. 2019. "Want to Improve Your Relationship? Start Paying More Attention to Bids." The Gottman Institute. February 11. https://www.gottman.com/blog/want-to -improve-your-relationship-start-paying-more-attention-to-bids/.

76 **"tempted to despise the wounded":** Boyle, Gregory. 2018. *Barking to the Choir: The Power of Radical Kinship.* New York: Simon & Schuster Paperbacks, p. 53.

83 **"no longer Gage":** Sapolsky, Robert M. 2023. *Determined.* New York: Penguin Press, p. 13.

83 **"the right thing to do":** Sapolsky, Robert M. 2017. *Behave: The Biology of Humans at Our Best and Worst.* New York: Penguin Books, p. 45.

87 **20 percent of our energy:** Clarke, Donald D., and Louis Sokoloff. 1999. "Circulation and Energy Metabolism of the Brain." Digital Research @ Fordham, January.

92 **when they are melting down:** Refer to the following websites for more resources: Ablon, Stuart. Think:Kids. https://thinkkids.org/; Greene, Ross. Lives in the Balance. https://livesinthebalance.org/.

97 **in his book *Self-Reg*:** Shanker, Stuart, and Teresa Barker. 2017. *Self-Reg: How to Help Your Child (and You) Break the Stress Cycle and Successfully Engage with Life.* New York: Penguin Books. Also, find more resources at https://self-reg.ca/.

98 **breaks down stress into five categories:** Shanker, Stuart, and Teresa Barker. 2017. *Self-Reg: How to Help Your Child (and You) Break the Stress Cycle and Successfully Engage with Life.* New York: Penguin Books, pp. 89–209.

102 flees the task: Shanker, Stuart. 2020a. *Reframed: Self-Reg for a Just Society.* Toronto: University of Toronto Press, p. 102.

102 activating our limbic brake: Shanker, Stuart. 2020a. *Reframed: Self-Reg for a Just Society.* Toronto: University of Toronto Press, p. 104–106.

104 we have three choices: Shanker, Stuart. 2020b. "The Science and Practice of Self-Reg." Presented at the Learning and the Brain: Social-Emotional Brains in Schools, November 8.

105 before and during exam season: Campbell, Denis. 2017. "Suicides by Young People Peak in Exam Season, Report Finds." *The Guardian.* July 12. https://www.theguardian.com/society/2017/jul/13/suicides-by -young-people-peak-in-exam-season-report-finds.

105 "The capacity for self-regulation": Steinberg, Laurence. 2015. *Age of Opportunity: Lessons from the New Science of Adolescence.* Boston: Houghton Mifflin Harcourt, p. 16.

110 any rhythm that soothes us: Perry, Bruce. 2015. Presented at the North Shore Academy Inservice, February.

114 slapping your hand on your opponent: "What Does It Mean to Tap Out in Wrestling?" n.d. Quora. Accessed September 25, 2023. https://www.quora .com/What-does-it-mean-to-tap-out-in-wrestling#:~:text=%E2%80 %9CTapping%20out%E2%80%9D%20%2D%20rhythmically %20slapping.

117 "not join their chaos": Knost, L.R. "Instagram." https://www.instagram .com/lrknost/reel/CxZMSR2sV2d/.

117 seventeen times per hour: Adolph, Karen E., Whitney G. Cole, Meghana Komati, Jessie S. Garciaguirre, Daryaneh Badaly, Jesse M. Lingeman, Gladys L. Y. Chan, and Rachel B. Sotsky. 2012. "How Do You Learn to Walk? Thousands of Steps and Dozens of Falls Per Day." *Psychological Science* 23 (11): 1387–94. https://doi.org/10.1177/0956797612446346.

119 Zones of Regulation: Kuypers, Leah M. 2011. *The Zones of Regulation: A Curriculum Designed to Foster Self-Regulation and Emotional Control.* Santa Clara, CA: Think Social.

119 the "zones" are associated with colors. Kuypers, Leah M. 2011. *The Zones of Regulation: A Curriculum Designed to Foster Self-Regulation and Emotional Control.* Santa Clara, CA: Think Social, p. 9.

121 we implemented "Mindful Minutes": We used the Calm Classroom curriculum and training. https://calmclassroom.com/.

122 **like our bank accounts:** Feldman Barrett, Lisa. 2021. *Seven and a Half Lessons about the Brain.* London: Picador, pp. 5–8.

124 **three additional weeks of instruction:** Pink, Daniel H. 2019. *When: The Scientific Secrets of Perfect Timing.* New York: Penguin Random House, p. 57.

124 **long or elaborate:** Pink, Daniel H. 2019. *When: The Scientific Secrets of Perfect Timing.* New York: Penguin Random House, pp. 60–63.

134 *At What Cost:* Gleason, David L. 2017. *At What Cost? Defending Adolescent Development in Fiercely Competitive Schools.* Middletown, DE: Developmental Empathy.

134 **"with their brain's development":** Personal conversation, 2018. For more information, see: http://developmentalempathy.org/about-us/.

144 **"driving a car at night":** E. L. Doctorow from Lamott, Anne. 1994. *Bird by Bird: Some Instructions on Writing and Life.* New York: Anchor Books, p. 18.

144 **"Hope begins in the dark":** Lamott, Anne. 2021. X (formerly Twitter). December 19. https://twitter.com/ANNELAMOTT/status/1472 606700288942085.

149 **defines trauma as:** Maté, Gabor, and Daniel Maté. 2022. *The Myth of Normal Trauma, Illness, and Healing in a Toxic Culture.* New York: Avery, p. 20.

149 **Complex trauma results from events that:** Peterson, Sarah. 2018. "Complex Trauma." The National Child Traumatic Stress Network. January 25. https://www.nctsn.org/what-is-child-trauma/trauma -types/complex-trauma#:~:text=Complex%20trauma%20describes %20both%20children.

149 **"The trouble with the word trauma":** Tronick, Ed, and Claudia Gold. 2020. *The Power of Discord: Why the Ups and Downs of Relationships Are the Secret to Building . . . Intimacy, Resilience, and Trust.* Melbourne, Australia: Scribe Publications, p. 145.

151 **Psychologist Dan Gilbert:** Gilbert, Daniel Todd. 2007. *Stumbling on Happiness.* New York: Harper Perennial, p. 62.

153 **"Our brains are map makers":** "The Ezra Klein Show: This Conversation Will Change How You Think about Trauma" on Apple Podcasts. Accessed October 15, 2023. https://podcasts.apple.com/us/podcast/this -conversation-will-change-how-you-think-about-trauma/id1548604447 ?i=1000532955898.

154 They designed a study: Felitti, Vincent J., Robert F. Anda, Dale Nordenberg, David F. Williamson, Alison M. Spitz, Valerie Edwards, Mary P. Koss, and James S. Marks. 1998. "Relationship of Childhood Abuse and Household Dysfunction to Many of the Leading Causes of Death in Adults." *American Journal of Preventive Medicine* 14 (4): 245–58. https://doi .org/10.1016/s0749-3797(98)00017-8.

155 an 87 percent likelihood: Stevens, Jane. (PACEs Connection. n.d. "PACEs Science 101 (FAQs)—Positive and Adverse Childhood Experiences." PACEsConnection. https://www.pacesconnection.com/blog/aces-101-faqs.

156 four or more ACEs: Swedo, Elizabeth A. 2023. "Prevalence of Adverse Childhood Experiences among U.S. Adults—Behavioral Risk Factor Surveillance System, 2011–2020." *MMWR. Morbidity and Mortality Weekly Report* 72. https://doi.org/10.15585/mmwr.mm7226a2.

156 Students with four or more ACEs: Burke Harris, Nadine. 2018a. "The Deepest Well: Healing the Long-Term Effects of Childhood Adversity." February 13. https://www.familyactionnetwork.net/events/the-deepest -well-healing-the-long-term-effects-of-childhood-adversity-3/.

158 70 percent greater likelihood: Dube, Shanta R., DeLisa Fairweather, William S. Pearson, Vincent J. Felitti, Robert F. Anda, and Janet B. Croft. 2009. "Cumulative Childhood Stress and Autoimmune Diseases in Adults." *Psychosomatic Medicine* 71 (2): 243–50. https://doi.org/10.1097/psy .0b013e3181907888.

158 life expectancy plummets by twenty years: Brown, David W., Robert F. Anda, Henning Tiemeier, Vincent J. Felitti, Valerie J. Edwards, Janet B. Croft, and Wayne H. Giles. 2009. "Adverse Childhood Experiences and the Risk of Premature Mortality." *American Journal of Preventive Medicine* 37 (5): 389–96. https://doi.org/10.1016/j.amepre.2009.06.021.

158 "as graphically as the human body": Maté, Gabor. 2018. *In the Realm of Hungry Ghosts: Close Encounters with Addiction.* London: Vermilion, p. 26.

164 "social isolation of solitary incarceration": Blum, Deborah. 2011. *Love at Goon Park: Harry Harlow and the Science of Affection.* New York: Basic Books, p. 214.

166 the brains of children who experience trauma: Ohio Department of Education, Holt and Jordan. n.d. *Trauma & Brain Development.*

174 "the impact of adverse childhood experiences": Burke Harris, Nadine. 2018a. "The Deepest Well: Healing the Long-Term Effects of Childhood

Adversity." February 13. https://www.familyactionnetwork.net/events
/the-deepest-well-healing-the-long-term-effects-of-childhood
-adversity-3/.

174 **Bessel van der Kolk:** "Bessel van der Kolk—How Trauma Lodges in the
Body, Revisited." n.d. The On Being Project. https://onbeing.org/programs
/bessel-van-der-kolk-how-trauma-lodges-in-the-body-revisited/.

174 **the impact of healthy relationships:** Perry, Bruce D., and Oprah Winfrey.
2021. *What Happened to You?* New York: Flatiron Books, p. 108.

174 **"by good things not happening":** Maté, Gabor, and Daniel Maté. 2022.
The Myth of Normal Trauma, Illness, and Healing in a Toxic Culture. New York:
Avery, p. 23.

175 **As poet Charles Finn wrote:** Finn, Charles. n.d. "Please Hear What I'm
Not Saying." Charles C. Finn. https://poetrybycharlescfinn.com/pages
/please-hear-what-im-not-saying.

176 **"The neural networks involved":** Perry, Bruce D., and Oprah Winfrey.
2021. *What Happened to You?* New York: Flatiron Books, p. 112.

188 **researching aqua dynamics:** Tang, Sindy. 2008. "The Rocket Swimsuit:
Speedo's LZR Racer." Science in the News. September 16. https://sitn
.hms.harvard.edu/flash/2008/issue47-2/.

188 **they instead looked to nature:** Brown, Sass. 2018. "Inspired by Nature:
Design That Imitates Life." The National. December 8. https://www
.thenationalnews.com/lifestyle/fashion/inspired-by-nature-design-that
-imitates-life-1.800318.

189 **"Trees are community beings":** Gill, Charlotte. 2012. *Eating Dirt: Deep
Forests, Big Timber, and Life with the Tree-Planting Tribe.* Vancouver: David
Suzuki Foundation/Greystone Books, p. 206.

189 **"the best tree it can be":** Wohlleben, Peter. 2018. *The Hidden Life of Trees:
The Illustrated Edition.* Vancouver: David Suzuki Institute/Greystone
Books, p. 16.

190 **"Your life will be unrecognizably different":** Sapolsky, Robert M. 2017.
Behave: The Biology of Humans at Our Best and Worst. New York: Penguin
Books, p. 273.

190 **"personality traits such as kindness are fixed":** Christakis, Nicholas A.
2019. *Blueprint.* New York: Little, Brown Spark, pp. 105–106.

192 **Robert Putnam's landmark book:** Putnam, Robert. 2000. *Bowling Alone: The
Collapse and Revival of American Community.* New York: Simon & Schuster.

192 described as a loneliness epidemic: "Our Epidemic of Loneliness and Isolation." 2023. The U.S. Surgeon General's Advisory on the Healing Effects of Social Connection and Community.

193 described millennials as the "loneliest generation": "Millennials Are the Loneliest Generation | YouGov." 2019. Today.yougov.com. July 30. https://today.yougov.com/society/articles/24577-loneliness-friendship -new-friends-poll-survey.

194 "Humans are world champion collaborators": Zaki, Jamil. 2019. *The War for Kindness: Building Empathy in a Fractured World*. New York: Crown, p. 6.

194 "Cooperation is a crucial predicate": Christakis, Nicholas A. 2019. *Blueprint*. New York: Little, Brown Spark, p. 14.

199 coined the term "psychological safety": Edmondson, Amy. 1999. "Psychological Safety and Learning Behavior in Work Teams." *Administrative Science Quarterly* 44 (2): 350–83. https://doi.org/10.2307/2666999.

200 "The behaviors that create psychological safety": Duhigg, Charles. 2016. "What Google Learned from Its Quest to Build the Perfect Team." *New York Times Magazine*. February 25.

201–202 Tom Boyce, a pediatrician and researcher: For a full and wonderfully readable account of his research, see: Boyce, Thomas. 2019. *The Orchid and the Dandelion*. London: Pan Macmillan.

204 reinforce or undermine classroom hierarchies: Boyce, Thomas. 2019. *The Orchid and the Dandelion*. London: Pan Macmillan, p. 151.

205 the impact of family dinners: The Family Dinner Project. 2012. "Benefits of Family Dinners—the Family Dinner Project." The Family Dinner Project. 2012. https://thefamilydinnerproject.org/about-us/benefits-of -family-dinners/.

214 Urie Bronfenbrenner, a Russian-American psychologist: Bronfenbrenner, Urie. 1979. *The Ecology of Human Development: Experiments by Nature and Design*. Cambridge, MA: Harvard University Press, p. 53.

217 *Stumbling on Happiness*, describes a study: Gilbert, Daniel Todd. 2007. *Stumbling on Happiness*. London: Harper Perennial, p. 20.

225 defines accountability differently: Merriam-Webster. 2019. "Definition of ACCOUNTABILITY." Merriam-Webster.com. https://www .merriam-webster.com/dictionary/accountability.

226 The word "discipline" comes from the Latin word, "disciplina": "What Does Discipline Mean?" 2020. Focus 3. January 28. https://focus3

.com/what-does-discipline-mean/#:~:text=The%20word%20%E2%80
%9Cdiscipline%E2%80%9D%20is%20from.

226 **modern definition of discipline:** "Discipline_1 Noun—Definition,
Pictures, Pronunciation and Usage Notes | Oxford Advanced Learner's
Dictionary at OxfordLearnersDictionaries.com." 2023.
Oxfordlearnersdictionaries.com. https://www.oxford
learnersdictionaries.com/us/definition/english/discipline_1#:~:text
=%2F%CB%88d%C9%AAs%C9%99pl%C9%AAn%2F-.

241 **his own research on childhood development:** Brendtro, Larry K., and
Martin Mitchell. 2015. *Deep Brain Learning: Evidence-Based Essentials in
Education, Treatment, and Youth Development.* Albion, MI: Starr
Commonwealth, p. 16.

241 ***Reclaiming Youth at Risk:*** Brendtro, Larry K., Martin Brokenleg, and Steve
Van Bockern. 2002. *Reclaiming Youth at Risk: Our Hope for the Future.*
Bloomington, IN: National Educational Service.

243 **Geoffrey Cohen defines belonging:** Cohen, Geoffrey L. 2022. *Belonging:
The Science of Creating Connection and Bridging Divides.* New York: W. W.
Norton, p. 5.

243 **"are more motivated to learn":** Cohen, Geoffrey L. 2022. *Belonging: The
Science of Creating Connection and Bridging Divides.* New York: W. W.
Norton, p. 213.

243 **a study of twelve thousand teenagers:** Cohen, Geoffrey L. 2022.
Belonging: The Science of Creating Connection and Bridging Divides. New York:
W. W. Norton, p. 232. Original source: Resnick, M. D. 1997. "Protecting
Adolescents from Harm. Findings from the National Longitudinal Study
on Adolescent Health." *JAMA: The Journal of the American Medical
Association* 278 (10): 823–32.

244 **journalist Eric Barker writes:** Barker, Eric. 2022. *Plays Well with Others.*
New York: Harper Collins, p. 223.

245 **"learning can only happen":** 2019. X (formerly Twitter). May 7. https://
twitter.com/BreneBrown/status/1125850064088391683?lang=en.

252 **"simple wisdom of Native culture":** Brendtro, Larry K., Martin
Brokenleg, and Steve Van Bockern. 2002. *Reclaiming Youth at Risk: Our
Hope for the Future.* Bloomington, IN: National Educational Service, p. 51.

252 **According to Csikszentmihalyi:** Csikszentmihalyi, Mihaly. 1990. *Flow:
The Psychology of Optimal Experience.* New York: Harper and Row.

252 in a state of flow: "Flow and Happiness." n.d. www.pursuit-of-Happiness .org. Accessed December 9, 2023. https://www.pursuit-of-happiness.org /science-of-happiness/getting-in-the-flow/#:~:text=In%20order%20for %20a%20flow.

253 Viktor Frankl wrote: Frankl, Viktor E. 1946. *Man's Search for Meaning.* Boston: Beacon Press, p. 166.

253 we create "Goldilocks" experiences: Pink, Daniel H. (2009) 2018. *Drive: The Surprising Truth about What Motivates Us.* Edinburgh: Canongate Books, pp. 118–19.

253 public speaker, Richard Curwin: Wikipedia Contributors. 2019. "Richard Curwin." Wikipedia. Wikimedia Foundation. February 3, 2019. https://en .wikipedia.org/wiki/Richard_Curwin.

256 a story from his book: Brendtro, Larry K., Martin Brokenleg, and Steve Van Bockern. 2002. *Reclaiming Youth at Risk: Our Hope for the Future.* Bloomington, IN: National Educational Service, p. 53.

256 responsibilities at early ages: For more on this, see Doucleff, Michaeleen. 2022. *Hunt, Gather, Parent: What Ancient Cultures Can Teach Us about the Lost Art of Raising Happy, Helpful Little Humans.* s.l.: Avid Reader Pr.

265 in favor of generosity: Pinker, Susan. 2015. *The Village Effect: Why Face-to-Face Contact Matters.* London: Atlantic Books, p. 49.

266 tells the story of a friend: Seligman, Martin E. P. 2011. *Flourish: A Visionary New Understanding of Happiness and Well-Being.* New York: Atria Paperback, p. 20.

267 summarizes the outcome this way: Achor, Shawn. 2011. *The Happiness Advantage.* New York: Random House, p. 52.

268 the Circle of Courage isn't met: Brendtro, Larry K., Martin Brokenleg, and Steve Van Bockern. 2002. *Reclaiming Youth at Risk: Our Hope for the Future.* Bloomington, IN: National Educational Service, pp. 62–65.

273 to change the world: Stevenson, Bryan. 2015. "American Injustice: Mercy, Humanity, and Making a Difference." Presented at the Family Action Network, March 23.

BIBLIOGRAPHY

Ablon, Stuart. n.d. "Home." Think:Kids. https://thinkkids.org/.

Achor, Shawn. 2011. *The Happiness Advantage*. New York: Random House.

Adolph, Karen E., Whitney G. Cole, Meghana Komati, Jessie S. Garciaguirre, Daryaneh Badaly, Jesse M. Lingeman, Gladys L. Y. Chan, and Rachel B. Sotsky. 2012. "How Do You Learn to Walk? Thousands of Steps and Dozens of Falls per Day." *Psychological Science* 23 (11): 1387–94. https://doi.org /10.1177/0956797612446346.

APA Dictionary of Psychology. 2014. "APA Dictionary of Psychology." Apa.org. https://dictionary.apa.org/behaviorism.

Baldwin, James. 1993. *Nobody Knows My Name: More Notes of a Native Son*. New York: Vintage Books.

Barker, Eric. 2022. *Plays Well with Others*. New York: HarperCollins.

"Bessel van der Kolk—How Trauma Lodges in the Body, Revisited." n.d. The On Being Project. https://onbeing.org/programs/bessel-van-der-kolk-how -trauma-lodges-in-the-body-revisited/.

Black, Tyler. 2022. "Children's Risk of Suicide Increases on School Days." *Scientific American*. August 22. https://www.scientificamerican.com /article/childrens-risk-of-suicide-increases-on-school-days/#:~:text=This %20should%20be%20common%20knowledge.

Blum, Deborah. 2011. *Love at Goon Park: Harry Harlow and the Science of Affection*. New York: Basic Books.

Bolton, Robert. 1979. *People Skills*. New York: Simon & Schuster.

Bowlby, John. 1951. "Maternal Care and Mental Health." *Bulletin of the World Health Organization Monograph Series 2*, 179. Geneva, Switzerland.

Boyce, Thomas. 2019. *The Orchid and the Dandelion*. Pan Macmillan.

Boyle, Gregory. 2018. *Barking to the Choir: The Power of Radical Kinship*. New York: Simon & Schuster Paperbacks.

Boyle, Gregory. 2021. *The Whole Language*. s.l.: Avid Reader Press / Simon & Schuster.

Breheny Wallace, Jennifer. 2019. "Students in High-Achieving Schools Are Now Named an 'At-Risk' Group, Study Says." *The Washington Post*, September 26. https://www.washingtonpost.com/lifestyle/2019/09/26 /students-high-achieving-schools-are-now-named-an-at-risk-group/.

Brendtro, Larry K., Martin Brokenleg, and Steve Van Bockern. 2002. *Reclaiming Youth at Risk: Our Hope for the Future*. Bloomington, IN: National Educational Service.

Brendtro, Larry K., and Martin Mitchell. 2015. *Deep Brain Learning: Evidence-Based Essentials in Education, Treatment, and Youth Development*. Albion, Mich.: Starr Commonwealth.

Bronfenbrenner, Urie. 1979. *The Ecology of Human Development: Experiments by Nature and Design*. Cambridge—, Mass. & London: Harvard University Press.

———. 2005. *Making Human Beings Human: Bioecological Perspectives on Human Development*. Thousand Oaks: Sage Publications.

Brown, Brené. 2012. "The Whole Hearted Family." Family Action Network. October 11.

Brown, Brené. 2012. *Daring Greatly: How the Courage to Be Vulnerable Transforms the Way We Live, Love, Parent, and Lead*. New York: Gotham Books.

Brown, Brené. 2019. X (formerly Twitter). May 7. https://twitter.com /BreneBrown/status/1125850064088391683?lang=en.

Brown, David W., Robert F. Anda, Henning Tiemeier, Vincent J. Felitti, Valerie J. Edwards, Janet B. Croft, and Wayne H. Giles. 2009. "Adverse Childhood Experiences and the Risk of Premature Mortality." *American Journal of Preventive Medicine* 37 (5): 389–96. https://doi.org/10.1016/j.amepre .2009.06.021.

Brown, Sass. 2018. "Inspired by Nature: Design That Imitates Life." The National. December 8. https://www.thenationalnews.com/lifestyle /fashion/inspired-by-nature-design-that-imitates-life-1.800318.

Buber, Martin, and Ronald Gregor Smith. 2002. *Between Man and Man*. Mansfield Centre Martino.

Burke Harris, Nadine. 2018a. "The Deepest Well: Healing the Long-Term Effects of Childhood Adversity." February 13. https://www.family

actionnetwork.net/events/the-deepest-well-healing-the-long-term
-effects-of-childhood-adversity-3/.

Burke Harris, Nadine. 2018b. *The Deepest Well: Healing the Long-Term Effects of Childhood Adversity*. Boston: Houghton Mifflin Harcourt.

Burstein, Brett, Holly Agostino, and Brian Greenfield. 2019. "Suicidal Attempts and Ideation among Children and Adolescents in US Emergency Departments, 2007-2015." *JAMA Pediatrics*, April. https://doi.org/10.1001 /jamapediatrics.2019.0464.

"Calm Classroom." 2019. Calm Classroom. https://calmclassroom.com/.

Campbell, Denis. 2017. "Suicides by Young People Peak in Exam Season, Report Finds." *The Guardian*. July 12. https://www.theguardian.com /society/2017/jul/13/suicides-by-young-people-peak-in-exam-season -report-finds.

Christakis, Nicholas A. 2019. *Blueprint*. New York: Little, Brown Spark.

Clarke, Donald D., and Louis Sokoloff. 1999. "Circulation and Energy Metabolism of the Brain." *Digital Research @ Fordham*, January.

Cohen, Geoffrey L. 2022. *Belonging: The Science of Creating Connection and Bridging Divides*. New York: W. W. Norton.

Cozolino, Louis J. 2013. *The Social Neuroscience of Education: Optimizing Attachment and Learning in the Classroom*. New York: Norton.

Csikszentmihalyi, Mihaly. 1990. *Flow: The Psychology of Optimal Experience*. New York: Harper and Row.

Deci, Edward L., Richard Koestner, and Richard M. Ryan. 1999. "A Meta-Analytic Review of Experiments Examining the Effects of Extrinsic Rewards on Intrinsic Motivation." *Psychological Bulletin* 125 (6): 627–68.

De Waal, Frans. 2020. *Mama's Last Hug: Animal Emotions and What They Teach Us about Ourselves*. London: Granta.

"Discipline_1 Noun—Definition, Pictures, Pronunciation and Usage Notes | Oxford Advanced Learner's Dictionary at OxfordLearnersDictionaries .com." 2023. Oxfordlearnersdictionaries.com. https://www .oxfordlearnersdictionaries.com/us/definition/english/discipline_1#:~:text =%2F%CB%88d%C9%AAs%C9%99pl%C9%AAn%2F-.

Doucleff, Michaeleen. 2022. *Hunt, Gather, Parent: What Ancient Cultures Can Teach Us about the Lost Art of Raising Happy, . . . Helpful Little Humans*. s.l.: Avid Reader Pr.

Dube, Shanta R., DeLisa Fairweather, William S. Pearson, Vincent J. Felitti, Robert F. Anda, and Janet B. Croft. 2009. "Cumulative Childhood Stress and Autoimmune Diseases in Adults." *Psychosomatic Medicine* 71 (2): 243–50. https://doi.org/10.1097/psy.0b013e3181907888.

Duhigg, Charles. 2016. "What Google Learned from Its Quest to Build the Perfect Team." *New York Times Magazine*. February 25.

Durose, Matthew, Alexia Cooper, Howard Snyder, and BJS Statisticians. 2014. "BJS Special Report Recidivism of Prisoners Released in 30 States in 2005: Patterns from 2005 to 2010." https://bjs.ojp.gov/content/pub/pdf /rprts05p0510.pdf.

Edmondson, Amy. 1999. "Psychological Safety and Learning Behavior in Work Teams." *Administrative Science Quarterly* 44 (2): 350–83. https://doi.org/10 .2307/2666999.

Feldman Barrett, Lisa. 2021. *Seven and a Half Lessons about the Brain*. s.l.: Picador.

Felitti, Vincent J., Robert F. Anda, Dale Nordenberg, David F. Williamson, Alison M. Spitz, Valerie Edwards, Mary P. Koss, and James S. Marks. 1998. "Relationship of Childhood Abuse and Household Dysfunction to Many of the Leading Causes of Death in Adults." *American Journal of Preventive Medicine* 14 (4): 245–58. https://doi.org/10.1016/s0749-3797(98)00017-8.

Finn, Charles. n.d. "Please Hear What I'm Not Saying." Charles C. Finn. https://poetrybycharlescfinn.com/pages/please-hear-what-im-not -saying.

"Flow and Happiness." n.d. www.pursuit-of-Happiness.org. Accessed December 9, 2023. https://www.pursuit-of-happiness.org/science-of -happiness/getting-in-the-flow/#:~:text=In%20order%20for%20a% 20flow.

Frankl, Viktor E. 1946. *Man's Search for Meaning*. Boston: Beacon Press.

Gilbert, Daniel Todd. 2007. *Stumbling on Happiness*. London: Harper Perennial.

Gill, Charlotte. 2012. *Eating Dirt: Deep Forests, Big Timber, and Life with the Tree-Planting Tribe*. Vancouver: David Suzuki Foundation/Greystone Books.

Gleason, David L. 2017. *At What Cost?: Defending Adolescent Development in Fiercely Competitive Schools*. Middletown, DE: Developmental Empathy.

Gneezy, Uri, and Aldo Rustichini. 2000. "A Fine Is a Price." *The Journal of Legal Studies* 29 (1): 1–17. https://doi.org/10.1086/468061.

Graham, Edward. 2015. "School Suspensions and the Racial Discipline Gap." JSTOR Daily. September 2. https://daily.jstor.org/school-suspensions -racial-discipline-gap/.

Grant, Adam, Jitendra Singh, Harbir Singh, Maurice Schweitzer, Michael Useem, and Peter Capelli. 2011. "The Problem with Financial Incentives— and What to Do about It—Knowledge@Wharton." Knowledge@Wharton. https://knowledge.wharton.upenn.edu/article/the-problem-with -financial-incentives-and-what-to-do-about-it/.

Greene, Ross. n.d. "Lives in the Balance." Lives in the Balance. https:// livesinthebalance.org/.

Greene, Ross W. 2005. *The Explosive Child*. New York: Quill; Enfield.

——. 2016. *Lost and Found: Helping Behaviorally Challenging Students (And, While You're at It, All the Others)*. San Francisco: Jossey-Bass.

"Greg Boyle—the Calling of Delight: Gangs, Service, and Kinship." 2019. The On Being Project. December 19. https://onbeing.org/programs/greg -boyle-the-calling-of-delight-gangs-service-and-kinship/.

Health (OASH), Office of the Assistant Secretary for 2023. "New Surgeon General Advisory Raises Alarm about the Devastating Impact of the Epidemic of Loneliness and Isolation in the United States." HHS.gov. May 3. https://www.hhs.gov/about/news/2023/05/03/new-surgeon-general -advisory-raises-alarm-about-devastating-impact-epidemic-loneliness -isolation-united-states.html.

Heath, Dan. 2020. *Upstream*. New York: Simon & Schuster.

Institute, The Gottman. 2021. "3 Ways to Make a Better Bid for Connection." The Gottman Institute. May 11. https://www.gottman.com/blog/3 -ways-to-make-a-better-bid-for-connection/#:~:text=Dr.

Junger, Sebastian. 2016. *Tribe*. New York: Twelve.

Karen, Robert. 1994. *Becoming Attached: First Relationships and How They Shape Our Capacity to Love*. New York: Oxford University Press.

Knost, L.R. n.d. "Instagram." www.instagram.com. Accessed November 26, 2023. https://www.instagram.com/reel/CxZMSR2sV2d/.

Kohn, Alfie. 1993. "Why Incentive Plans Cannot Work." *Harvard Business Review*. September. https://hbr.org/1993/09/why-incentive-plans -cannot-work.

Kolk, Bessel van der. 2014. *The Body Keeps the Score: Mind, Brain and Body in the Transformation of Trauma*. London: Penguin Books.

Kuypers, Leah M. 2011. *The Zones of Regulation: A Curriculum Designed to Foster Self-Regulation and Emotional Control.* Santa Clara, CA: Think Social.

Lamott, Anne. 1994. *Bird by Bird: Some Instructions on Writing and Life.* New York: Anchor Books.

———. 2021. "https://Twitter.com/ANNELAMOTT/Status/14726067002 88942085." X (formerly Twitter). December 19. https://twitter.com /ANNELAMOTT/status/1472606700288942085.

Lehrer, Jonah. 2017. *A Book about Love.* New York: Simon & Schuster Paperbacks.

———. 2009. *How We Decide.* Boston: Houghton Mifflin Harcourt.

Maté, Gabor. 2018. *In the Realm of Hungry Ghosts: Close Encounters with Addiction.* London: Vermilion.

Maté, Gabor, and Daniel Maté. 2022. *The Myth of Normal Trauma, Illness, and Healing in a Toxic Culture.* New York: Avery.

Merriam-Webster. 2019. "Definition of ACCOUNTABILITY." Merriam-Webster .com. https://www.merriam-webster.com/dictionary/accountability.

Merrick, Melissa T., Derek C. Ford, Katie A. Ports, and Angie S. Guinn. 2018. "Prevalence of Adverse Childhood Experiences from the 2011–2014 Behavioral Risk Factor Surveillance System in 23 States." *JAMA Pediatrics* 172 (11): 1038. https://doi.org/10.1001/jamapediatrics.2018.2537.

"Millennials Are the Loneliest Generation | YouGov." 2019. Today.yougov.com. July 30. https://today.yougov.com/society/articles/24577-loneliness -friendship-new-friends-poll-survey.

Ohio Department of Education, Holt and Jordan. n.d. *Trauma & Brain Development.*

Perry, Bruce D. 2011. *Born for Love: Why Empathy Is Essential—and Endangered.* New York: Harper Paperbacks; Enfield.

Perry, Bruce D. 2015. Presented at the North Shore Academy Inservice, February.

Perry, Bruce D., and Oprah Winfrey. 2021. *What Happened to You?* New York: Flatiron Books.

Peterson, Sarah. 2018. "Complex Trauma." The National Child Traumatic Stress Network. January 25. https://www.nctsn.org/what-is-child-trauma /trauma-types/complex-trauma#:~:text=Complex%20trauma%20describes %20both%20children.

Pink, Daniel H. (2009) 2018. *Drive: The Surprising Truth about What Motivates Us.* Edinburgh: Canongate Books Ltd.

———. 2018. *When: The Scientific Secrets of Perfect Timing*. New York: Penguin Random House LLC, Copyright.

Pinker, Susan. 2015. *The Village Effect: Why Face-to-Face Contact Matters*. London: Atlantic Books.

Putnam, Robert. 2000. *Bowling Alone: The Collapse and Revival of American Community*. New York: Simon & Schuster.

"Research Proves Your Brain Needs Breaks." 2021. www.microsoft.com. April 20. https://www.microsoft.com/en-us/worklab/work-trend-index /brain-research.

Resnick, M. D. 1997. "Protecting Adolescents from Harm. Findings from the National Longitudinal Study on Adolescent Health." *JAMA: The Journal of the American Medical Association* 278 (10): 823–32. https://doi.org/10.1001/jama .278.10.823.

"Richard Davidson—a Neuroscientist on Love and Learning." n.d. The On Being Project. https://onbeing.org/programs/richard-davidson-a -neuroscientist-on-love-and-learning-feb2019/.

Ryan, Richard M., and Edward L. Deci. 2000. "Intrinsic and Extrinsic Motivations: Classic Definitions and New Directions." *Contemporary Educational Psychology* 25 (1): 54–67. https://doi.org/10.1006/ceps.1999 .1020.

Sapolsky, Robert M. 2017. *Behave: The Biology of Humans at Our Best and Worst*. New York: Penguin Books.

———. 2023. *Determined*. New York: Penguin Press.

Schwartz, Barry. 1982. "Reinforcement-Induced Behavioral Stereotypy: How Not to Teach People to Discover Rules." *Journal of Experimental Psychology: General* 111 (1): 23–59. https://doi.org/10.1037/0096- 3445.111.1.23.

———. 2012. "The Paradox of Choice." Workshop. Winnetka Community Center. May 1.

Seligman, Martin E. P. 2011. *Flourish: A Visionary New Understanding of Happiness and Well-Being*. New York: Atria Paperback.

Shanker, Stuart. 2020a. *Reframed: Self-Reg for a Just Society*. Toronto: University of Toronto Press.

———. 2020b. "The Science and Practice of Self-Reg." Presented at the Learning and the Brain: Social-Emotional Brains in Schools, November 8.

Shanker, Stuart, and Teresa Barker. 2017. *Self-Reg: How to Help Your Child (and You) Break the Stress Cycle and Successfully Engage with Life.* New York: Penguin Books.

Siegel, Daniel J. 2012. *Mindsight: Change Your Brain and Your Life.* Melbourne, Australia: Scribe Publications.

Skinner, B. F. 2002. *Beyond Freedom and Dignity.* Cambridge, MA: Hackett.

Steinberg, Laurence. 2014. *Age of Opportunity: Lessons from the New Science of Adolescence.* Boston: Mariner Books, Houghton Mifflin Harcourt.

Stevens, Jane. 2015. "Adverse Childhood Experiences Study—the Largest, Most Important Public Health Study You Never Heard of—Began in an Obesity Clinic." ACEs Too High. June 3. https://acestoohigh .com/2012/10/03/the-adverse-childhood-experiences-study-the-largest -most-important-public-health-study-you-never-heard-of-began-in-an -obesity-clinic/.

Stevens, Jane. PACEs Connection. n.d. "PACEs Science 101 (FAQs)—Positive and Adverse Childhood Experiences." PACEsConnection. https://www .pacesconnection.com/blog/aces-101-faqs.

Stevenson, Bryan. 2015. "American Injustice: Mercy, Humanity, and Making a Difference." Presented at the Family Action Network, March 23.

Swedo, Elizabeth A. 2023. "Prevalence of Adverse Childhood Experiences among U.S. Adults—Behavioral Risk Factor Surveillance System, 2011–2020." *MMWR. Morbidity and Mortality Weekly Report* 72. https://doi.org /10.15585/mmwr.mm7226a2.

Tang, Sindy. 2008. "The Rocket Swimsuit: Speedo's LZR Racer." Science in the News. September 16. https://sitn.hms.harvard.edu/flash/2008 /issue47-2/.

"The Ezra Klein Show: This Conversation Will Change How You Think about Trauma." n.d. Apple Podcasts. Accessed October 15, 2023. https://podcasts .apple.com/us/podcast/this-conversation-will-change-how-you-think -about-trauma/id1548604447?i=1000532955898.

The Family Dinner Project. 2012. "Benefits of Family Dinners—the Family Dinner Project." The Family Dinner Project. 2012. https:// thefamilydinnerproject.org/about-us/benefits-of-family-dinners/.

The MEHRIT Center. 2019. "Self-Reg with Dr. Stuart Shanker." https://self-reg. ca/.

Tough, Paul. 2014. *How Children Succeed: Confidence, Curiosity and the Hidden Power of Character*. London: Arrow Books.

Tronick, Ed, and Claudia Gold. 2020. *The Power of Discord: Why the Ups and Downs of Relationships Are the Secret to Building . . . Intimacy, Resilience, and Trust*. Melbourne, Australia: Scribe Publications.

Tronick, Edward. "Tronick's Still Face Experiment." YouTube. https://www .youtube.com/watch?v=f1Jw0-LExyc.

Ury, Logan. 2019. "Want to Improve Your Relationship? Start Paying More Attention to Bids." The Gottman Institute. February 11. https://www .gottman.com/blog/want-to-improve-your-relationship-start-paying -more-attention-to-bids/.

Vaillant, George E. 2012. *Adaptation to Life*. Harvard University Press.

———. 2015. *Triumphs of Experience: The Men of the Harvard Grant Study*. Cambridge, MA: Belknap Press of Harvard University Press.

Watson, John B. 1928. *Psychological Care of Infant and Child*. New York: W. W. Norton.

Weir, Kirsten. 2014. "The Lasting Impact of Neglect." www.apa.org. American Psychological Association. June. https://www.apa.org/monitor/2014 /06/neglect.

"What Does Discipline Mean?" 2020. Focus 3. January 28. https://focus3 .com/what-does-discipline-mean/#:~:text=The%20word%20%E2%80 %9Cdiscipline%E2%80%9D%20is%20from.

"What Does It Mean to Tap Out in Wrestling?" n.d. Quora. Accessed September 25, 2023. https://www.quora.com/What-does-it-mean-to-tap-out-in -wrestling#:~:text=%E2%80%9CTapping%20out%E2%80%9D%20%2D %20rhythmically%20slapping.

Wikipedia Contributors. 2019. "Richard Curwin." Wikipedia. Wikimedia Foundation. February 3. https://en.wikipedia.org/wiki/Richard _Curwin.

Winnicott, D. W. (1971) 2005. *Playing and Reality*. London; New York: Routledge.

Wohlleben, Peter. 2018. *The Hidden Life of Trees: The Illustrated Edition*. Vancouver; Berkeley: David Suzuki Institute.

Zaki, Jamil. 2019. *The War for Kindness: Building Empathy in a Fractured World*. New York: Crown.

INDEX